THE T̲
OF THE̲

A STUDY OF THE
SERMON ON THE MOUNT

by

L. G. SARGENT

THE CHRISTADELPHIAN

404 SHAFTMOOR LANE

BIRMINGHAM, B28 8SZ

1981

THE TEACHING OF THE MASTER

CONTENTS

I. THE PREPARING OF THE TEACHER

1

THE WORD SPOKEN AND THE WORD MADE FLESH

A word is the expression of a mind, and words are a channel through which power is exercised; originating in the mind of one, that power can flow forth to many who are influenced by a thought or who obey a command. The grand assumption of Scripture is that behind all that men can know there is an eternal Mind whose spirit fills the universe, and when the mind of the Eternal is expressed the power is without limit, and the result instant and infallible.

Between the word and the work of God, therefore, the connexion is so close that David can treat them as parallel.[1] When a man speaks, the expression of his mind and the accomplishment of his purpose are, as it were, linked only by a thread which may easily snap; with God, the utterance and the end are one: the " word that goeth forth out of his mouth " shall not return void, but shall accomplish that which He pleases.[2] And thus " by the word of the Lord were the heavens made; and all the host of them by the breath of his mouth . . . He spake, and it was done; he commanded, and it stood fast."[3]

The race of mortal men who in due time spread over His earth could only know God as He expressed Himself in terms their minds could grasp. His " eternal power and divinity " they might read writ large in the works of creation,[4] but the way He wished them to live and His

[1]Psa. 33 : 4 ; [2]Isa. 55 : 11 ; [3]Psa. 33 : 6-9 ; [4]Rom. 1 : 20.

purpose to redeem men from sin and death and " bring many sons unto glory " could be known only by the words He might speak, and those words would be in themselves a power working on recipient minds to effect His purpose with them.[5] In many parts and in many ways, therefore, He spoke[6]; but throughout the record in which it is written, its origin is emphasized : it is " the word of the Lord "[7]; the word " came " as a power not of themselves to Elijah, to Isaiah, to Jeremiah,[8] and to all the prophets who spoke as they were " moved " or " borne " by the Holy Spirit.[9] So separate was this revelation from any impulse or will of the prophet—and sometimes so contrary to his human desires—that it could be described as "the words of God's holiness".[10] So strongly was the word conceived as actively effecting God's will that it could be spoken of as though it were an object going forth from God and functioning as His agent.[11] The word was " God-breathed ",[12] and as an " out-breathing " going forth from God it could be spoken of as though it had taken on an objective existence.

Though given in many parts and in many ways, the revelation of God was thought of as a whole. But its essential unity was established when all its manifoldness was gathered up in one full and perfect revelation. As the Eternal Spirit " moved upon the face of the waters " in God's creative work, so now the Holy Spirit came upon a virgin of the House of Israel, and the power of the Most High overshadowed her, and the babe who was born in Bethlehem in consequence was called the Son of God.[13] God, therefore, who had spoken

[5]Rom. 1 : 16-17 ; [6]Heb. 1 : 1 ; [7]1 Sam. 3 : 21, etc. ; [8]1 Kings 21 : 17, 28 ; Isa. 38 : 4 ; Jer. 1 : 2 ; [9]2 Peter 1 : 21 ; [10]Jer. 23 : 9 ; [11]Isa. 9 : 8 ; cf. Psa. 147 : 15 ; [12]2 Tim. 3 : 16 ; [13]Luke 1 : 35.

through many prophets, at last spoke in one, and that one a Son.[14] But the antecedents of that Son went back far beyond the day of his conception; beyond even the first of the prophets or the first angelic message; it is John the beloved disciple who shows that that Logos which combines mind, reason, thought, and utterance, had its origin " in the beginning " and was " with God ", and was inseparable from His own being.[15] That Logos, says John, " became flesh, and tabernacled among us (and we beheld his glory, glory as of the only begotten of the Father), full of grace and truth ."[16] As God had revealed Himself in the past through the word spoken through prophets, so now He revealed Himself in one who was the living embodiment of His own mind, " the brightness of his glory " and the impress of His nature upon human flesh.[17] As with the word which was sent from God, so Jesus could say of himself, " I proceeded forth and came from God "[18]; both the word spoken and the word made flesh were expressions of the mind of God through the working of His eternal Spirit, for, says Jesus, " neither came I of myself, but he sent me ". But so transcendent was this revelation that he could also say, " He that hath seen me hath seen the Father ".[19]

Because in this manner the Father was revealed in him, Jesus could speak of himself as not merely true but " the Truth "[20], and by the choice of this term he expressed in a particular way the same principle of the continuity of God's revelation. The rarity of purely abstract terms is one of the distinguishing marks of Hebrew thought, and even where abstract terms appear in the English version it will often be found that they include in their meaning an active quality which dif-

[14]Heb. 1 : 2 ; [15]John 1 : 1 ; [16]verse 14 ; [17]Heb. 1 : 3 ; [18]John 8 : 42 ; [19]John 14 : 9 ; [20]John 14 : 6.

ferentiates them sharply from the intellectual abstractions which are so common, for instance, in Greek thought. Truth in the Old Testament is not so much a standard of comparison as a mode of behaviour, and especially is this the case with the truth of God. The work that is " in truth " (to use an example from the Psalm quoted above) is work marked by the steadfastness of God. His truth is His self-consistency which takes the form of faithfulness in His dealings with men. The living God, therefore, is Himself the standard of truth ; and this quality is the ground of man's dependence upon God ; that which may be depended upon is the idea radically suggested by the Hebrew words. So Jacob could say, " I am not worthy of all the truth which Thou hast showed to thy servant ",[21] when by it he meant the quality of God as revealed in His actions. So Micah could say, " Thou wilt perform the truth to Jacob ".[22] This idea of truth as essentially active explains the remarkable frequency with which it is joined with mercy throughout the Old Testament. By the example of God, moreover, His children are required to " walk in truth ",[23] an idea carried over into the New Testament[24] and particularly notable in the writings of John.[25]

In Christ we see the full revelation of God's word, the perfect expression of His active truth. Not only does Christ speak truth, he is truth ; he is the Word which with unfailing power is accomplishing God's ends ; and so in the last vision, when he is seen going forth with the heavenly armies to subdue all the world to righteousness, he is called " Faithful and True " and

[21]Gen. 32 : 10 ; [22]Micah 7 : 20 ; [23]1 Kings 2 : 4 ; 3 : 6 ; Isa. 38 : 3 ; Psa. 26 : 3 ; 86 : 11 ; [24]cf. Eph. 4 : 17-24 ; [25]2 John, verse 4 ; 3 John, verses 3, 4 ; 1 John 1 : 6.

his name is called " The Word of God ".[26] How, then, does Christ himself regard the earlier writings? The final answer, as of so much else in Jesus, is the Cross ; because it was written in Moses, the Psalms, and the Prophets, it was binding upon him to suffer ;[27] because he came to do the will of God, he took upon himself all that was prescribed to him in the roll of the Book,[28] and was obedient even to death, and that the agonizing and shameful death of the cross.[29] We have also his many express declarations of the authority of Scripture ; and one such saying must be carefully considered in a study of the Sermon on the Mount.[30]

Conviction in such a field, however, is shown most fully and deeply by intimate knowledge and the assurance with which Scripture is used ; and in a sense this is true even of the Son of Man. One special aim of the present study, therefore, has been to examine the use of the Old Testament in the Sermon. Many terms Jesus uses had gained a wealth of meaning as they passed through the hands of prophets and psalmists ; in many the content had been wrought out in the experiences of Israel's history. It can be shown that this fullness of meaning is carried forward by Jesus into his own revelation. The New Testament words can be followed back to their Hebrew originals through the Greek version of the Old Testament—a work in which a writer who can lay no claim to scholarship must depend on concordances, commentaries, and such-like scholarly aids. The words can then be examined in their various contexts, and their development and associations traced. In following a word's growth, aid may sometimes be found in later and uninspired writings, such as the Apocrypha, while

[26]Rev. 19 : 11, 13 ; [27]Luke 24 : 26-27 ; 46-47 ; [28]Psa. 40 : 7-8 ;
[29]Phil. 2 : 8 ; [30]Matt. 5 : 17-19.

Rabbinical writings may show the idea which the term would be likely to suggest to a Jewish audience in the time of Christ ; it is from this point of view alone that these are occasionally referred to by way of illustration. The tracking to their origins of parables, figures of speech, turns of phrase, will also show how thoroughly the mind of " the man Christ Jesus " was steeped in Holy Writ. This study of the Sermon therefore becomes to some extent a study in literary sources, but with infinitely more than a literary significance.

The purpose of the Sermon is to show the children of the Heavenly Father how they may " walk in truth ". But they can only be shown the road they are to go if there is clear perception of the end they are to reach. Teaching on the conduct of life must be founded on judgments—explicit or implied—as to the nature, meaning and ends of life ; and in that respect no teaching in Scripture or out of it rests more firmly on its foundations than the Sermon on the Mount. The words of Jesus are marked by all the sublime assurance concerning God, man, life, death, judgment, the Kingdom of God, and immortality, which might be expected from one in whom God's truth is embodied ; and any study of the Sermon, to be adequate or even reasonable, must therefore be largely a theological study.

All great literature has form, and one of the tests of greatness is that the form is not arbitrarily imposed on the substance, but is itself a part of the meaning : the full quality of the thought can only be conveyed in such a mould. There is no reason to suppose that the form will be any less fitting when the words are those of the Holy Spirit, instead of human genius. Now, the Sermon has definite form. In fine oratory, where clear thinking is matched by emotional power, the sentences tend to fall into balanced and rhythmic clauses, and in Hebrew this tendency is heightened into a poetic technique; the regularity and recurrence which distinguish poetry from prose are to be found in the sense more than in the sound. On this principle there were developed the varied and sometimes intricate parallelisms of Old Testament poetry; and translation—probably even double translation, from Aramaic to Greek and Greek to English—does not conceal the employment of the same forms in the Sermon. To aid the reader in appreciating this structure, at the head of a chapter will be found the passage to which it relates, set out in lines and indented so that the eye can readily pick out the lines which correspond with one another, and showing also the grouping of lines into stanzas or strophes which often have a well-marked climax. Added to parallelism, Hebrew poetry (in the view of present-day scholars) shows regularity in the number of accents to the line, in this resembling the Early English alliterative verse as distinct from the more sophisticated metrical verse from Chaucer onwards. The lines fall into patterns, suited to the mood and subject-matter of the poem. It can hardly be mere coincidence that when the Sermon is rendered back from Greek into Aramaic it frequently reveals the same verse-forms that are used in the Old Testament. While translation back into the original tongue must be largely conjectural, and we cannot assume that by this means we recover Christ's own words, the fact that these forms come to light in different parts of the Sermon does suggest that they must have been present in the spoken word. The Sermon is a poem, and it should be read as a poem.

13

GROWTH IN WISDOM

The Preacher of the Sermon on the Mount had lived in a Jewish town through a boyhood which was normal in all its outward circumstances. He had been " subject " to his mother and his presumed father ; he had grown through babyhood, boyhood and youth, developing mentally as he increased in " stature ". In the eyes of those around him he was unique only in the increase of " wisdom " which accompanied his advance in years, and in the grace of character which won the favour of God and man.[1]

But that wisdom is clearly said to have been a thing of growth. It fed on the education in the word of God which a Jewish child received ; and we may imagine how well it was nurtured from the time the child could speak by Joseph and by that " handmaid of the Lord " who had been chosen to be " blessed above women " for so precious a trust. Growth mentally and physically was an essential part of his experience in bearing our nature.

Nazareth, to which the family had been led, had its own part to play in the training of the Teacher. From the ridge of the hill under which the town lay the boy Jesus could gaze for thirty miles in three directions over country which has been described as " a living map " of the history of his people. Prominently before him was the cone of Mount Tabor, where Barak had gathered his forces for the overthrow of Sisera.

> So let all thine enemies perish, O Lord :
> But let them that love him be as the sun
> when he goeth forth in his might.[2]

[1]Luke 2 : 51-52 ; [2]Judges 5 : 31.

In the valley of Jezreel, to the south, Gideon began his pursuit of the Midianites after his army had been reduced deliberately at the stream from the well of Harod from 32,000 to a mere skirmishing party of 300, in order that Israel should not say, " Mine own hand hath saved me ".[3]

Bounding the view beyond were the mountains of Gilboa, scene of the defeat of Saul. To a mind filled with the history of Israel, those heights would call up the whole tragedy of the king who became haunted by the knowledge of his own rejection and filled with hatred of the successor whom God had chosen. It was the story of a man who by worldly standards was not irreligious, but who was lacking in the faith which could make the word of God a living reality in his life. Weakness in trust has in him its retribution ; the ground of trust is removed, and as a result rebellion against the Divine judgment finds an outlet in the murderous pursuit of David ; and " stubbornness " leads at last to the seeking of consolation in the witchcraft which stands in antithesis to the God who has forsaken him. In beautiful contrast to Saul was the forefather of the Lord, whose faith was as true as a sheep's in its shepherd, and who, in spite of one great sin, remained in his contrition " the man after God's own heart ". David is the most profoundly God-conscious man in the Old Testament.

Jezreel, beyond the hill Moreh which divides the two arms of the valley as they descend to the Jordan, was the scene of the downfall of Ahab. That king was the type of the " double-minded man, unstable in all his ways ", who yielded to the single-minded pride of Jezebel. Looking down on the Plain of Esdraelon, Jesus would recall when even the fertile soil watered by the

[3] Judges 7 : 2.

Kishon and its streams had been as iron, and the sky over it as brass. Through that Plain king, prophet and the attendants of Baal journeyed to Carmel to decide the great issue : " How long halt ye between two opinions ? If the Lord be God, follow him : but if Baal, then follow him ". An echo of that challenge was to be found later in Jesus' own words on that other Mount : " Ye cannot serve God and Mammon ".

From her palace in Jezreel Ahab's queen sent the threat which drove Elijah to exile in the hills of the Negeb ; and there under the slender shelter of a broom he was fed with " a cake baken on the coals ". When Jesus hungered after forty days' fasting, he would not forget that angelic ministration to Elijah which for the time was withheld from himself. And while as a youth he looked across to the hills of Samaria his mind would travel with the prophet far beyond Beersheba to " Horeb, the mount of God ". For him once again the strong wind would break in pieces the rocks, the earthquake heave, and the fire rage ; and then the " still, small voice " would command the prophet to embark on a new mission, with the assurance that even in Israel there was a remnant of " seven thousand " in whom the word of the Lord dwelt. The purpose of the Kingdom had not perished. In small things and among humble folk its seed would grow secretly, bringing forth fruit for the harvest of God's glory ; for the day would come when the proclamation should go forth : " The Lord reigneth ".

Sheltering to the south of Moreh was Shunem, where a godly woman had made provision for the man of God. In that home, as to Sarah of old, a son was born, a child was given—a witness to the power of

16

God over life and begettal; a foreshadowing in some degree of the purpose to be fulfilled with a virgin in Bethlehem. Did that Son think of these things as he looked from the hill above Nazareth? But the child in Shunem died; and again the power of God was shown—this time in a foretaste of that day when death shall be swallowed up in victory. Did Jesus know then that he too would bring joy by raising the dead when in him the kingdom drew near, and that in the end the power of resurrection to eternal life would be in his hands?

With such memories and visions we may imagine him looking down on the Plain of Esdraelon, growing in wisdom as he garnered the lessons of God's working in Israel of old. We, in our feebler way, may gather a few of those lessons even in the glance at Israel's history which we have taken : the reality of God; the certainty of His victory in the earth; His power to save by many or by few, and the glory that must be to Him alone; His rejection of those whose ears are not open to His word; His choice of those who " hunger and thirst after righteousness ", and His forgiveness even when they grievously fail; His claim to the whole of man's heart, and His repudiation of a divided allegiance; His care for those who love Him even when He leads them through the wilderness; His power to work unseen through the poor and the few; His power to accomplish His purpose through " a root out of a dry ground " and to bring life from death; and, as a corollary to this last, the assurance that man cannot destroy the life, and the awe that belongs to Him who can. Esdraelon and its surrounding hills summarized in their history the controversy between God and fallen man, and foreshadowed the triumph of the righteousness of God

17

through the Seed of David and in His saints. In the Divine provision it was no mere chance that the rich significance of the scene could enter into the soul of the growing lad in Nazareth.

One of the delights of the Sermon is the variety and abundance of its allusions to every-day life. The situation of Nazareth, as well as the periodic visits to Jerusalem from his twelfth year onward, had contributed to this side of Jesus' growth in wisdom. Between Tabor and the hill on which Nazareth stood, the great highway from Damascus emerged on to the Plain and crossed to the southern hills. By this route men had travelled to Egypt since the days of Abraham. From the northern edge of the hill could be seen the highway between Acre and the Decapolis along which Roman legions marched and Roman officials made their way. From the fords of the Jordan Arab caravans journeyed across the Esdraelon. Sir George Adam Smith says: " It was up and down these roads that the immortal figures of the Parables passed. By them came the merchantmen seeking goodly pearls, the king departing to receive his kingdom, the friend on a journey, the householder arriving suddenly upon his servants, the prodigal son coming back from the far country." Galilee was fertile, thickly populated, and with an abundant and busy life. It would have been thriving but for the burden of taxation and political uncertainty. Much of its traffic, and many of its companies of pilgrims going up for the feasts, passed over the plain from the foot of the hill from which Jesus could look down.

Add to these scenes the experience of an oriental town—no mere village—with all its chaffering business and cross-currents of passion and rumour. Add the daily toil in the home of a craftsman—a worker in wood who would also be a builder in a small way. From all these and much more, Jesus drew his knowledge of human life and the range of his illustrations. In the Sermon alone he has references to the home—light, salt, the lamp on its stand, the bushel measure, the kinds of food a child might ask for and a father give ; to working life—the requirements of good building, dangers to the flock, minor accidents such as getting a speck in the eye ; to the customs of the market place—the haggling with vociferous oaths, the corn measure well or scantily filled ; to social customs and conditions—salutation, public and demonstrative alms-giving, prayer or fasting, the use of abusive epithets in anger, the insulting blow, the habit of storing wealth in perishable forms ; to legal procedure—the local council, the Sanhedrin, the plaintiff, the judge, the court officer, the prison, the exacting of pledges, the demand for State service ; to nature— birds, flowers, sun and rain, trees good or worthless, the habits of dogs or swine ; to familiar scenes—the city on the hill, the beaten track to the main gate and the obscure door in the wall. He had observed them all, and knew how to use them to make his words live.

3

WISDOM PERFECTED THROUGH TRIAL

Yet it was not in Nazareth, but in the wilderness of Judea, that Jesus underwent the final preparation for his work. The Son of Man who is the Captain of salvation had to be " made perfect through sufferings " ; and before even he brought the message of salvation he " suffered, being tempted " in the wilderness. While for him this was not the end but the beginning of the suffering by which he was fitted to become the "Great High Priest ", it was the completion of his training for the work he was to do "in the days of his flesh ". For in that temptation all the wisdom he had gained in a sinless life in the knowledge of God was put to the test ; and, proving victorious, it was strengthened like tempered steel to be the ground both of his teaching and of his own obedience " even to death ". For, whatever view may be taken of some of the questions surrounding the temptation, one thing is fundamental : he " was tempted ". He knew temptation as a fact, and conquered it in the power of the Word ; and this was part of the experience by which he was " made perfect " in order that others may be " made perfect " through him. As he " tasted of death for every man " so also he tasted of temptation ; and as through death he obtained an eternal redemption—for himself, that it might be for others—so through temptation he gained a victory for himself that others might share its fruits.

Unbelief had been the source of man's first disobedience ; and as a result mankind had become imprisoned in disobedience—in " a refusal to yield ".[1] But God's word was vindicated by belief and obedience in the very sphere of human nature where it had been denied : it was upheld by the willing submission of one who yielded himself as the Servant of the Lord because his ears were opened. Immediately before his temptation he, the sinless one, had identified himself with human nature by submitting to baptism : " Suffer it to be so now, for thus it becometh us to fulfil all

[1]Rom. 11 : 32, *Rotherham.*

righteousness ". But even his recognition by God as the Beloved Son does not relieve him from being driven forth into the wilderness.

The fundamental issue which determines all the others is faced in the first temptation : " If thou be the Son of God, command that these stones be made bread ". The implication may be expressed in this way : " If you are the Son of God, all things are for you as the Heir, and all the purpose of God depends upon you as the Saviour. You therefore have a title— as heir—and a duty—as the pivot of God's purpose— to use the powers of the Spirit to supply your own needs." The answer comes from Deut. 8 : 2-5 : " . . . Man doth not live by bread only, but by every word that proceedeth out of the mouth of the Lord doth man live."

The wilderness wandering was a Divine education in which Israel were to learn two truths. The first was that things seen are not the ultimate reality. They came into existence by the word of God, which said " Let there be light . . . Let the earth bring forth . . . " By the same word they can be controlled, supplied, withheld, or destroyed. That word is therefore the substratum on which the whole creation rests. Life must depend, literally and finally, not upon bread but upon a man's acceptance of the Word of God, and with that all things needful for his life shall be added ; for the word which proceeds from God is the unchanging reality in a world of change. If Jesus himself is the pivot of God's purpose, it is because in him the Word had become flesh, and only through the Word can the purpose be fulfilled. The purpose of God does not depend on him, Jesus of Nazareth, but on God who anointed him and the Word of God which is embodied in him.

Christ's first answer therefore established the truth that God is the Reality without whom nothing is real, the Eternal without whom nothing abides; and it declares man's entire dependence upon Him. But it does more. If the first truth Israel was to learn was their relation to God, the second was God's relation to them. If He made them know in the wilderness their utter dependence on Him for very existence, He did so with the far-seeing love of a Father who imposes discipline for the training of His son. These profound lessons of the Exodus are inwrought in every part of the Lord's teaching in the Sermon on the Mount.

The temptation to throw himself from the topmost point of the Temple into the rocky depths of the Kidron Valley implied proving to the world his Messiahship by one decisive act. " Why not show the whole nation at one stroke that God has chosen you and given His angels charge over you? " The answer was in the words of Deut. 6 : 16 : " Ye shall not tempt the Lord your God, as ye tempted him in Massah ". In their clamour for water the Israelites had sought to put God to the test, saying " Is the Lord among us or not? " They had issued a challenge to God, and by seeking to impose upon Him a mode of behaviour which they had devised, they were making God subservient to their own wills. They were telling God what to do, on pain of their disbelief in Him if He did not do it. As the supreme Reality of the universe, it is not God but men who are to be put to the test, for Exod. 15 : 25 says : "There he proved them ".

Nor is He to be made subject to men's own desires ; they are to be conformed to Him, not He to them. It was this lesson which Moses distilled from their experience when he reviewed their history at the end of their wanderings. In his answer to the second temptation, therefore, Christ vindicated the supremacy of God by refusing to attempt to make God's will serve his own.

Westward from the hill of Nazareth Jesus had caught the gleam of the illimitable sea, whose islands should wait for God's law : and his eye had followed the way across the plain by which the fathers had travelled to mysterious lands. We need not wonder that to such a mind the view from a high hill would unfold " all the kingdoms of the world, and the glory of them ". All are to be his when the kingdoms of this world become the kingdom of the Lord and His Christ. Must that end be reached only through ages of the suffering of the peoples? The suggestion in the last temptation was that he might avoid the agony of the cross and cut short the travail of man by taking the rule to himself there and then. But that would be to take the glory to himself, and set up a new object of veneration. By an act of self-exaltation he would become his own God. How then should God be glorified? The Father's name could only be glorified through the way of the cross with its repudiation of human nature, and the preparation of a people through " much tribulation ". From the same part of Deuteronomy he cites the words : " Thou shalt fear the Lord thy God, and him shalt thou serve ".[2] God's is the Kingdom, and the glory and the worship are His alone ; and His must be the means by which it is established.

[2] 6 : 13.

Out of the threefold temptation which appealed basically to the desire of the flesh, the desire of the eyes, and the pride of life, Jesus emerged to proclaim the reality, supremacy and sanctity of God. These had been the foundation of his life from the day when as a boy of twelve he said : " Wist ye not that I must be about my Father's business ? " Yet even for him the very object of the temptation was that the truth he had never failed to follow should gain an intenser power by trial. It is these principles which had been challenged when the first Adam disobeyed, for sin is in its nature the denial that God is true to His own word, or even that He exists. It was these principles which were upheld by the obedience of the Second Adam. His ministry begins with the triumphant assertion of the reality of God in his own life, and ends with the proclamation of that reality to the world from the vantage point of the Cross. The principles he maintained glow throughout his sayings, and nowhere with a clearer light than in the Sermon on the Mount. From the hill of temptation he went forward to the hill of the Sermon and on to the hill of transfiguration and the hill of crucifixion with a mind calm and clear, filled with the zeal of the Lord's House, yet with an inward peace which permeated his words. " My peace ", he could say, " I give unto you."

His taking his seat upon this hill in Galilee where he summoned his disciples around him must therefore be seen not as an isolated incident but as a part of his whole life. It is a passage within a context—and the context is the revelation of God in Christ. The context is the Word which was from the beginning, and which became flesh in order that the flesh might be perfected through the suffering of which only flesh is capable.

" When he had sat down, his disciples came unto him ".[3]   By delivering his teaching from the Mount he claims comparison with Moses, to whom the Lord had said : " I will raise them up a prophet from among their brethren, like unto thee, and will put my words in his mouth ; and he shall speak unto them all that I shall command him.   And it shall come to pass, that whosoever will not hearken unto my words which he shall speak in my name, I will require it of him. "[4] " We have found him of whom Moses in the law, and the prophets, did write ",[5] says Philip after that first wonderful night spent at Jesus' lodging place.   " I do nothing of myself ", said Jesus ; " but as my Father hath taught me, I speak these things. "[6]   " The Father which sent me, he gave me a commandment, what I should say, and what I should speak.   And I know that his commandment is life everlasting : whatsoever I speak, therefore, even as the Father said unto me, so I speak. "[7]   But Moses received the Law standing before God, and descended from the Mount to deliver it to the people.   The One who is greater than Moses is seated, and delivers the Law in the Mount as the very voice of God.   With a direct allusion to the Lord's emphatic " I will require it " in Deuteronomy, Jesus declares that the man who receives not his words " hath one that judgeth him : the word that I have spoken, the same shall judge him at the last day ".[8]   The result of that judgment is clearly foreshown in a thought common to Jesus and Deuteronomy : the commandment is life ; therefore, and inexorably, the persistent rejection of the commandment is death.[9]

[3]Matt. 5 : 1 ;   [4]Deut. 18 : 15-19 ;   [5]John 1 : 45 ;   [6]John 8 : 28 ; [7]John 12 : 49-50 ;   [8]John 12 : 48 ;   [9]cf. Deut. 30 : 15-19, 20.

Jesus, like Moses on Pisgah, looks from the height over the ravine of time into the future Kingdom of God. Like Moses at Sinai, he declares the commands he had received of God. Like Moses in " the Arabah over against Suph ", he lays life and death before them in the " blessings " of the Kingdom.[10] The decisiveness of the choice is all the greater because there is no catalogue of curses in the words of Jesus : their absence points to a grave reality. While life in the ancient Kingdom was conditional upon a continuing obedience, life in the future Kingdom will be given for a faith already proved. No disobedience will mar it, because the disobedient will have perished in a destruction from which there can be no release. " Wide and broad is the way that leads to destruction ", says Jesus," and many there are who go in at it. How narrow is the gate, and straitened the way, that leads to life ! And few are those who find it. "[11] It is not mildness of disposition but a stern logic which impels Jesus to open the discourse with blessings only.

[10]Deut. 1 : 1, R.V. ;   [11]Matt. 7 : 13-14, cf. R.V. and R.V. marg., etc.

II. THE PEOPLE OF THE COVENANT

1

THE KINGDOM OF HEAVEN (Matt. 5 : 3)

Jesus sets before his disciples the portrait of a character : and the character is his own. Not even in Jesus could that character be perfected without training and effort : and both have reached a climax in the Temptation, from which he emerges with that absorption in and dependence on the will of God which the Beatitudes define and the remainder of the Sermon illustrates.

The Beatitudes are not a list of attributes which may be shown one by one in different people, any of whom may thereby qualify for the Kingdom of God. They describe a single personality seen from different sides ; but the continual emphasis on the plural pronouns—" they shall inherit ", " they shall see God " —proclaims that while the perfect example of this character is to be found in Jesus alone, it is also the character of each member of the class of people who are to find their true home in his Kingdom. They, and they alone, can be its citizens.

No single English word quite conveys the twofold meaning of king's rule and king's realm which the word rendered " kingdom " contains. Nor would it be correct to say that it meant to those who heard Jesus only a political dominion. Its secular use is illustrated when in Rabbinic writings " the kingdom " means the Roman government in Palestine. But its religious use can best be seen in connection with the Shema. Twice daily, when he lay down and when he rose up,[1] the devout Jew recited the words of Deut. 6 : 4-5, " Hear, O Israel ; the Lord our God is one Lord : and thou shalt love the Lord thy God with all thine heart . . ." ; in thus acknowledging God's sovereignty and his own responsibility under it he was said to take on him " the yoke of the kingdom of heaven ". This wide sense of the word was rooted in the Old Testament. David says of God Himself : " The Lord hath established his throne in the heavens ; and his kingdom ruleth over all . . . Bless the Lord, all ye his works, in all places of his dominion. "[2] It is true that this passage is prophetic, coming as a climax in the Psalm of Redemption, but this does not alter the sense, which is clearly : " The Divine sovereignty rules throughout His dominion ".[3] To the oriental mind " kingdom " is a highly personal conception, the sovereignty of a particular monarch, and only in a secondary sense is it the land over which that sovereignty extends.

At the same time the sovereignty must be exercised somewhere. It is to the unique history of the people of God's own possession[4] that we must look for an understanding of the Kingdom as a Bible term. In that record the sovereignty first embraces the covenant-people who are constituted " a kingdom of priests " while still in the wilderness, but also includes the land which is given them to inherit. They were on a journey ; their goal was to enter into the land for which God had brought them out of Egypt. And while it was not only for the sake of the land of Canaan that they were redeemed from bondage—for He " bare them on eagles'

[1]Deut. 6 : 7 ; [2]Psa. 103 : 19-22 ; [3]cf. also 2 Chron. 13 : 5 ; Psa. 22 : 28 ; also the parallelism of " kingdom " with " power " in Psa. 145 : 11 ; [4]Exod. 19 : 5.

wings " in order that He might bring them unto Himself[5]—yet it is also true that without the land sanctified by God's choice and assured by His promise the Kingdom was incomplete. With the coming of David on " the throne of the Lord ", the Kingdom finds its heart in the place of God's choice which becomes His habitation, " the city of the Great King."

A kingdom, then, comprises—first, the rule of a king : secondly, the relation between the king and his subjects ; and thirdly, the land they inhabit and over which his law is in force. But the relation may exist before even a settled territory has been gained ; and in Israel the kingdom as a political entity rested on the foundation of the covenant. Without the covenant there would have been no kingdom ; certainly not the Kingdom of God. It is for this reason that, while the rule is intensely personal, this kingdom has a constitution in a fuller sense than any of the surrounding nations. The covenant includes in its terms a system of law penetrating every part of national and individual life, and the administration of that law is in the hands of an appointed priesthood.

The oriental idea of sovereignty is emphasized by the contemporary phrase " the kingdom of the heavens ", which is so characteristic of Matthew. It is the Kingdom of Him who is enthroned in the heavens, and the metonymy is used by Jewish custom to avoid direct mention of God. While Jesus is not bound to the custom, it would be in accord with his practice to conform to it in general, and Matthew's phrase may represent his actual words, while the other evangelists paraphrase it as " the Kingdom of God " for the benefit of non-

[5]Exod. 19 : 4.

Jewish readers. The two expressions are strictly equivalent.

We need not stress the fact here that Jewish thought of the Kingdom always looked forward in the spirit of the prophetic hope to the day when " the Lord shall be king over all the earth ". This would be the " appearing " or " revelation " of God's Kingdom : and so the Targum renders " The Lord shall be King " by the words, " The Kingdom of God shall be revealed ". With the land under the dominion of Rome, the contrast between the " kingdom of the world " and the " kingdom of the heavens" was painfully manifest. The Zealots, indeed, contended that " the yoke of the Law " freed them from " the yoke of the kingdom " (that is, the foreign government) ; but there were others, such as Simeon, who in meekness waited eagerly for that " consolation of Israel " which would also be the manifestation of God's kingship to the world. When the Galilean people, suffering under a burden of taxation and illegal exactions, wanted to make Jesus a king by force because he had fed them with bread in the wilderness, they betray the material side of the popular hope.

In the teaching of Jesus the Kingdom of the Heavens is the subject of an announcement.[6] This is to be " published abroad ".[7] While it was a message of good news, it also called for repentance.[8] A number of verbs are used which imply that the kingdom is a coming dispensation : to be " nigh at hand " ; to come ; to appear ; to be seen.[9] The Kingdom of God is an order under which men are placed, because the patriarchs

[6]Matt. 4 : 23 ; 24 : 14, where it is simply " the Kingdom " ; Luke 4 : 43 ; [7]Luke 9 : 60, R.V. ; [8]Matt. 4 : 17 ; [9]Luke 21 : 31 ; Matt. 6 : 10 ; Mark 9 : 1 ; Luke 22 : 18 ; 19 : 11 ; 9 : 27.

and prophets can be seen as its subjects; and in it men may recline at table (A.V. " sit down ") ; and may eat and drink.[10] A man may be great, greater, greatest, less, least in the Kingdom ; yet in it all the righteous shall " shine forth as the sun ", in accordance with Dan. 12 : 3.[11]

The Kingdom may be " shut against men " by unfaithful teachers who prevent their access to it by misleading them.[12] On the other hand men may be invited to it ; and may enter into it.[13] In the days of Jesus' flesh it was at hand ; it was in their midst ; it had " come upon " them.[14] It could even force itself upon men[15] and, correspondingly, forceful men could seize it ; or as Luke had it, could force their way into it.[16] Yet men might be " not far " from it, fitted or unfitted for it, worthy or unworthy.[17] The Kingdom can be sought earnestly, or striven for.[18] It can be given ; but it must first be accepted or received before men can take possession of it as an inheritance.[19] It belongs to those who receive it, whether by way of title or in actual possession.[20] It had been prepared or made ready.[21]

The disciples entrusted with the message are given " the keys of the kingdom of heaven ".[22] But there will also be a day when " the door of the marriage chamber " is closed against " foolish virgins " ; and

[10]Luke 13 : 28 ; Matt. 8 : 11 ; Luke 13 : 29 ; Matt. 26 : 29 ; Luke 22 : 30 ; [11]Matt. 5 : 19 ; 18 : 1, 4 ; 11 : 11 ; 5 : 19 ; 13 : 43 ; [12]Matt. 23 : 13 ; [13]Matt. 22 : 3, etc. ; 5 : 20 ; 7 : 21 ; 18 : 3 ; 19 : 23, etc. ; [14]Matt. 10 : 7 ; Luke 17 : 21 ; Matt. 12 : 28 ; [15]Matt. 11 : 12 ; the verb is active, not passive as in A.V., the usage being illustrated by an inscription of B.C. 24 ; [16]Luke 16 : 16 ; [17]Mark 12 : 34 ; Luke 9 : 62 ; 20 : 35 ; [18]Matt. 6 : 33 ; 13 : 45 ; Luke 12 : 31 ; [19]Luke 12 : 32 ; Mark 10 : 15 ; Matt. 25 : 34 ; [20]Matt. 5 : 3 ; 19 : 14 ; [21]Matt. 25 : 34 ; [22]Matt. 16 : 19.

people may be " cast forth ",[23] or be expelled.[24] The " sons of the kingdom " may either be those who claim it by descent and may be cast forth, or those in whose hearts the message concerning it springs to life, and who are therefore sons by faith.[25]

From these expressions we may gather the meaning which the word has on the lips of Jesus. It is a future order in which the promises to the fathers will be fulfilled ; and those who are admitted to share their blessings will be their spiritual kin. It has a historical basis, for the claim of the descendants of Abraham to be " sons of the kingdom " is acknowledged historically while it is rejected on spiritual grounds. That men may enter this Kingdom through faith is the substance of the message of Good News ; and because fitness for the Kingdom is determined by faith and the character which faith develops, the Message is at the same time a call to repentance. Acceptance of the message in a child-like spirit of faith is acceptance of " the Kingdom ". With the coming of the King, " the Kingdom " was among them. His presence brought the powers of the kingdom into their midst, and brought also an invitation so pressing, an opportunity so urgent, that " the King-dom " might be said to force itself upon men. Yet they had of their own freewill to accept the call ; and while men of earnest simplicity might be said to press into it, " the Kingdom " also overtook with something akin to calamity those who were not in a state of mind to receive it.

" The Kingdom ", then, has a threefold meaning. First and last it is the future reign into which men may enter through judgment, and this must govern all

[23]Matt. 25 : 10 ; Luke 13 : 25 ; Matt. 22 : 13 ; Luke 13 : 28 ; [24]Matt. 8 : 12—a different word is used ; [25]Matt. 8 : 12 ; 13 : 38.

secondary meanings. But it is also the power, authority, sovereignty, vested in the King; and in this sense the Kingdom was in their midst when he was among them, searching and testing them by their response to him. Further, the Kingdom is the message through which men become related to the future order. The use of " Kingdom " in this sense is something more than a metonymy, because the message is an operative power working among men to prepare the materials out of which the future Kingdom is to be formed; and the relation to the Kingdom of those who accept the message is more than a hope : it is a covenant. Because covenant and kingdom are inseparable for the people of God, the present possessive can be used even of the time of their probation : " theirs is the Kingdom ". The ground of their blessedness is their relation to God and His King.

The primary meaning of the Kingdom as the future order makes its citizens tent-dwellers in the world of today. They belong to it no more than the Fathers belonged to the settled polity of Canaan; and Isaac, surrendering his wells and leaving the fertile plain for the bare hills of Beersheba to avoid strife, sets the pattern for their lives.[26] By this light they see a marked antithesis in the Lord's sayings. The people of the Covenant are contrasted with the environment in which they live as aliens; their qualities are the opposite of those who seek success in the world. And their present is no less sharply contrasted with their future; in the Kingdom it is they who will be exalted. These clear logical contrasts—between the saints and the world, and between their present and their future—give form to the Beatitudes and a foundation to the whole discourse.   [26]Gen. 26 : 12-23.

2

THE FUTURE CITIZENS (Matt. 5 : 3)

Blessed are the poor in spirit :
For theirs is the kingdom of heaven.

" Blessed is the man . . ." say the first and many
subsequent Psalms. Always the idea conveyed is " O
the happiness of the man . . . ! " The word used is 27
times rendered " blessed " and 18 times " happy ", and
implies a happiness which is consequent upon straightness, rightness, uprightness, for the same word also
means " to be straight or right ". It is found in the
name Asher ; and the forerunner of all later usage
seems to be in Moses' blessing of the people : " Happy
art thou, O Israel : who is like unto thee, a people
saved by the Lord ? "[1] Only men are said to be " blessed"
in this sense. For praise and adoration to God, and for
God's benediction upon men, there is a quite different
word. The same distinction is preserved in Greek.

Blessedness is happiness raised to bliss ; and in this
term the " man of sorrows " describes a supreme joy.
Jesus does not only say that the poor in spirit shall be
happy when, like his Master, he has " endured the
cross " for the joy set before him ; he says that such a
man is happy now. The condition of those whom he
describes is the best that men can have, because they
are the true Israel of God ; and they may find joy in the
knowledge of their privilege. Even in " the days of his
flesh " there was a strong and holy joy in him who was
" acquainted with grief ". It was reflected from the
future day of his glory ; but it was even more a joy in
the fellowship with his Father which he already possessed,
and which his entry into his Kingdom would only con-

[1]Deut. 33 : 29.

firm. That joy will be shared in some measure by all who are truly followers of him.

Who are the " poor in spirit " ? The expansion in Matthew of the blessing which occurs in Luke as " Blessed are ye poor " recalls Isa. 66 : 2 : " To this man will I look, even to him that is poor and of a contrite spirit, and that trembleth at my word ". The contrast implied in those words is not with the rich but with the proud and hardened heart. The Hebrew word rendered " poor " does not of itself mean those who are in penury ; it means those who are humbled or bowed down ; especially those who are bowed down by ill-treatment and by being deprived of their rights. As the people in that condition were so often the poor suffering under the arrogance of the rich, the term came to denote the class who were in poverty. This class would be the special care of a righteous king, and above all of the Messiah.[2] The term can be applied to Israel in the wilderness when they are viewed as the congregation of God, so that Psa. 68 : 10 says of that time, "Thou didst prepare of thy goodness for the poor".

This and some other words " came gradually to imply more than persons who were merely in some kind of social subjection or material need : they came to denote the godly poor, the suffering righteous, the persons who, whether ' bowed down ', or ' needy ' or ' reduced ', were the godly servants of Jehovah. It is evident that in ancient Israel, especially in later times, piety prevailed more among the humbler classes than among the wealthier and ruling classes."[3]   " Poor " thus came to be almost synonymous with the God-

[2]Psa. 72 : 2, 4, 12 ; cf. Jer. 22 : 16 ; [3]DRIVER, in *Hastings' Dictionary of the Bible*.

fearing class, the " remnant " who would be saved out of the judgment coming upon Israel.[4]

The Greek in Matt. 5 : 3 properly implies one who is destitute, but as the LXX show considerable freedom in their choice of equivalent for the various Hebrew words for " poor " and " meek ", it would be unwise to press the classical meaning too closely. The Aramaic which underlies it denoted " those who are oppressed by the tyrannical power of evil and who long for the intervention of God. The poor are primarily the faithful men and women who are oppressed by the present world order."[5] They were men and women " looking for the city which hath the foundations, whose Builder and Maker God is ".[6] While no single English word can cover it, the attitude of mind is beautifully indicated in the phrase " waiting (in the sense of an expectant looking) for the consolation of Israel ".[7]

The sacrifices of God are a broken spirit ; and Isaiah had uttered the daringly beautiful paradox that " the high and lofty One that inhabiteth eternity " finds His dwelling with the humble spirit, and will revive him in the day when He shall declare the perfection of peace to the far off and the near, and will heal them.[8] To be poor, in these words of Jesus, is not an accident of circumstance but a quality of life : a life which is not centred in possession and not rooted in the present world order—not even to the extent of trying to overturn that order, for the political zealot and the rebel are as much immersed in the world as is the conserver of things as they are. And this word " poor ", like the whole group of sayings, has its direct

[4]Zeph. 3 : 11-13 ; [5]HOSKYNS & DAVEY, *The Riddle of the N.T.* ; [6]Heb. 11 : 10 ; [7]Luke 2 : 25 ; [8]Psa. 51 : 17 ; Psa. 34 : 18 ; Isa. 57 : 15, 19 ; cf. ch. 26 : 3 and margin A.V.

source in the Hebrew prophets. Jesus focuses in one phrase all this teaching which runs through the words of the ancient seers, and has its beginning in the lives of the patriarchs : this God-given insight into the paradox that the Creative Power, because He is Almighty, must needs find only in the lowly hearted those able to be received into kinship with Himself; and for that reason these—and not any who rest on privilege or a secret self-sufficiency—are they who shall find their abiding home in the Age to Come. It is these who are the " babes " whom Jesus contrasts with the " wise and prudent " ; because they are not sheathed in a hard shell of self-sufficiency, they are able to learn of him who is " meek and lowly in heart ".[9]

[9]Matt. 11 : 25-30.

3

JOY FOR THE MOURNERS (Matt. 5 : 4)

Blessed are they that mourn :
For they shall be comforted

Those who mourn are not those who are mournful, who might only wish " to be seen of men to fast ". The blessed are those who mourn for Zion because only in God do they find a true resting place. Their home is in Him, and not in the world as it is ; and when His day comes they shall be given " the oil of joy for mourning, the garment of praise for the spirit of heaviness ".[1] " I will restore comforts to him and to his mourners " is

[1]Isa. 61 : 3 ;

said of the man of " a contrite and humble spirit ", and is connected with the promise of reconciliation contained in the words, " Peace, peace, to him that is far off, and to him that is near ".[2]   The tears with which the Israelites sow their seed, described in Psa. 126, are caused by " captivity " or oppression ; the laughter which afterwards fills their mouths is occasioned by the Lord's deliverance.   There is a captivity which all the people of God suffer until His kingdom and righteousness are in the earth. They are the prisoners of the world ; but more than that, they are in the bonds of sin or death. They are weighed down by the contrast between the glory of God and the evil of the world—and the weakness of their own flesh.[3] And the symbol of the reign of evil is the downtreading of God's " holy habitation ". In the day when Zion shall be exalted the Lord will "turn their mourning into joy, and will comfort them, and make them rejoice from their sorrow ".[4]   They are strengthened now by the knowledge that their Lord is leading them to that day.

In Isa. 61 : 1-3 it is the work of the Anointed to comfort all that mourn. But to think only of a gracious return for bygone sorrows would be to miss the pith of the prophecy. The Redeemer who will come to Zion says through the prophet : " The spirit of the Lord God is upon me ; because the Lord hath anointed me . . ."[5] The giving of the good message, binding up the brokenhearted, liberating the bondsmen and prisoners, and turning grief into praise, are the work of God Himself through One whom He has set apart ; and that work

[2]Isa. 57 : 15, 18, 19 ; cf. Eph. 2 : 14-18 ; [3]Twice Paul uses the verb " to mourn " of sorrow for sin in the ecclesia : 1 Cor. 5 : 2 ; 2 Cor. 12 : 21 ; [4]Jer. 31 : 13 ; [5]Isa. 59 : 20-61 : 1.

has an aim and consummation far outstretching the happiness of men. It is " that they might be called oaks of righteousness, the planting of the Lord, that he might be glorified ".[6]

The whole context of these words in Isa. 61 and 62 is filled with pictures of earthly blessedness. Even the Land itself is not a mere neutral mass on whose inert surface the building of the new Kingdom is laid. Isaiah apostrophizes the city of Zion when he says : " Thou shalt no more be termed Forsaken ; neither shall thy land any more be termed Desolate . . . the Lord delighteth in thee, and thy land shall be married. For as a young man marrieth a virgin, so shall thy sons marry thee : and as the bridegroom rejoiceth over the bride, so shall thy God rejoice over thee ".[7] Richer expression than that never could be given to the essential poetry of men's vital union with one significant land ; and the more intense the poetry is, the stronger and more tangible must be the basis from which it springs.

Words from this prophecy Jesus uses as the foundation of his own " words of grace "[8] in the Sermon on the Mount, as he did on at least two other critical occasions in his life. One was when in the Synagogue at Nazareth he declared himself to be the Anointed One in the prophets by quoting such part of the prophecy as applied to that stage of his work, and saying, " This day is this scripture fulfilled in your ears ".[9] The other was when the disciples of John came with the inquiry " Art thou he that should come, or look we for another? "[10] Jesus replied by citing the witness of his works in the very words of prophecies from Isaiah,

[6]Isa. 61 : 3 ;   [7]Isa. 62 : 4-5 ;   [8]Luke 4 : 22 ;   [9]Luke 4 : 16-21 ;
[10]Matt. 11 : 2-6 ; Luke 7 : 19-23.

including an allusion to this passage, and ended by identifying with himself that " tried foundation stone" which, while a source of sanctuary to the faithful, should also be a " stone of stumbling " to Israel. When, therefore, Jesus takes his seat on the mount and pronounces " blessed " the poor, the meek, and the mourners, he does what he alone can do ; he speaks as the Anointed of the Lord in whom the Kingdom has come near ; the making of the pronouncement is a Messianic act.

With all this in view Paul can write to the Thessalonians : " Now our Lord Jesus Christ himself, and God, even our Father, which hath loved us, and hath given us eternal comfort and good hope through grace, comfort your hearts, and stablish you in every good word and work".[11] Eternal comfort came to the disciples through the assurance of God's purpose in the risen Christ. The time would come to these disciples who heard the words on the Mount when they would " weep and lament " while the world rejoiced in its seeming triumph over the King of the Jews. But their sorrow then would be as birth pangs of a new joy, for he who was to be taken from them said, " I will see you again, and your heart shall rejoice, and your joy no man taketh from you".[12] The joy brought by the knowledge that " the Lord had risen indeed " was an earnest of the joy of the future age when Zion shall be " a crown of beauty in the hand of the Lord, and a royal diadem in the hand of thy God".[13]

[11]2 Thess. 2 : 16-17 ; [12]John 16 : 20-23 ; [13]Isa. 62 : 3.

4

THE HERITAGE OF THE MEEK (Matt. 5 : 5)

Blessed are the meek :
For they shall inherit the earth.

While the poor are those who have been humbled, the meek are humble in themselves. They are not the weak, but the teachable ; and so " the meek will he guide in judgment : and the meek will he teach his way . . . The secret of the Lord is with them that fear him, and he will show them his covenant ".[1] Solomon says, " Surely he scorneth the scorners, but giveth grace unto the lowly ".[2] In these the same word is used as for the " meek " in Psa. 37 : 11, whose inheritance of the earth is promised both in the Psalm and in the Beatitude. Meekness is first a disposition towards God ; an awe of Him which results in confident dependence on Him as righteous and faithful. But humility towards God has its effect in a forgiving and self-abnegating spirit towards men. That quality is shown above all in the example of Christ, by whose " meekness and gentleness " Paul can " beseech " the Corinthians.[3]

To inherit means to enter into possession. " He that putteth his trust in me shall *possess* the land, and shall *inherit* my holy mountain ", runs an illuminating parallelism in Isaiah 57 : 13. The verb is interwoven with the entire history of Israel, and it draws its meaning from the promise that God will be a God to them, and they shall be His people. Actual dwelling in the Land is the literal groundwork of that Divine Covenant.

This heritage, says Jesus, God gives to the meek ; the people whose heart is not set in possessions shall receive the everlasting possession, and this possession will

[1]Psa. 25 : 9-14 ; [2]Prov. 3 : 34 ; cf. James 4 : 6 ; 1 Peter 5 : 5 ; [3]2 Cor. 10 : 1 ; cf. Eph. 4 : 2 ; Jas. 3 : 17 ; 1 Peter 3 : 4.

be on the face of the land. Two consequences follow :
that those who are not meek and who now possess it will
no longer be there ; and that the hope of the meek is in
a bodily life lived in material surroundings, and not in
the survival of death by an intangible ego. And with
those very obvious deductions from a simple statement,
we are face to face with the basic things in religious and
philosophical belief : things which determine not only
our ideas but what our objects in life are, and how we
try to carry them out.

The deductions become sure conclusions on reading
the 37th Psalm, with which the saying of Jesus corresponds almost word for word. The theme of the Psalm,
reiterated and expanded with the most varied imagery,
is that the wicked will vanish as utterly as yesterday's
smoke, while the righteous will remain, founded and
sure in the favour of God. It forcibly recalls the sayings
of Jesus and of John the Baptist that the tree which
does not bear good fruit will be " hewn down and cast
into the fire " ;[4] and nowhere else in Scripture—and
that is saying a great deal—are the two radical ideas
of the transience of the wicked and the ultimate permanence of the righteous contrasted more decisively.

It would be easy to explore at length in the Psalms
this idea that God " will not for ever suffer the righteous
to be moved ", but will bring the wicked " down into
the depth of the pit " :[5] the point which must be made
plain is that this clearly expressed antithesis of the
transient and the abiding rests on an equally clear
teaching on what human nature is. To understand
what the spiritual aims of Jesus were when he quoted
Psa. 37 : 11 it is essential to know what the words mean
[4]Matt. 3 : 10 ; 7 : 19 ; [5]Psa. 55 : 22-23 ; cf. modern versions.

in their setting in the mental world of the Old Testament. The radical alternatives of transience and permanence are as truly the basis of his teaching as of the Psalmist. For those who hear his words there is either the life of the Kingdom of God in the coming Age, or there is utter destruction. The standard of judgment which decides their future—" whosoever heareth these sayings of mine, and doeth them "—is the standard of the Psalms and the Prophets. Life is not a thing possessed as of native right : it is in the hand of God, to maintain or to end it : "Behold, all souls are mine ; as the soul of the father, so also the soul of the son is mine : the soul that sinneth, it shall die".[6] It is the reality of that stark opposition between death and life which gives such driving urgency to the Gospel of Jesus. This opposition is implied in his blessing on the meek ; for the words cannot be divorced from their Old Testament context.

" They shall inherit " was well understood in contemporary speech to refer to Messiah's day. In Zephaniah it is said that the " remnant " of the Lord's " nation " shall " inherit " the lands which His judgments have left desolate ;[7] and earlier in the chapter this " remnant " have been addressed with the words : " Seek ye the Lord, all ye meek of the earth, which have wrought his judgment ; seek righteousness, seek meekness : it may be ye shall be hid in the day of the Lord's anger ".[8] " I will cause the remnant of this people to possess (R.V. : inherit) all these things ", says Zechariah.[9] While we are told the Hebrew terms do not necessarily mean " to take possession of a paternal estate ", the idea of the legal title as heir is clearly

[6]Ezek. 18 : 4 ; [7]Zeph. 2 : 9, R.V. ; [8]verse 3 ; [9]Zech. 8 : 12.

brought out in one of James's many allusions to the
Sermon : " Hath not God chosen the poor of this world
rich in faith, and heirs of the Kingdom which he hath
promised to them that love him? "[10]   Peter's first letter
also is permeated with the words of his Master ; and,
in exhorting the brethren to give " blessing " for
railing, he adds : " Knowing that to this ye were called,
that ye should inherit a blessing ".[11] The fulfilment of
the promise is in the vision of John : " Thou hast made
us unto our God kings and priests, and we shall reign
on the earth ".[12] The possession into which they are
to enter is the result of sonship because they are "joint-
heirs " with the Son ; for " he that overcometh shall
inherit all things ; and I will be his God, and he shall
be my son ".[13]

The man who overcomes is the man rich in faith.
Because he receives the experiences of life in faith, he is
humbled by them instead of being embittered. Because
he sees the vision of God's glory, he mourns over present
darkness.   Because he worships God alone, he is not
only humbled but humble. The quality of life which he
manifests is only possible because God is to him the
ever-present Reality. The character fit for the kingdom
is exactly that displayed in the Lord's victory over
temptation. He himself is the poor in spirit and the
meek one when he says : " Man doth not live by bread
alone . . . thou shalt not tempt the Lord thy God . . .
thou shalt worship the Lord thy God, and him only
shalt thou serve."

[10]James 2 : 5 ; [11]1 Peter 3 : 9 ; [12]Rev. 5 : 10 ; [13]Rom 8 : 16-17 ;
Gal. 4 : 7 ; Rev. 21 : 7.

5

THE FEAST OF THE KINGDOM (Matt. 5 : 6)

Blessed are they that hunger and thirst after righteousness :
For they shall be filled.

One of the Proverbs reads in the American Jewish version : " The hunger of the labouring man laboureth for him : for his mouth compelleth him ".[1] The needs of a healthy appetite give zest to work, and with the effort, appetite gains a keener edge. So it is with things of the mind : strong desire for spiritual food makes the work of gaining it seem light, while the effort in turn sharpens the desire. But hunger is not always healthy in this world : too often " the famished crave in vain their fill ". And though in the word of God a rich feast is always open to those who will turn their minds to it, the spiritually minded also suffer a sense of deprivation. Like David, when he had fled into the wilderness of Judea, they can say :

> My soul thirsteth for thee, my flesh longeth for thee,
> In a dry and weary land where no water is ;
> So have I looked upon thee in the sanctuary,
> To see thy power and thy glory.[2]

Though for himself he may " taste and see that the Lord is good ", it is precisely as his own spiritual sense grows that the godly man becomes more aware of the gulf between the holiness of God and the corruption of man. There is a hunger which must always remain unfilled until " the mouth of them that speak lies " is " stopped ",[3] a thirst which will never be quenched until God's name is hallowed in the earth. In only one place could a present satisfaction be found for that

[1]Prov. 16 : 26 ; [2]Psa. 63 : 1-2 ; [3]Psa. 63 : 11.

hunger, and it was the place which God had chosen to manifest Himself. To the courts of the Temple the worshipper might go to perform his appointed service, knowing that within the sanctuary the Lord shone forth over the mercy seat between the Cherubim. That holy place where atonement was made year by year was the assurance that in the end, as surely as He lives, " all the earth shall be filled with the glory of the Lord " in the day when the world is reconciled to Him.

To come in this way to the sanctuary is to be brought through the mediation of the priesthood into the presence of the Great King, and that idea of appearing in audience in a royal presence is in the mind of the levitical Psalmist.[4] It is in the sanctuary that the Israelite gains a true sense of values which gives him contentment in life.[5] But because of the imperfection in the world and in himself, even the spiritual satisfaction to be found there is imperfect, and only a foretaste of a fullness to come. For the final satisfaction of all his hunger he looks to the coming day, and that is a time when neither David nor the Levites will any longer be barred by the flesh from entry into the Most Holy itself. No longer will they approach only so far into the Divine Presence, and then only through the offices of the priesthood. As God spoke with Moses " face to face ", and " the similitude of the Lord did he behold ", so David will see, without any veil between, the fullness of the Divine glory.

As for me, I will behold thy face in righteousness :
I shall be satisfied, when I awake, with thy likeness.[6]

How often in Psalms and Proverbs bodily hunger and its satisfaction are made figures of the spiritual life

[4]Psa. 42 : 2 ;   [5]Psa. 73 : 17 ;   [6]Psa. 17 : 15 ; 22 : 25-26.

46

may be gathered from these examples : and when Jesus employs the same imagery we can be assured that he had these Scriptures in mind. Nor would he think of these only, for Isaiah uses the same figure ; and as in the Psalms, so also in the prophets, the satisfaction of the hungry and thirsty belongs to the coming day when the poor are exalted and blessing is poured out upon the meek.[7]

Because His bounty is bestowed on those whose character wins God's approval, it must be preceded by a judgment which separates them from the world and vindicates them in the eyes of men ; and so to those rebellious descendants of Abraham who " forsake the Lord, and forget his holy mountain ", the word comes through the prophet : " Behold, my servants shall eat, but ye shall be hungry : behold, my servants shall drink, but ye shall be thirsty : behold, my servants shall rejoice, but ye shall be ashamed . . . For behold, I create new heavens and a new earth, and the former things shall not be remembered nor come into mind ".[8]

Examination of the setting of such sayings invariably leads back to the prophecies of the Anointed of the Lord. It is through the Messiah that the hungry will be satisfied. The one who is addressed in, for instance, Isa. 49 : 7-10, is clearly the suffering Servant of Isaiah 53 and elsewhere, who is also the Anointed in Isaiah 61, and the Messianic ruler in the day when the righteousness of Zion shall go forth as brightness ; and with this recurring figure in the prophecy Jesus deliberately identifies himself.[9] It is because he is given for the purpose of " a covenant of the people " that he is able to

[7]Isa.41 : 17-20 ; 44 : 3-4 ; 49 : 7-10 ; [8]Isa. 65 : 2, 11, 13-18 ; [9]Isa. 62 : 1 ; Matt. 16 : 21 ; 17 : 22-23 ; 20 : 17-19, etc. ; Luke 24 : 25, 26, 27, 44-48.

bring release to those in bondage, to slake for ever their hunger and thirst ; for he shall lead them beside those streams of Isa. 49 : 10, which recall so vividly the " waters of rest " beside which the shepherd Psalmist was led by the Lord, his everlasting Shepherd.[10] While Jesus already gives to those who seek him a liberation from the fear of death and a satisfying of hunger for the righteousness of God, yet manifestly this vision of the prophet cannot be realized as a whole until it is fulfilled in God's kingdom.

" If any man thirst ", says Jesus, " let him come unto me, and drink " ; " No man cometh unto the Father, but by me " ; " I am the bread of life ; he that cometh unto me shall never hunger ; and he that believeth in me shall never thirst ".[11] In all these sayings, and in his repeated words, " Come unto me ", Jesus is making conscious use of the prophecy of Isaiah 55, with its summons to " everyone that thirsteth ". But he had already done no less in the Sermon on the Mount, when in uttering the blessing on those who hunger he tacitly presented himself as the one through whom the blessing would be fulfilled.

Beyond doubt it is the teaching of Jesus that that " bread of life " which is himself is literally the means of living : the point of the metaphor is that without that food there can be no life beyond this transient mortality. But those who feed on him he will raise up at the last day ; they will be accounted worthy to " attain that age ", and will be " children of the resurrection " ; and from that point in time they cannot die any more.[12] To bring God's purpose with them to fruit His word has gone forth ; that word in due time took tangible form

[10]Psa. 23 : 2 ; [11]John 7 : 37 ; 4 : 14 ; 6 : 35 ; 14 : 6 ; [12]John 6 : 39-40 ; Luke 20 : 35-36.

and " was made flesh " in Christ Jesus ; and faith in him is " seed to the sower, and bread to the eater ", building up a new manhood for the life of the Age to Come.[13]

In this prophetic imagery which is so deep-rooted in the Old Testament we have the source of all Jesus' sayings which liken the Kingdom to a banquet. These are the words he is recalling when he says that " many " shall come from the east and the west, and recline at table (for such is the meaning of to " sit down ") in the Kingdom with Abraham, Isaac and Jacob, when the " children of the kingdom " shall be cast forth into the outer darkness.[14] The same prophecy is reflected in his promise to those who shall " eat and drink " at his table in his kingdom.[15] And it is also in mind when he retorts with the Parable of the Great Supper to one who said : " Blessed is he that shall eat bread in the kingdom of God ".[16]

The likening of the Kingdom to a banquet conveys a threefold thought. First, those who eat of it are filled ; they are completely satisfied ; every spiritual desire is met, every need supplied. Secondly, the meal is a communion ; all who partake—King, fathers, Israelites, or those who were " afar off " and have been " made nigh "—are joined in an unbreakable fellowship. Thirdly, it is a ritual feast—a Feast of Tabernacles— which the Lord will make on His holy mountain, when He will " destroy the face of the covering cast over all peoples " ; for He will have " swallowed up death in victory ".[17] In its fullest meaning, therefore, the promise of the Beatitude, " they shall be filled "—or " satisfied to the full "—is a prophecy of the Kingdom. And they

[13]cf. Isa. 55 : 8-13 ;   [14]Matt. 8 : 11-12 ;   Luke 13 : 29 ;   [15]Luke 22 : 30 ;   [16]Luke 14 : 15-24 ;   [17]Isa. 25 : 6-8.

are to find their satisfaction not merely in an ethical rectitude, but specifically in the righteousness of God. There is nothing self-centred in their desire : not even the sublimated self-centredness of desiring above all that *they* shall be righteous. They yearn for *God's* righteousness to be manifested, *His* holiness to be vindicated, in an earth filled with His glory. It is the desire for the appearing of the Branch of Jesse on whom the spirit of the Lord shall rest, who shall judge the poor with righteousness, and reprove with equity for the meek of the earth ; for " righteousness shall be the girdle of his loins, and faithfulness the girdle of his reins ".[18]

Yet they too are embraced in this desire : they cannot wish for the righteousness of God to be manifest in the earth unless they long for it to be fulfilled in themselves. Looking forward in the spirit to that future day, the prophet finds his satisfaction in the prospect of his own righteousness, both individually and as a part of a larger whole : " I will greatly rejoice in the Lord, my soul shall be joyful in my God ; for he hath clothed me with the garments of salvation, he hath covered me with the robe of righteousness. . . . For as the earth bringeth forth her bud, and as the garden causeth the things that are sown in it to spring forth ; so the Lord God will cause righteousness and praise to spring forth before all nations ".[19]

While the meek, the merciful, and the rest, are called blessed for qualities which they already possess, Christ does not say : " Blessed are the righteous " ; he pronounces men blessed who have an unsatisfied longing for righteousness. But if this righteousness of

[18]Isa. 11 : 1-5 ; [19]Isa. 61 : 10-11.

God is genuinely desired for the future day of His glory, it is no less desired within this present life. It is impossible to desire righteousness in the abstract, or as something which happens only in the Millennium; and it is impossible to desire it for others and not for oneself. The line between deathfulness and deathlessness for the body is sharp; we shall be changed " in a moment, in the twinkling of an eye ". But there can be no such instantaneous change for the mind: in character we only become what we constantly and strongly desire to be, and the becoming begins now. To those reborn in Christ Peter says: " As newborn babes, desire the sincere milk of the word, that ye may grow thereby "[20]; and the R.V. reads: " long for . . . that ye may grow thereby unto salvation ". Spiritual hunger and thirst is for present righteousness because it is for the future, and the beginnings of the future are in the present; and hunger for righteousness is hunger for the food of righteousness, which is the Word. And the food is found in him who says: " I am the bread of life ".

Those words are the Lord's own exposition of the parable he had enacted in feeding the multitude. Often in the Gospels the action of Jesus, or his comment on the action of others, illustrates the sayings of the Sermon on the Mount: and the Feeding of the Five Thousand illustrates the blessing on the hungry. To feed the flock is the function of a shepherd; only he, as the Good Shepherd, can give the food of eternal life, because the food he offers is himself. Those who " hunger and thirst after righteousness " must come to him. Yet even this saying reflects his own character; the reason he can feed others is that he himself has hungered after righteousness, and because he could say: " My meat is to do the

[20] I Peter 2 : 2.

51

will of him that sent me, and to finish his work ".[21]
Through " the travail of his soul " he becomes the
Passover Lamb on whom all may feast, and his blood
poured out becomes the emblem for them not of death
but of life. He can satisfy the hungry because he himself is "satisfied " with life evermore and fullness of joy
in the presence of God.[22]

Some may think that this saying is concerned with
" righteousness " in the sense of right conduct, and not
with the theological concept of salvation. They may say
that to follow our contemplation to the point which we
have is to detach the saying from its bearing on daily
life and lose it in a metaphysical cloud. The first answer
is that in so doing we have followed the Scripture. We
have examined the Old Testament use of words in the
conviction that here we find the meaning in which Christ
would use them ; and we have tested this conclusion
by comparison with his words and acts in other parts of
the Gospel record. As a result, we find ample evidence
that we cannot confine his thought to a merely ethical
channel. A further reply is that the criticism misconceives
the nature of " righteousness ", as though it were
primarily conduct between man and man, and chiefly
had reference to this life. Righteousness is life lived with
the vision of God and His purpose constantly before
our eyes ; hunger for righteousness is such a desire for
that purpose to be accomplished in the world and in
ourselves that it becomes the controlling power in our
character and conduct. His is indeed a purpose of goodness, mercy and truth, and demands the same qualities
in those who would be associated with it ; but there can
be no divorce between the conduct of life and the

[21]John 4 : 34 ; [22]Isa. 53 : 11 ; Psa. 16 : 11 ; Psa. 91 : 16.

purpose of God in Christ which gives it meaning, any more than there can be a divorce between the loving self-sacrifice of Christ and the object for which that sacrifice was made.

With that last thought our contemplation may be brought to a focus. As men of old found their satisfaction in the sanctuary where God made Himself manifest, so we may come week by week with the assurance which Christ has given : " Where two or three are gathered together in my name, there am I in the midst of them ". We may partake of emblems he himself has given, which represent him as the bread and wine of life. As in these emblems we look back to his sacrifice, by his own words we also look forward to his Father's Kingdom, when he will drink anew of the fruit of the vine.[23] And in this rite we may see the embodiment for him and for all who follow him of the blessing of those who hunger and thirst after righteousness : " for they shall be filled".

[23]Matt. 26 : 29.

6

MERCY FOR THE MERCIFUL (Matt. 5 : 7)

Blessed are the merciful :
For they shall obtain mercy.

The root of the saying is to be found in words of David :

> Therefore hath the Lord recompensed me according to my righteousness,
> According to the cleanness of my hands in his eyesight :
> With the merciful thou wilt show thyself merciful ;
> With an upright man thou wilt show thyself upright ;
> With the pure thou wilt show thyself pure ;
> And with the froward thou wilt show thyself froward.
> For thou wilt save the afflicted people ;
> But wilt bring down high looks.[1]

God is always the same, and the qualities He shows towards men are constant, and will be experienced in human life. Yet those qualities are not always revealed in the present age ; and David in this Psalm stands on the ground of his past experience of God to look forward to a day when God will "save the afflicted". The Psalm, drawing on the events of the Exodus for its imagery, foreshadows the day described in Habakkuk in language which echoes David's, and looks to God's visible intervention when He will vindicate both the qualities embodied in His Memorial Name,[2] and the man who reflects those qualities and whom therefore He loves. Seen against the background of Law, Psalms

[1]Psa. 18 : 24-27 ; [2]Hab. 3 ; Exod. 34 : 6-7.

and Prophets, the expression " to obtain mercy " is bound up with God's covenant, and carries the thought forward to the days of God's Kingdom and righteousness.

What the quality of mercy is in the sense in which Jesus uses the term may best be found from examining the two occasions on which he quotes Hosea 6 : 6 : " I will have mercy, and not sacrifice ". The enquiry will lead back, not only to the immediate context of the words in Hosea, but to the wider use of the word rendered " mercy " (*hesed*) both in Hosea 6 : 6, and Psa. 18 : 25. Also frequently rendered " lovingkindness ", it can be applied (1) to God's attitude towards men ; (2) to men's attitude towards God ; and (3) to men's attitude towards one another. As used of God, it is specifically associated with His covenant. Dr. N. H. Snaith points out that out of 43 cases in the Old Testament in which the noun *hesed* is linked by a copula with another noun, in 23 it is associated with firmness, truth, faithfulness ; in seven with covenant ; and in four with righteousness. Out of 18 cases in which *hesed* occurs in a parallelism, in nine the other member of the parallelism is one of the words meaning faithfulness, and in four a word for righteousness. A classic example is Micah 7 : 20, where " the truth to Jacob " is paralleled with " the mercy to Abraham ", and both are equivalents for the Abrahamic covenant. In such a connexion *hesed* might fairly be rendered " covenant-love ".[3]

The same word is used in Hosea 6 : 4 of Israel's attitude to God, when He tells them : " Your *goodness* is as a morning cloud ". The words quoted by Jesus follow in the same context, the theme of which is,

[3]N. H. SNAITH, *Distinctive Ideas of the O.T.*

" They have not known the Lord ".[4]   The context leaves it beyond doubt that the " mercy " which God desires is an affectionate fulfilment of the covenant with Him : " I desired mercy . . . but they have transgressed my covenant ".   By contrast, God's " mercy " towards Israel is shown in His faithfulness in the covenant against all provocation.   When Jeremiah, in a chapter which contains many echoes of Hosea, says : " I have loved thee with an everlasting love : therefore with lovingkindness have I drawn thee ",[5] he shows that love is the motive and lovingkindness (*hesed*) the expression of it in a certain constant relation.

The LXX frequently render " lovingkindness " by " mercy ", and so the latter meaning is carried over into the New Testament, but it is easy to see that neither in Greek nor in English can any one word bear all the meaning which the term has in the Old Testament.   Jesus would probably speak to the Pharisees in Aramaic, and might make the quotation in the original Hebrew ; his meaning, therefore, need not be limited by the Greek.

That the context of Hosea 6 : 6 was in his mind when he quotes the words in Matt. 9 : 13 is certain : Israel in Hosea 6 : 1 confess the need of healing : " Come, and let us return unto the Lord : for he hath torn, and he will heal us " ; and Jesus says, " They that be whole need not a physician, but they that are sick . . . for I am not come to call the righteous, but sinners to repentence".   What were the circumstances in which these words were spoken ?   It was at Matthew's feast, and in reply to the criticism of Jesus' habits addressed by the Pharisees to the disciples.   Matthew

[4]Hosea 5 : 4 ;   [5]Jer.31 : 3.

was one of the despised class of collectors of tolls and dues on behalf of the wealthy *publicani*, who farmed the taxes from the government ; and Matthew had left his toll-booth at the call of the Master, " Follow me ". At the earliest opportunity he held a dinner to mark the closing of his old life, and to celebrate his joy at the opening of a new life in the company of Jesus. He was one of the " sons of the bridechamber " who rejoiced while the " bridegroom." was with them ;[6] and his rejoicing took the form of gathering together as many as he could of his old companions and people of his own class to meet Jesus. In accordance with oriental custom, others came uninvited as onlookers at the feast. The Pharisees, so punctilious in their legal observances, found a stumbling-block in the Teacher's friendly intercourse with " publicans and sinners " ; but such men knew their need of salvation, while the Pharisees were blinded by confidence in their own righteousness. One at least of the despised class had shown something more. Matthew had revealed his " lovingkindness " towards Christ in obeying the summons to follow him ; and that " lovingkindness " overflowed to his former associates when he brought them near to his Lord. It was among the tax-gatherers and fishermen that this true " mercy " —God-ward as well as man-ward—was to be found. The Pharisees might go as they would to the feet of their rabbis, but they never learnt this love which alone can bind men to God.

The second time that Jesus uses Hosea's words is when again he is accompanied by the " sons of the bridechamber ", but this time he compares them to the companions of David—and therefore implies that he is

[6]Matt. 9 : 15.

the Seed of David. It was when the Pharisees objected
because the disciples plucked ears of corn on the
Sabbath, and Jesus recalled to them " what David did
when he was an hungred, and they that were with him ".[7]
In their midst was a greater than David, who is even
Lord of all. The priests, too, in the Temple " profaned
the Sabbath " in the very act of carrying out the Law's
own requirements, and were " guiltless ". One greater
than the Temple was in their midst, because in him the
God of the Temple was made manifest. Why did they
not recognize him? Because they did not know what
this meaneth, " I will have mercy and not sacrifice ".
They had substituted their own " righteousness which
is of the law " for love towards God, and therefore they
could not recognize the love of God revealed in His
own Son, whom He had sent into their midst ; and so
they condemned the Lord's disciples when they were
as guiltless as the priests carrying out the service of God
in the Temple. But he was recognized by these open-
hearted men who gave up their all to follow him.
These disciples were not always merciful in the narrower
sense ; they might in their zeal earn Christ's rebuke by
wanting him to call down fire from heaven on his
adversaries. But they knew their Lord and Christ
because they had hearts not blinded by self-righteousness. Knowing their need, they could know God's love
extended to meet their need, and could answer with
their own affection towards God and His Son. And
from that point they could grow into the fullness of
mercy towards men when they went forth at the risk
of their lives with the message of life in Christ's name,
knowing that " he that converteth a sinner from the
error of his ways shall save a soul from death ".[8]

[7]Matt. 12 : 1-8 ; [8]James 5 : 20.

These, then, were the men of God's covenant.
They were men of " lovingkindness " who by that
quality were enabled to know and to receive the lovingkindness of God revealed in Christ Jesus.   Yet his
lovingkindness comes to them in a form which they
can never return—though they may reflect it to men
frail as themselves : for it is the compassion with which
the Lord " pitieth them that fear him ".   To these
men God " showed himself merciful " because they
had eyes to see and ears to hear.   They " obtained
mercy " through forgiveness of sins when they com-
panied with Christ, and will receive mercy in full when
they share in " the mercy to Abraham " in the day of
resurrection : for " the mercy of the Lord is from everlasting to everlasting upon them that fear him " : they
will be embraced in the eternal covenant of God.   Yet
at their best theirs was only a pale reflection of the
quality of their Master, who is perfect in love towards
God and men.

The covenant-mercy must first of all take the form
of forgiveness, since men are sin-stricken and need to be
healed : therefore the love of God comes to them as
mercy in the more conventional sense of the word.   But
man does not by nature want mercy : he wants power.
The desire to obtain mercy is not a thing native to his
own spirit, for the desire is an acknowledgement of that
Eternal One who is wholly other than ourselves.   Left to
grow untramelled, the " I " that is in us seeks to assert
itself ; and if a man begs mercy from another who has
more power than he, his object is to preserve himself
or to adapt himself to that which he cannot control.
That is why men's religion leans to magic, by which
they seek to gain power over or effect an adjustment to

the unseen world ; or to a wish-fulfilment belief in the continuity of their own being ; or to the imaginative projection of their own self-assertion into some despotic Baal or Chemosh. " Let us make us a name " puts in a phrase one of the leading motive forces in human nature, either as individuals or in combination. When desolation comes on their works, a philosophy recognizing their own littleness may be forced on them by facts outside themselves. But this alone is not enough to bring them to see God : faith in the God of mercy needs that " I " to be broken down from inside ; the soil for a responsive relationship to grow between the Eternal God and man is a broken and a contrite heart.

Both the need and the fact of mercy recur in the Bible literally from Genesis to Revelation, and in a way which marks out its message as standing apart from all beliefs which have been evolved out of man's own consciousness. " While we were yet sinners " God so loved the world that He gave His only begotten Son to " die for the ungodly ", in order that whoever turned to believe on him " might not perish, but have eternal life " ; and just as there is no basis for the hope of eternal life in Christ unless the death from which he saves is really death, so there is no basis for the concept of God's mercy except in a frank and full admission of the concept of sin. And it is just this reality of man's indebtedness to God which calls for his forgiveness towards his debtors.[9] The saying of the Lord, therefore, carries us beyond any merely human conception of man, and by placing man in his right relation to God, places him also in his right relation to other men.

[9]Matt. 6 : 12, 14 ; 18 : 21-35.

The Lord's saying, therefore, searches out a man and lays him bare. By recalling his own need for mercy it shows him a lonely atom of powerless flesh, naked before the light of God. The line of thought we have been considering deals with a man as an individual brought to know his need and therefore changed in his attitude to other individuals. But the recipient of God's mercy is no longer an isolated fragment of humanity; he is brought into the Covenant. He becomes an integral part of a whole—the commonwealth of Israel, the household of God, the Body of Christ. And therefore the saying which brings home to him his terrible isolation opens up the way to a new union in the Divine fellowship on which the Kingdom of God will be founded. By breaking down the self-sufficiency of the individual soul, God welds men and women into the Temple in which they are " living stones ". And at this point we return to the thought that the " mercy " and the " covenant " of God are inseparable ideas ; and we do not doubt that the fullness of meaning which the Old Testament reveals was in the mind of the Lord Jesus when he spoke of the mercy which the merciful would obtain.

7

STANDING BEFORE THE KING (Matt. 5 : 8)

Blessed are the pure in heart :
For they shall see God.

The qualities which make up the character of the disciple grow from stage to stage, and the order in which the blessings are given reveals a relationship between them. It is those who have been humbled from outside themselves by the training of life who develop meekness as an inward grace. Meekness is selfless ; from it there springs a reaching out to that which is beyond ourselves —a hunger and thirst after righteousness. In " loving-kindness " these qualities are fused into unity and warmth ; and at that level the disciple may attain the " purity " of a heart at one with itself. From purity comes an inward peace which flows out into his communion with others.

The Lord's words in Matt. 5 : 8 agree with the LXX. of Psa. 24 : 4 (the only place in the version where the exact Greek expression occurs). Here David declares that the man who will stand in the Lord's holy place is " he that hath clean (that is, innocent) hands, and a pure heart "—a heart at once " choice " and " clear ", as the same word is rendered in two successive verses in the Song of Solomon.[1] It has been said that of the Hebrew words denoting purity this adjective " is the least tinged with the idea of ceremonial uncleanness ", and it is used in an ethical sense also in Job 11 : 4 and Psalm 19 : 9 ; it only occurs seven times altogether.

The words which Jesus quotes derive their force from their place in the thought of the Psalm as a whole.

[1] Songs 6 : 9,10.

It is a poetic meditation on the principle that the Lord will be sanctified in them that come near Him, and before all the people will He be glorified : and from this follows the conclusion that the earth will ultimately be filled with His glory.[2] This is a faith of which the ground is to be found in God's creative power. Who will prove to have an abiding place at the heart of God's purpose? Will it not be those who sanctify Him by their " clean hands and pure heart "? But now comes a remarkable step in the thought : for the blessing which that man will receive from the Lord will be " righteousness from the God of his salvation ". Without attempting to impute to the word " salvation " all the meaning it gathers from the New Testament, it is still a striking fact that this man of seemingly flawless character needs to have righteousness ascribed to him or declared by the graciousness of God. The same truth is implied in the fact that the spiritual race, the " generation " of the true Israel, of which this man is a type, are called seekers after God. " This ", says the Psalmist, " is the generation of them that seek thee, that seek thy face " ; and they are the true seed of Jacob. Jesus lays hold of the words and carries the thought to its conclusion. He says that to those who knock it shall be opened ; those who ask shall receive ; the pure in heart shall find God whom they seek. Nor is the seeking theirs alone ; God, who is spirit, seeks them to worship Him in spirit and in truth.[3]

But Psalm 24 : 4 is not the only passage to which the Lord's saying may bear an allusion. The same phrase occurs once again (and only once) in Psalm 73 : 1, which the R.V. renders : " Surely God is good to

[2]Lev. 10 : 3 ; Num. 14 : 21 ; [3]John 4 : 23.

Israel, to such as are pure in heart." This is the conclusion of Asaph after wrestling with the problem of the prosperity of the arrogant, which had proved so great a stumbling block that " his feet were almost gone ". And the point is that only the " pure in heart " can perceive the purity of God which is revealed in His ultimate dealings with man ; for as David said—and again a cognate word is used—" With the pure thou wilt show thyself pure ".[4]

At this point we reach the centre of the Master's teaching. A pure life can only come from a pure heart, just as good fruit can only grow on a sound tree. Only if the heart is whole and clean will life be lived constantly as in the sight of God, because no other heart can hold the stong desire to know or be known by Him. Without the woven vesture of a pure life, no man is fitly clothed to enter the Royal Presence, or he will find himself like the man at the marriage feast, without a wedding garment. In this saying Jesus joins issue finally with the interpretation of righteousness which made it a matter of outward acts punctiliously performed : unless the acts express the heart, they are rotten fruit from a corrupt tree, and however pleasing they may look in skin or texture, they will prove rotten when they are put to the test.

Only twice afterwards in the New Testament do we find the expression " a pure heart ", and both are in Paul's letters to Timothy. In 1 Tim. 1 : 3-5 the apostle commissions Timothy to " charge some that they teach no other doctrine ", and goes on to explain the object for which such a charge is given : " the end of the charge is love out of a pure heart, of a good conscience, of faith unfeigned ". In 2 Tim. 2 : 22, he

[4] Psa. 18 : 26.

exhorts, " Follow after righteousness, faith, love, peace, with them that call on the Lord out of a pure heart ". In the last especially we cannot fail to see an allusion to the Sermon ; and we can scarcely add to the apostle's exposition of what " purity of heart " means.

" Happy are these thy servants, which stand continually before thee ! " said the Queen of Sheba to Solomon. It was reckoned the great privilege of the " seven princes of Persia and Media " that they " saw the King's face ".[5] David can apply to the Lord this language of oriental court etiquette, and say, " The upright shall behold his face ".[6] And so in the language of Jesus, the promise that the pure in heart " shall see God " implies also seeing His Kingdom, for they will see Him enthroned in rule.[7]

To see the King means to be accepted in His presence, and for frail human nature that is impossible without reconciliation. Job, in the most sublime utterance of his faith, declares that God Himself will at the last act the part of his kinsman and will vindicate him, rising up in judgment " over the dust " of the grave ; and in that day, says Job, " from my flesh shall I see God ".[8] Then God will no longer seem to be his adversary : Job's assurance that his eyes shall behold God is the assurance also that they will be at one. It is in this sense that Elihu takes up the expression when he says that " if there be a messenger, an interpreter, one among a thousand " to declare unto man God's uprightness, then God will say " I have found a ransom ", and part of the restoration of the suffering man is that " he shall see God's face with joy ".[9]

[5] Esther 1 : 14 ; [6] Psa. 11 : 7, with R.V., Jewish, and commentators ; see also Psa. 17 : 15 ; 140 : 13 ; [7] cf. Isa. 52 : 8, R.V. ; [8] Job 19 :25-27, cf. R.V. and margin, and commentators ; [9] Job 33 : 23-26 ; Isa. 33 : 17.

Later in the New Testament Christ's expression is expanded in two notable ways. First, him whom they are to see enthroned is God manifest in His Son. Paul has an undoubted allusion to the Sermon (for reasons which will be even more apparent when we consider the next saying) in Heb. 12 : 14 : " . . . Holiness, without which no man shall see the Lord ". What Lord? This letter has already spoken of Jesus as Lord :[10] may we not conclude that " the Lord " whom they shall see is the Son who is the brightness of God's glory when he is enthroned in power? In Rev. 22 : 4 the very words of Esther 1 : 14 and Psa. 11 : 7 are used in reference to " the throne of God and of the Lamb ", when it is said ; " His servants shall do him service, and they shall see his face ". Whose face shall they see? The occupant of the throne, who is God manifest in the Lamb. And John says of the Lamb : " We know that when he is manifested, we shall be like him, for we shall see him as he is ".[11]

The other direction in which the idea is expanded is that to " see God " is not only a future blessing ; the pure in heart have even in the days of their flesh a knowledge of him denied to others. The thought is brought out by contrast in 1 Thess. 4 : 5, where the impure heart results from ignorance of God and excludes knowledge of Him : " Not in the passion of lust, even as the Gentiles which know not God ". But in this channel of thought also we are led back to God's manifestation ; if disciples can even now see God it is because they see His reflection in Christ, and because in Christ the vail which interposed for the Israelites is done away. " We all, with open face, beholding as in

[10]Heb. 2 : 3 ; 7 : 14 ; [11]1 John 3 : 2.

66

a mirror the glory of the Lord, are transformed into the same image from glory to glory." " The light of the knowledge of the glory of God shines in the face of Jesus Christ ".[12]

[12]2 Cor. 3 : 18 ; 4 : 6.

8

THESONS OF GOD (Matt. 5 : 9)

Blessed are the peacemakers :
For they shall be called the sons of God.

Peace is the product of that transformation which is referred to at the end of the last chapter. It is a peace coming from " the wisdom which is from above ", for it has its origin in the Father of lights from whom all good gifts come.[1] He recognizes as His sons those who reflect His character as it is revealed in Christ by being not merely peaceable but makers of peace : for Paul is appealing to a principle in the Father's nature when he says, " God is not the author of tumult, but of peace ".[2] " The God of peace begets children of peace, whose actions are peace."[3]

Synonyms which may often be interchangeable can at will be distinguished by a particular nuance of meaning. Two Greek words which may be represented respectively by " son " and " child " afford an example. John can convey a special tenderness by writing to the believers as " little children ", and he emphasizes their dependence on the Father when he says : " Beloved,

[1]James 1 : 17 ; [2]1 Cor. 14 : 33 ; [3]H. OLSHAUSEN, *Commentary on the Gospels.*

now are we children of God."[4] But the term " son ",
while it maintains to the full the bond with the Father,
at the same time defines the son as an individual with a
standing and character of his own ; and he is all the
more recognizable as an individual by the very fact of
likeness to his father. " The God of peace " is a favourite
expression of Paul's. So also is the Hebraic expression
" sons of God ", often in the sense of moral kinship
as well as of " adoption " through forgiveness of sins.

Light is thrown on the thought in the saying by
Isa. 58, where " the house of Jacob " are reproached for
being the opposite of peacemakers : they " fast for strife
and contention ", and hence they do not fast so as to
make their voice to be heard on high.[5] But " if thou
draw out thy soul to the hungry, and satisfy the afflicted
soul, then shall thy light rise in darkness, and thine
obscurity be as the noonday ".[6] Here is the antithesis to
strife : the true fast for which God calls is the life of
mercy out of a pure heart which brings peace : a peace
which is not merely the absence of contention but a
positive upbuilding in love. For the result to which it
leads with God's blessing is restoration, rebuilding :
" They that be of thee shall build the old waste places :
thou shalt raise up the foundations of many generations ;
and thou shalt be called, The repairer of the breach, the
restorer of paths to dwell in ".[7] " The repairer of the
breach "—what better synonym for a peacemaker? If
the tabernacles of David which have fallen are to be
raised again so as never to fall, their foundation must
be more than stone : they must rest on lives filled with
lovingkindness, and their pillars must be set in spiritual
peace. And the message of Isaiah is surely that it is not

[4] I John 3 : 2, R.V. ; not " sons ", as in A.V. ; [5] verse 4 ; [6] verse 10 ;
[7] verse 12.

God alone who makes the peace of the Kingdom ; it is men whose lives have been peace who repair the breach. The peacemaker is not one who plasters over a crack so that it does not show, nor one who takes the easy line of surface amiability. Peace is made by the love which builds up ; and the metaphor is true whether we think of building up a damaged wall with new stones or building up the breach in an injured body with living tissue. If the picture which Isaiah calls up is the rebuilding of the broken city, it is because for him the material and the spiritual are parts of one whole. With such full-blooded thoughts would the word " peacemakers " have been filled in the mind of Jesus : those who edify in love now are building for the house of God in His kingdom, and are " repairers of the breach ". Their lives and influence are as constructive as those who live for " strife and contention " are destructive, and the construction is carried over into that Kingdom where mere destructiveness will have no place.

But in this and every other sense the supreme Peacemaker is the Son of God himself : and to him the word is applied in its only other occurrence in the New Testament, Col. 1 : 19-20 : " For it pleased (the Father) that in him should all fullness dwell : and, having made peace (or " making peace ") through the blood of his cross, by him to reconcile all things unto himself ". " He is our peace " : and it is because he is " the repairer of the breach " that in him " all the building fitly framed together groweth unto an holy temple in the Lord ".[8] And as he became the author of salvation so also he became the author of peace, and the prototype of all his brethren who are peacemakers, because in some tiny

[8]Eph 2 : 14, 21.

degree they reflect that quality in which he must for ever be supreme.

The fullest exposition of the Lord's thought is found in a passage in James which—by a perversion which would be ludicrous were it not painful—is used more often than not to justify strife. " First pure, then peaceable ",[9] does not mean that peace is only to be attained when opposition is crushed. The " first " is not a note of time, as though you could be " pure " this week and " peaceable " next, when the other people are eliminated. Such naive philosophy belongs not to Christ but to Hitler, who at last could find only a barren peace in a suicide's death. He may be credited with having sincerely wanted peace—once all disagreement with him had been liquidated. Like most perversions of Scripture, this is made possible by quoting a fragment—a mere splinter—away from its context. For what James is saying is that peace comes from the pure heart as strife comes from the impure.

" Bitter jealousy and faction ", James says, has its source in a wisdom which does not " come down from above ".[10] Its origin is earthly, its character is that of the human mind, and its outcome is the disorganization which in the language of the time could be called " demon-like " ; " for where jealousy and faction (or ambitious rivalry) are, *there* is confusion and every vile deed ".[11] With a little play upon the word demon-like, we may say, *There* is pandemonium. Here is a sad picture indeed of the working of the fleshly mind in the ecclesias ; and it corresponds closely (especially when we read on to ch. 4) with the " works of the flesh " described in Gal. 5 : 19-20.

[9]James 3 : 17 ; [10]verse 15 ; [11]verse 16.

In contrast to this dark picture, James portrays the wisdom which has its origin from " the Father of lights ", and so (to recall again Gal. 5) yields " the fruit of the spirit ". Its prime quality from which all others follow is that it is " pure ". Once again James is more concerned with the thought than the words of his Master, for he uses a different word for " pure ", not conveying the idea of cleansing or catharsis, but more nearly related to (though not identical with) the " holiness " or " sanctification " of Heb. 12 : 14 ; it " denotes freedom from any kind of defilement ", and is the positive side of keeping oneself " unspotted from the world ".[12] The word may be used of merely ceremonial purity[13], but on the moral level it is the purity enjoined by Paul to Timothy.[14] But James uses it of the " perfect freedom from inward stain or blemish " which is also the meaning of John when he applies the word to the Son who is the manifestation of the Father : " Every man that hath this hope in him purifieth himself, even as he is pure ".[15] Peter, too, uses the verb in a passage which reflects the mind of the Lord and illuminates the language of James : " Seeing ye have purified your souls in your obedience to the truth unto unfeigned love of the brethren, love one another from the heart fervently ".[16] Those who obey that injunction will be peace-makers indeed.

James crowns his thought with a manifold allusion to the Sermon : " And the fruit of righteousness is sown in peace of them that make peace "[17] The whole chapter, with its starting point in the warning against the ambition to be teachers,[18] is parallel to the Lord's warning against " false prophets " who will bring

[12]James 1 : 27 ; [13]as in John 11 : 55 ; Acts 21 : 24, 26, etc. ; [14]1 Tim. 4 : 12 ; 5 : 2 ; [15]1 John 3 : 3 ; [16]1 Peter 1 : 22, R.V. ; [17]James 3 : 18 ; [18] 3 : 1.

destruction and confusion among the flock. In verses 11-12 James introduces two similes—the spring which pours water out of the crevice of the same kind as that which wells from the source deep in the ground ; and the tree which bears fruit " after its kind ", and not after another kind. The latter is a favourite simile of the Lord's which is found first in Matt. 7 : 16-18. These two figures have remained in James's mind and coloured his choice of language : and now he returns to the tree as a metaphor. There is a tree which is righteousness, and righteousness is its fruit. The sowing of that fruit is an unobtrusive work, but it is done by the " peace-makers " who are " pure in heart ".[19] The growth may be " secret " and unobserved : but the product in the end is " trees of righteousness, the planting of the Lord, that he may be glorified ". But there is a condition for this planting in which God works with and through men : it is done " in peace ", for strife is destructive of the very seed of righteousness.

Nothing, however, could be further from the thought either of Jesus or of James than a mere tolerance of wrong doing or wrong teaching. Their very object is to exhort to discrimination. Beware of false teachers, says Jesus—and the passage is the reverse side of the blessing on the peacemakers, for these are strifemakers and destroyers of life ; you can distinguish them, he says, by what they produce. Beware of yourselves, says James ; do not all strive to be teachers : discriminate between the sweet and the bitter that issues from your mouths, and if need be change the source from the wisdom that is from beneath to the wisdom that is from above. Both Jesus and James grieve over conflicting teachings in the

[19]James resolves the single word of Matt. 5 : 9 into a phrase, but where he gets it from cannot be in doubt.

Church and the contention which results ; and both trace them to a moral rather than an intellectual source. The distortion begins in the heart before it is reflected in the mind : the root of heresy is in self-love. And who, looking over the sadly chequered history of the Household of God, would venture to deny that the root cause of much of the " wars and fightings " has been emulation, envying, or—to put it bluntly—jealousy? We cannot be judges of the hearts of men : but we are called on to be judges of their fruits—and of our own.

Paul, too, mentions that which is bitter in a context concerned with purity and peace. The " root of bitterness " in Heb. 12 : 15 is an allusion to the " root which beareth gall and wormwood "—the man or family practising idolatry—in Deut. 29 : 18. That root is defiling, says Paul. " Follow after peace with all men, and the sanctification without which no man shall see the Lord. "[20] The order is changed, but the idea is the same as in the Beatitudes. Clean, sanctified, purified : the terms vary, but the thought is one : the pure in heart shall see God, and they are the peacemakers.

[20]Heb. 12 : 14.

9

REJOICING IN THE NAME
(Matt. 5 : 10-12)

Blessed are they which are persecuted for righteousness'
sake :
For theirs is the Kingdom of Heaven.

Blessed are ye, when men shall revile you, and persecute you,
And shall say all manner of evil against you falsely, for
my sake.

Reioice, and be exceeding glad :
For great is your reward in heaven :
For so persecuted they the prophets which were before you.

The happiness of the Beatitudes is not so much a
state of mind as a condition of privilege. Yet there is one
point in the series of sayings at which Jesus calls on those
who are destined for the Kingdom to know their
happiness and rejoice in it : and—by a remarkable
paradox—it is at the climax, when he calls " blessed "
those who suffer persecution for his sake.

The three verses in which he does so, 10-12, are
deeply penetrated by the language of Isaiah. In particular there are allusions to Isa. 51 : 7-8. In Isa. 50
it is shown that the instrument of the Lord's salvation
will suffer more than even the " children " whom he
comes to save,[1] the " afflicted " or " poor " of verse 13.
Because his ear is open to command, and he is not
rebellious,[2] he is able to say : " I gave my back to the
smiters, and my cheeks to them that plucked off the
hair : I hid not my face from shame and spitting ".[3]
He sets his face like a flint because it is the Lord Eternal
who justifies him, while those who condemn him shall

[1] 49 : 25 ; [2] 50 : 5 ; [3] verse 6.

" wax old as a garment : the moth shall eat them up ".[4]
And as the Servant is not alone in suffering, so his
endurance is not only for his own sake : it is an encourage-
ment to the man who fears the Lord and " obeys the
voice of his servant " to " trust in the name of the
Lord, and stay upon his God ".[5]   For if the heavens
and the earth are to be shaken so that the dwellers
on the earth vanish with it, the things which are
unshakable shall remain for those who receive a Kingdom which cannot be moved : " My salvation shall be
for ever, and my righteousness shall not be abolished ".[6]
And it is in this setting, and in the light of the example
of the suffering Servant (for his very words about the
perishing garment and corrupting moth are taken up
again), that the message comes :

> Hearken unto me, ye that know righteousness,
> The people in whose heart is my law ;
> Fear ye not the reproach of men,
> Neither be ye afraid of their revilings.
> For the moth shall eat them up like a garment,
> And the worm shall eat them like wool :
> But my righteousness shall be for ever,
> And my salvation from generation to generation.[7]

What is startling in Matt. 5 : 11 is that Jesus
equates suffering " for righteousness' sake " with
suffering " for my sake " : who is this who identifies
righteousness with himself, and himself with righteousness ?   Isaiah provides the answer, for the whole setting
of the words alluded to in Matthew is Messianic : it
concerns the Kingdom, and the Servant who must
needs suffer and enter into his glory ; and it declares
that as with the teacher (who has " the tongue of the

[4]verses 7, 8, 9 ;   [5]verse 10 ;   [6]Isa. 51 : 6 ;   [7]Isa. 51 : 7-8.

learned ") so must it be with those who obey his voice.[8]
Let it be noted that those who " obey the voice of his
servant " are also those who " follow after righteousness " ;[9] the identification which Jesus takes to need no
explaining is already made in Isaiah.

But the point can be carried further : " for my
sake " sounds like an echo of Isa. 66 : 5, where the
Lord Himself is the speaker : " Hear the word of the
Lord, ye that tremble at his word ; Your brethren
that hated you, that cast you out for my name's sake,
said, Let the Lord be glorified : but he shall appear
to your joy, and they shall be ashamed ". " For my
name's sake " is actually the reading of Matt. 5 : 11 in
the Old Syriac, which P. P. Levertoff says " is probably
not a variant, but an idiomatic rendering ". In any
case, the expression is found on the Lord's lips in
Matt. 10 : 22 ; 19 : 29 ; Mark 13 : 13 ; Luke 21 : 12, 17.
Only one could speak in this way : and that is he who
is the salvation of the Lord embodied in flesh, and who
bears his name. He himself tells the disciples, in the
very words of Isaiah, " Ye shall be hated of all men for
my name's sake ".[10]

In verse 12 there is a direct reference to the
prophets which may be something more than a historical allusion ; it shows how fully Jesus was thinking
of the prophetic word. " Rejoice and exult ", says
Jesus, as though the gladness of the coming festival of
the Kingdom were already yours : for the word has a
festal ring illustrated in the accounts of Hezekiah's
passover and the dedication of the rebuilt wall of
Jerusalem.[11] The rejoicing is in praise and to the glory

[8]cf. Matt. 10 : 24-25 ; [9]Isa. 50 : 10 ; 51 : 1 ; [10]Matt. 10 : 22 ;
[11]2 Chron. 30 : 23 ; Neh. 12 : 27, A.V., gladness.

of God. Such also is the " joy of their Lord " when he celebrates his entry into the Kingdom which he has received and in which he invites the " good and faithful servants " to share.[12]

Their reward is " in the heavens "—that is, with God, laid up as a treasure in the Divine purpose, for the Kingdom is " prepared from the foundation of the world ".[13] In Peter's phrase, the reward is " reserved in heaven " ; the thought is exactly that of David : " Oh how great is thy goodness, which thou hast laid up for them that fear thee ".[14] In the light of Old Testament turns of speech, it is clear that Matt. 6 : 19-20 is an expansion of the " reward in heaven " of 5 : 12.

In a similar way Jesus can use another familiar Old Testament figure, the book of God in which are written the names of those who " live unto him ".[15] Thus he can tell the disciples to rejoice that their names are " written in heaven ".[16] Like so many of the vital images of the Old Testament, this goes back to Moses, who prays to God—rather than that Israel should be unforgiven—" Blot me, I pray thee, out of thy book which thou hast written ".[17] Isaiah can say of the " remnant ", " He that is left in Zion, and he that remaineth in Jerusalem, shall be called holy, even every one that is written among the living (margin : to life) in Jerusalem ".[18] Unquestionably the meaning is eternal life, the life of the Kingdom. So Jesus interprets it, and carries on the figure.

The saying left a mark on its hearers which was ineffaceable. When they were discharged by the Sanhedrin, the apostles " departed from the presence of the

[12]Matt. 25 : 21, 23 ; [13]Matt. 25 : 34 ; [14]1 Peter 1 : 4-6 ; Psa. 31 : 19 ; [15]Luke 20 : 38 ; [16]Luke 10 : 20 ; [17]Exod. 32 : 32 ; [18]Isa. 4 : 3.

council, rejoicing that they were counted worthy to suffer for the Name ".[19] Peter says : " If you suffer for righteousness sake, happy (blessed) are ye " ; and, " Inasmuch as ye are partakers of Christ's sufferings, rejoice ; that when his glory is revealed, ye may be glad also with exceeding joy ". Again, in the next verse : " If ye be reproached for the name of Christ, happy (blessed) are ye ".[20]

Was James, the Lord's brother, also among the hearers? Nowhere are there more allusions to the Sermon than in his letter. " Take, my brethren, the prophets, who have spoken in the name of the Lord, for an example of suffering affliction, and of patience. Behold, we count them happy (blessed) which endure." " Count it all joy when ye fall into manifold trials. " " Blessed is the man that endureth temptation : for when he is tried, he shall receive the crown of life. "[21] The allusions are obvious. Paul, too, reveals his acquaintance with the teaching of the Master.[22]

With these verses we complete the study of the Beatitudes. It has been extensive and detailed because in these sayings we have the foundation on which the discourse is built. To trace the roots of the words of Jesus in their ramifications through the soil of the Old Testament is much more than a fascinating literary research. It is to discover that in these brief sayings is the quintessence of the prophets ; a distillation of the Hope of Israel.

[19]Acts 5 : 41, R.V. ; [20]1 Peter 3 : 14 ; 4 : 13, 14 ; [21]James 5 : 10-11 ; 1 : 2, 12 ; [22]Rom. 5 : 3 ; 2 Cor. 2 : 10 ; Col. 1 : 24 ; 2 Tim. 2 : 12 ; Heb. 10 : 34.

10

THE BELIEVERS AND THE WORLD
(Matt. 5 : 13-16)

Ye are the salt of the earth :
But if the salt becomes tasteless,
With what shall it be salted?

For nothing has it strength any longer
But to be cast out,
And to be trodden under foot of men.

Ye are the light of the world :
A city cannot be hid
That is set on a hill.

Neither do men light a lamp,
And put it under a bushel,
But on the lampstand,
And it shineth unto all that are in the house.

So let your light shine before men
That they may see your good works,
And glorify your Father which is in heaven.

The character of the citizens of the Kingdom of God, who are embraced in His covenant, has been portrayed in the Beatitudes. In the address recorded in Luke 6 : 20-26, similar blessings are accompanied by woes pronounced on the " rich ", those who " are full now ", those who " laugh now ", those of whom all men speak well ; for they too will experience a reversal of fortune. Having received their consolation now, they have nothing but condemnation and its consequent mourning to come. Their treasure is not in heaven ; as James tells them, with a clear allusion to the words of Jesus, they have " laid up their treasure in the last days ".[1] Those who trust in riches will then find their gold corrupted and their garments moth-eaten.[2] That on which they have depended will fail them utterly.

In Matt. 5 : 3-12, however, this class are only referred to indirectly, when the blessings on those who are persecuted and reviled show how the people of God will stand in relation to the world around them. This thought provides the background for two sayings which follow, when Jesus shows what the disciples are to be in themselves, and towards the world.

" Ye ", he says emphatically, " are the salt of the earth." Salt in a warm climate is a necessity of life. Being abundant in the land of the Salt Sea, it was freely used in food and medicine, and even with animal fodder.[3] Any meal would include salt in some form, and so to partake of a meal with a man was to " eat salt " ; and the sharing of a meal meant—as among the Bedawin to-day—to enter into a fellowship.[4] A covenant was accompanied by a sacrificial meal, and " a covenant of salt " was of peculiar sanctity and durability. God gave " the kingdom over Israel to David for ever, even to him and to his sons by a covenant of salt ".[5]

Doubtless from this association with a covenant, salt entered largely into ritual use. As a condiment it represented zest in contrast to insipidity ; as a preservative it was an emblem of incorruptibility as against the inconstancy of human nature ; and by use it became the symbol of faithfulness. " Every oblation of thy meal offering shalt thou season with salt ; neither shall thou suffer the salt of the covenant of thy God to be

[1]James 5 : 3, R.V. ;   [2]4 : 15-17 ; 5 : 1-3 ;   [3]See Isa. 30 : 24 ;   R.V. margin ;   [4]cf. Ezra 4 : 14 ; R.V. ;   [5]2 Chron. 13 : 5 ; cf. Num. 18 : 19.

lacking from thy meal-offering : with all thine oblations thou shalt offer salt. "[6] It is possible also that salt was used in the preparation of the incense, as the words rendered " tempered together " in the A.V. of Exod. 30 : 35 are by some rendered " seasoned with salt ".[7]

To the man of the world meekness, poorness of spirit, and the rest, are the insipid virtues of the feeble, the undervitalized, the inferior ; they are the mark of the " slave morality ". To Jesus exactly the reverse is true : the men of God are not insipid but " salty " ; it is they who have savour and strength of character. When human pride brings rivalry among the disciples he can tell them to " have salt in themselves, and have peace with one another ".[8] The salt of humility gives the savour of peace. But this potent quality of life does not belong to men by nature. How is it attained? Only by the self-discipline which is self-sacrifice—even to the extent of cutting off the offending hand or plucking out the wayward eye. This salt is a sacrificial quality and is only gained by " presenting your bodies a living sacrifice ".

The great sacrifice in which the new covenant was to be sealed was not yet offered, and could not, at that stage, enter into the teaching of Jesus, though it might be present to his mind. Nevertheless, he is undoubtedly teaching that the people whose " is the Kingdom " must be the true covenant-people of God, and the description of them as salt links them with " the salt of the covenant of thy God ". Underlying all the Sermon is the continual contrast between the true Israel and the false : " *Theirs* is the Kingdom " means " *theirs*—and not others " ; and so now, with an emphatic

[6]Lev. 2 : 13 ; [7]cf. margin, R.V. and American Jewish Version ; [8]Mark 9 : 50.

pronoun, he says, " *Ye* are the salt . . . ".

But the threatened fate of Israel was a reminder that salt remains salt only so long as it retains its potency. True salt, indeed, will remain chemically the same whether dry or in solution ; but the imperfectly purified substance in daily use in Palestine might in practical experience " become tasteless " through the effect of damp. A little salt might be useful as manure, either spread on the land, or added to " the dunghill " ;[9] but the refuse from spoilt rock salt was good for nothing but to be thrown on the track where it was trampled in. Salt which had deteriorated in the Temple store might be used to make the steps less slippery in wet weather, or on the sloping ramp up to the altar, which became dangerous through being covered with blood. In any case it was " trodden under foot of men ", a striking type of rejection : they are as dust underfoot.

Such salt was said to have become " saltless ".[10] This was the state " Israel after the flesh " were approaching ; and R. F. Weymouth, in a footnote to his *New Testament in Modern Speech*, says : " The second sentence of verse 13 is our Lord's first recorded pre-diction of the divine rejection of his fellow-countrymen— a rejection then so near—consequent on their failure to respond to their divine election." Still more was it a lesson to the disciples that if one generation were rejected, so could another be ; their standing as the people of God depended on a continuing " saltness ", not on an arbitrary selection ; " because of unbelief they were broken off, and thou standest by faith "— faith with all that it implies of the quality of life.[11] Heb. 6 : 4-8 is a pointed commentary on the same idea.

[9]Luke 14 : 35 ;   [10]Mark 9 : 50, literally ;   [11]Rom. 11 : 20.

The saying refers to the whole of the qualities which Jesus has said are blessed; but it has a special bearing on the last of the Beatitudes. Will they remain constant to him under persecution for his name's sake? The question is not only whether they will continue to profess that name, but whether they will remain truly, and not merely nominally, the covenant people of God by retaining the " salt of the covenant " in their lives. Without the spirit of Christ in its meekness and purity they are none of his, and fit only to be " cast forth ". It was with this in view that the disciples so often emphasized the need for suffering meekly under reproach and persecution.[12] When Jesus uses salt as a figure in Luke 14 : 25-35, this responsibility of discipleship and the need for constancy in the undertaking is the most prominent idea. Here in the Sermon the thought behind the figure comprehends all the meanings he gave it elsewhere.

The implied contrast with those who were " Jews outwardly " is even more apparent when Jesus says, " Ye are the light of the world ", for this was unquestionably the function assigned to Israel of old. Moses, exhorting Israel to keep the commands of God, says : " For this is your wisdom and your understanding in the sight of the peoples, which shall hear all these statutes, and shall say, Surely this great nation is a wise and understanding people ".[13] Jews themselves recognize that this " contains in substance the idea of the missionary purpose of Israel's existence ", and that this is " frequently emphasized in Prophetic and Rabbinic literature."[14] But this missionary purpose is implied at a

[12]Rom. 12 : 17-21 ; James 5 : 7 with verse 12 ; 1 Peter 3 : 8-9, 14-17 ; 4 : 12-14, etc. ; [13]Deut. 4 : 6-8 ; [14]J. H. HERTZ, *Pentateuch and Haftorahs*.

still earlier point, when they are told that if they keep the covenant they shall be not only " a holy nation " but " a kingdom of priests ".[15] For whom are they priests? Priesthood implies a two-sided relationship —not only to God but to men. As a man " taken from among men and ordained for men in things pertaining to God ", a priest is both a teacher and an intercessor. These were the functions of the Levitical priesthood towards the twelve tribes ; and though the analogy cannot be pressed to apply to peoples outside the covenant who have no appointed means of approach to God, the Priestly Kingdom must have some function towards the peoples of the earth. That function was to be a witness to God by observing His laws, and thus to teach by example. Indeed, an analogy drawn from the Household of Faith would suggest that intercession was not excluded, for Paul exhorts that " supplications, prayers, intercessions, and giving of thanks, be made for all men ", on the ground that God, who is " our Saviour ", willeth that all men should be saved, and come to the knowledge of the truth.[16] The purpose of God that all the earth should be filled with His glory was inherent in all His dealings with Israel ; and Moses, as Paul shows, looks forward to the day when all nations will rejoice in the Lord.[17] In the accomplishment of that purpose Israel were chosen as God's spearhead ; and so the Lord could say of them through Isaiah : " This people have I formed for myself, that they might set forth my praise ".[18] The purpose for which they were chosen from among the nations was never at any stage for their own sake alone ; it was in order that through them the blessing of Abraham

[15]Exod. 19 : 5-6 ; [16]1 Tim. 2 : 1-4 ; [17]Num. 14 : 20-21 ; Deut. 32 : 43 ; Rom. 15 : 9, 10 ; [18]Isa. 43 : 21, R.V.

might come upon all families of the earth, and that by this means God should be glorified.

For this end, Israel was as " a city set on a hill ". Placed in a land unique in its geographical situation, they were at the meeting point of the rival cultures of the ancient world, on the passage way of its traffic, and the battleground of its clash of forces. David and Solomon raised the kingdom to a brief eminence ; and the visit of the Queen of Sheba is both an example of what its influence might have been and a type of those Gentile " kings " who will come to " the brightness of Zion's rising " when, at last, her Divine destiny is fulfilled.[19] But even when power and prosperity had gone, the world could not be blind to the distinctiveness of Jewish life so long as the Law was observed and the Temple worship maintained.

Two dangers beset Israel throughout their history. The first was that they would cease to be holy ; becoming like the nations around them, they would no longer have any witness to bear. The other was that they would cease to be priestly ; becoming self-righteous, they would cease to bear to others the witness they had. The filching away of the Court of the Gentiles for the trade in sacrifices and exchange of money in which the House of Annas had a vested interest, was a symptom of Jewish failure on the second of these counts in the Lord's day. But whether they showed to the world the love of God, or their own selfish hatred, they could not be hid.

Commentators have pointed out that Safed, visible from the supposed scene of the delivery of the Sermon and nearly three thousand feet above sea level, would

[19] Isa. 60 : 3.

very well answer the description of " a city set on a hill " ; while Tabor, familiar to the Lord throughout his life in Nazareth, was also probably crowned with buildings in his day. But another city even more fitting as an illustration might have been in his mind. When he was a boy of twelve coming to his first Passover, if the pilgrims from Nazareth took the route through Perea they would toil up the steep and dangerous road from Jericho. As they breasted the mount of Olives there would burst on his eyes one of the most remarkable sights in the world. High on the hill of Zion, gleaming all the whiter by contrast with the shadowed cliffs of the grim Kidron Valley, he would see the snowy limestone of Herod's Temple flashing with gold. No imaginative boy would forget the experience. What picture must it have left on the vivid mind of the boy who a few days later was to be found asking questions of the rabbis in the Temple? That picture would be renewed year by year until he was thirty as he came up regularly for the feasts. There, in all its beauty and significance, was the city which was the very embodiment of Israel's life and purpose. The day would come when he would weep for the desolation that was to come upon it ; and when he would take the disciples over that valley of the shadow to the slope of Olivet, there to tell them, as the sun went down behind Jerusalem, the signs when these things should come to pass.

His disciples, too—this remnant, this other Israel— would inherit the duty of witness to the world. They could not be hid ; as a community of believers they would be seen, known and judged. But they could hide their light, and whether they would be seen to the glory of God would depend on the light shown by each individual member. The saucer lamp burning all night was the sign of life in every home. For the lamp to be put out was a synonym for the extinction of the household.[20] To put the lamp under the household bushel measure would be a futile act which no one in his senses would do. The earthenware lamp would be placed on a three-forked branch of a tree cut and inverted to form a stand : and thus lifted up, in the humble one-roomed dwelling its glimmer would " give light to all that were in the house ". Similarly in the bridal procession each of the virgins carried her lamp on a pole fitting into a hollow cup which would contain the reserve supply of oil. And beyond all this homely illustration Jesus would not be unmindful of another symbol—the seven-branched lampstand which illumined the Holy Place.

The community of believers who are in Christ Jesus is represented by the golden lampstand fed by the two olive trees in Zechariah's vision. Dr. Thomas says : " Without this light-bearing body, the world in all ages and generations from apostolic times until now, would have been in lightless outer darkness. The One Body has been the golden seven-branched lightbearer in all the gloomy period of the times of the Gentiles." While this is true, it must not be overlooked that in the words of Jesus the light represents works rather than words.

It is a paradox that men should both persecute the disciples for righteousness' sake and yet glorify God for their good works, yet it is true to experience. Men— sometimes the same men—both reproach and respect the

[20]Prov. 13 : 9 ; cf. Psa. 132 : 17 ; 1 Kings 15 : 4.

righteous, and the genuinely Christlike character never fails to win some admiration. But a particular light is thrown on the passage by an allusion of Peter's, when he exhorts the " sojourners of the Dispersion " to " have their behaviour seemly "[21] among the Gentiles, " that wherein they speak against you as evildoers, they may, by your good works, which they shall behold, glorify God in the day of visitation ".[22] Calumny, as the Lord had foretold, was a common experience of believers, and Suetonius uses the very expression " evil-doers " of the Christians ; but Peter says that the people who have " spoken against " them may one day " end by glorifying God " for them. " A day of visitation " will come (the phrase is without the definite article) ; visited by God's grace, their conversion will be aided when they look back and recognize the true character of the lives they have witnessed ; they will find beauty in the very thing they had vilified. There was a man who watched the stoning of Stephen, and yet lived to " glorify God " for the martyr's witness. If, however —as is possible—Peter is thinking of the final " visitation " of God's judgment in the " last day ", the idea is not substantially changed : it is still that the converts will rejoice in the influence on their own lives of conduct they had once despised. But these results can only follow if the works of believers have been good, gracious, beautiful—" honest " in the Latin sense which is now almost lost from English ; for twice in the one sentence Peter uses his Lord's word. That beauty of life can come only by reflection from a life more beautiful ; its motive power is a love which has an origin beyond human nature. " A new commandment " their Master gave them, that as he had loved them, so they should

[21]good ; A.V. " honest " ; [22]1 Peter 2 : 12, R.V.

love one another ; and he added, " By this shall all men know that ye are my disciples, if ye have love one to another ".[23] By this a light would shine whose source none could mistake. And in this Jesus is truly the revelation of the Father ; for the point of his saying in the Sermon is that men will not fail to recognize the Father's likeness in the children, and so glorify—not them—but Him.

With this we reach the end of the first section of the Sermon. Jesus has pictured for the disciples the character which has its foundation in faith in God as Father, and in a clear conviction in His Kingdom and His righteousness. This character is revealed in the very conditions of evil which exist in the interim before the Kingdom is established ; in those conditions the character must retain its unfailing savour which belongs to the covenant with God. And behind this teaching on the way of life is the fact that the pattern character which he paints is his own. It must be so, for he is the King, the Anointed of the Lord, and from him the Kingdom must take its character and its law ; by him the ground of citizenship must be defined. The Messiahship of Jesus is nowhere stated in the Sermon on the Mount, but it pervades all the teaching. Who else could set forth the basis of citizenship in the Kingdom? For this reason, claims which could be made only of the Messiah are taken for granted as needing neither assertion nor demonstration ; they are not incidental to the Sermon, but inherent in it. From the first of the " blessings " onwards this is a manifesto which could have been issued by the King of the Age to come, and no one else.

[23]John 13 : 34-35.

III. THE WAY OF THE PILGRIM LIFE

1

THE NEW LAW AND THE OLD (Matt. 5 : 17-19)

*Think not that I am come to destroy the law and the
prophets :*
I am not come to destroy, but to fulfill.

For verily I say unto you :
Till heaven and earth pass away,
One jot or tittle shall in no wise pass away from the law
Till all be accomplished.

*Whosoever therefore shall break one of these least
commandments,*
And shall teach men so,
    Shall be called least in the Kingdom of Heaven :
But whosoever shall do and teach them,
    He shall be called great in the Kingdom of Heaven.

By what " works " are the believers in the Messiah
to show the " light " which reveals their citizenship of
his coming Kingdom? What law will govern those
" works " and guide their steps in pilgrimage? What
relation will this law bear to the law of the Kingdom of
old? To these questions, which arise from what has
gone before, Jesus goes on to provide answers.

How radical is the issue with which Jesus confronted the world then, and confronts it now, is proclaimed in his first words. " Think not ", he says,
" that I came to destroy the law . . . ". The construction
recurs in Matt. 10 : 34, and implies that some had
thought or might be likely to think it. Why should

they? Not only because of the arresting note of authority in his teaching, but because he had come; for " I came " (or rather, " I am come ") is a form of words implying nothing less than that he is one in whom there will be a new dispensation. It is as though he said, " *My Advent* is not for this object, but for that ". It brings to mind Psa. 40 : 7 : " Then said I, Lo, I am come " (R.V.). " To destroy " combines the ideas of *to pull down*, and *to undo*, and appears to have its source in the law concerning vows where the husband may " make void " or " of none effect " a vow undertaken by his wife.[1]   Hence the word has the meaning " to annul ". This was in effect what the Pharisees were doing when they made the word of God " powerless " (or " repealed " it—Moffatt) by their traditions. By contrast, Jesus comes not to annul but to confirm— and more, to fulfil it. For the moment, not his actions but his teaching is in question, and it is to this the saying must have primary reference. In his teaching will be found the fulness of law and prophets—for he explicitly includes both equally as is emphasized by the disjunctive " or " rather than the conjunctive " and " : " the law, or the prophets ". The passive " to be fulfilled " is one of the characteristic words of Matthew, and is found on the lips of the Lord in Matt. 26 : 54, where—as so often elsewhere—it carries the thought that he himself is the fulfilment of the Word of God. Doubtless in the mind of Jesus there could be no separation between his teaching and his life. He said in the Nazareth synagogue, " This day is this Scripture fulfilled in your ears " ; and to fulfil the law and prophets would mean for him the life culminating in the perfect sacrifice. But in this place the primary meaning which

[1] Num. 30 : 8-16.

the words would convey—and must have been intended to convey—to the listening disciples must be kept in view.

To this statement he adds another which is prefaced by " Amen, I say unto you . . . ". The use of " amen " as an asserveration of the truth of what is to follow is peculiar to Jesus ; according to scholars, no true parallel is to be found in Rabbinic writings. Normally, a man said " amen " to confirm something spoken by another, whether a statement, an oath, a benediction, or a prayer. With Jesus, the word is equivalent to " yea " or " truly " : which sometimes stand for it in Luke where Matthew and Mark have " amen " either in identical sayings or similar sayings on different occasions. When, however, we compare Jesus' usage with Isa. 65 : 15-19, we may well conclude that Jesus meant to convey that his word is truth as God is true : for in this passage—to which, as we have seen earlier, the Beatitudes are so closely related—it is said that the Lord God " shall call his servants by another name : that he who blesseth himself in the earth shall bless himself by the God of Amen[2] ; and he that sweareth in the earth shall swear by the God of Amen . . . For, behold, I create new heavens and a new earth . . ." The conclusion is that Jesus was " swearing by the God of Amen " while reverently avoiding the Divine Name or the form of an oath, which he condemned ; and this gives added point to Rev. 3 : 14, where he speaks as being himself " the Amen, the faithful and true witness ".[3]

And with this we come for the first time to one of the most notable expressions of the Sermon, " I say unto

[2]A.V. : truth ;   [3]See also 2 Cor. 1 : 20 ;   R.V.

you ". In that emphatic " I " he claims an independent authority which challenges the question, " Who then are you? " If the claim has any validity there can be only one answer : " The prophet of whom God said through Moses, ' I will put my words in his mouth, and he shall speak unto them all that I shall command him '."[4] That Prophet would speak as Moses spoke, as one with whom God spoke face to face, and who could therefore come with His direct command. As Moses had said of the Prophet, " to him shall ye hearken ", so the Father said of Jesus, " This is my beloved Son, in whom I am well pleased ; hear ye him ".[5] In those three words is a commission of un-bounded authority ; even in the days of his flesh Jesus could say, " All things have been delivered unto me of my Father ".[6]

Yet, so far from being in conflict with the law, this bringer of the new dispensation declares the law's lasting validity. The language in which he does so has close affinity with Isa. 65 : 17, already quoted ; but it is an actual quotation from Isa. 51 : 6 : " Lift up your eyes to the heavens, and look upon the earth beneath : for the heavens shall vanish away like smoke, and the earth shall wax old like a garment, and they that dwell therein shall die in like manner : but my salvation shall be for ever, and my righteousness shall not be abolished ". The whole passage needs to be studied, noting specially that it is concerned with a " law going forth " which is to be " a light of the peoples "—that is, the Gentiles.[7]

This law Jesus identifies with the " salvation " and " righteousness " of God — a connexion which . it is important to bear in mind when we come to verse 20 ;

[4]Deut. 18 : 18 ;   [5]Matt. 17 : 5 ;   [6]Matt. 11 : 27 ;   [7]" Peoples " (plural) is R.V.

93

and therefore he declares that one *yod* or one " little horn " shall *in no wise* pass away from the law until all be accomplished, or come to pass. The form of the saying is proverbial, and the Rabbis give examples of absurd and even blasphemous meanings which could be read into Scripture by confusion between pairs of Hebrew letters which differed only by a " tittle ".

When Jesus says he had not come to nullify the law, he uses a term which " stands for what might have been the powerful and decisive purpose of a prophet or reformer " ; but when he says in verse 19, " Whosoever shall break one of these least commandments ", the word means to relax or loosen, and " stands for the lesser acts of disciples tending in the same direction ".[8] Such behaviour might show a disparagement of the commands which would weaken their force, and would lead in time to their " teaching men so ". As they treated the word of God, so He would treat them, and their standing in the Kingdom of God would suffer accordingly. But he who maintains the commands in practice and precept (for to " do " is to " make ", to " practise "), this man (he is singled out for emphasis) " shall be called great in the kingdom of heaven ". The words receive emphasis from the action of Jesus in the first incident recorded by Matthew after the Sermon— the command to the healed leper, " Show thyself to the priest and offer the gift that Moses commanded, for a testimony unto them ".[9] Most of the incidents of this eighth chapter directly illustrate the Sermon, and seem to have been chosen and arranged for that object.

How are we to understand the words of Jesus in view of the independence with which he sometimes

[8]HORT, *Judaistic Christianity* ;   [9]Matt. 8 : 4.

treats the Law? To answer we must ask : What is the nature of the law itself? Along with its ritual aspects, it is a civil and criminal system for the administration of a national society. It is designed for citizens of a state, and to be administered through state judges ; and it must be so framed that it can be applied by a human judiciary. It must therefore deal—in the main, at any rate—with external acts on which judges can decide as matters of fact. Such a law must at some points represent a compromise between essential principle and practical application.

Yet it is incorrect to think of the Law of Moses as merely prohibitive or concerned only with overt acts. One of the ten commandments which form its kernel is " Thou shalt not covet ", which searches the mind and emotion ; and when one of the objects not to be coveted is " thy neighbour's wife ", the way is already prepared for the condemnation of adultery " in the heart ". When Jesus says, " Love thy neighbour as thyself ", he is quoting the law verbatim.[10]   The law which says, " Thou shalt not kill ", says also, " Thou shalt not hate thy brother in thine heart "[11]—and no judge could discern whether that law was broken unless hatred led to breach of some other clause in a malicious act. In the same verse the law imposes a responsibility to " rebuke thy neighbour, and not suffer sin upon him ", or " bear sin because of him ". Cause of offence is to be removed by a frank approach, so that the offender does not go on in error and the offended does not harbour resentment. It is exactly in the spirit of this command that Jesus lays down the course to be followed by a believer in endeavouring to restore to unhindered

[10]Lev. 19 : 18 ; [11]Lev. 19 : 17.

fellowship with God and his brethren a brother who has injured him.[12]

Most of this nineteenth chapter of Leviticus—to name no other part of the law—is concerned with the conduct of life in ways where no external authority could impose it : and in this the Law is unique as a code. Faith is its motive force ; without faith a man would not observe laws for which he could not be judged by a visible tribunal ; and without faith he could not hope to bring the springs of conduct in the heart into obedience to the will of God. For all the law is " briefly comprehended " in two positive principles, " Thou shalt love the Lord thy God . . . Thou shalt love thy neighbour as thyself " ; and as only God can judge love, the whole law rests on the foundation of faith in the invisible God.

This summary of the Law Jesus confirms. When in the Sermon he repeatedly uses the formula, " Ye have heard . . . but I say unto you ", he is in large measure criticizing the current interpretation of the Law, rather than the Law itself. But that is not the whole truth. He does not scruple to modify an actual provision in regard to the " bill of divorcement " (which he says elsewhere Moses gave them " for the hardness of their hearts "). Clauses which offer protection against harsh and oppressive treatment by a creditor he abrogates so far as his disciples are concerned ; and in so doing, he repudiates for them the justice which is the essential principle of the Law as a judicial system. His own command, " Swear not at all ", is deliberately contrasted with the Law, " Thou shalt perform unto the Lord thine oaths "—even if illustrations which he gives are taken

[12]Matt. 18 : 15-20.

from current practice by which the force of the law was evaded. We are compelled to say that the terms of the Law itself may come under his scrutiny, and therefore the saying that " not one jot or tittle shall pass " cannot be interpreted with legal literalness. Yet if, on the other hand, it is not a legal definition but a proverbial hyperbole, that does not imply that Jesus meant any the less by it ; such a saying is not overstatement, but statement belonging to a different realm of thought and meaning. In that wider realm and on that higher level its meaning is not partial and relative, but absolute. And here the wider sense of the term " law " as applied to the Scriptures must be borne in mind : *torah* (instruction) is applied not only to the legislative code, but to the whole of God's revelation.

No discussion of Jesus' attitude to the Law would be adequate without some reference to the Sabbath, for this was the point at which his conflict with the religious authorities was continually brought to a focus. It is a mistake, however, to think that Jesus relaxed Sabbath law : his appeal is to what is " lawful ".[13] No doubt in that he is taking up their own term and returning it on their own heads[14] ; but essentially the claim of Jesus is that by " doing good ", " saving life ", or making a man " every whit whole "[15] on the Sabbath day, he is not overriding the Sabbath law but fulfilling it. It was in fulfilment of all that the Sabbath means, and as an earnest of all that it foreshadows, that Jesus on the Sabbath day healed men and women of their infirmities. He eased the shackles of mortality in which the children of Adam are held, and foreshowed the complete deliverance which is offered through him. In this he

[13]Mark 3 : 4 ; [14]Mark 2 : 24, etc. ; [15]John 7 : 23.

was working the works of the Father[16] and acting as the
" Son of man " who is " Lord even of the Sabbath
day ".[17]   The controversy over Sabbath-keeping,
therefore, turns on Rabbinical interpretation ; but the
real issue underlying the conflict was Jesus' claim to be
Son of Man.

Jesus' attitude to the Sabbath, however, may help
to an understanding of his attitude to the Law, even on
the points where he supersedes its terms.   He relaxes
nothing.   So far from making the Law easier, " He
sharpens the edge of every precept, and enlarges the
scope of every principle.   There is an intensity in the
Sermon on the Mount which is appalling : it searches
the conscience as with an electric ray ".[18] He lays bare
the spiritual aim of the Law, and reveals the height and
breadth of its demands, which must surpass all the
limits of a formal code.   " Behind the law in its original
form lay a divine purpose for the law, and the fulfilment
of the law, in this pregnant sense of the word fulfilment,
was an accomplishment of that divine purpose. "[19]
The best comment on the Sermon is in the words of
Paul, that great interpreter of " the spirit of Christ " :
" Love worketh no ill to his neighbour :   therefore love
is the fulfilling of the law ".[20] More literally : " Love is
the fulness of law " : law in itself attains completion in
every jot and tittle where love reigns.   " The whole law
in one word has been summed up, in the (word) : Thou
shalt love the neighbour of thee as thyself".[21]

If love cannot pass away, can the law of love? Yet
Jesus brings in a note of time with the word " until ",
corresponding with the imagery of the " passing away "

[16]John 5 : 17 ; [17]Matt. 12 : 8 ; [18]J. STALKER, *The Ethic of Jesus* ;
[19]HORT, *Judaistic Christianity* ;   [20]Rom. 13 : 10 ;   [21]Gal. 5 : 14.
Interlinear Greek-English N.T. (1958).

of heavens and earth which he has borrowed from Isaiah. In view of this context the words can hardly be a poetic synonym for " never ", because Isaiah prophecies " a new heavens and a new earth ", in which " the former things shall not be remembered ", but in which the " salvation " and " righteousness " embodied in a new " law " will prevail.[22]   At what point, then, is the validity of the Law to cease?

Heb. 8 : 13 applies Isaiah's simile (" wax old like a garment ") to the old covenant, which was being replaced with the new covenant in Christ. With the change of covenant, there must be a change of law ; and by implication it is the " heavens and earth " of the Mosaic dispensation which pass away. In 2 Peter 3 : 5-13, Isaiah's imagery is applied to the " heavens and earth " which were destroyed by the Flood, and to the worldly society of men to be destroyed by the judgments of Christ's coming. The " kingdom of men " would also seem to be the " heaven and earth " of the Lord's Mount of Olives discourse.[23] In Revelation, it was the " heaven " of Pagan Rome which " departed as a scroll when it is rolled up " under the sixth seal ; but the fleeing away of " heaven and earth " and the coming of " a new heaven and a new earth " belong to the end of the Millennium and the coming of " God, all and in all " to dwell with men.[24] Here, then, are three " passings " of " heaven and earth " : (1) The end of the Mosaic order ; (2) The end of the kingdom of men ; (3) The end of mortality and the order of things which belong to it in the completed work of redemption. Isaiah's language is capable of manifold application :

[22]Isa. 65 : 17 ; 51 : 4-6 ; [23]Matt. 24 : 35 ; [24]Rev. 6 : 14 ; 20 : 11 ; 21 : 1-5.

may not the Lord's use in Matt. 5 : 18 comprehend all its meanings?

Jesus was "made of a woman, made under the law". In his life the Law received its "fulness", for he showed perfect love to God in obedience even to death, and perfect love to men, in that "greater love hath no man than this, that a man lay down his life for his friends".[25] "All the law and the prophets"[26] thus find their fulfilment in his love : and this includes the ritual and sacrifices of the Law, for these have their meaning in love to God which brings recognition of man's fallen state in God's eyes. Through this loving obedience he offers the perfect sacrifice in which all ritual sacrifice is both "completed" and "accomplished". When he is raised up, Jesus passes beyond law into that divine nature where law is transcended in perfect union with God. He is no longer "under law" because he is no longer "in the flesh" : for him those Mosaic heavens which had overarched him, that Adamic earth of which he had formed part, have passed away. So, too, for those who are "in Christ", the Mosaic order has come to an end, and they are called to "stand fast in the freedom wherewith Christ has made them free". Yet they are still in the flesh, and called upon to "mortify their members which are upon earth" ; they cannot, therefore, be "without law to God", but must be "under law to Christ",[27] and Christ's law is the re-affirmation of the law of love given through Moses. They are "dead to the law through the body of Christ"[28] ; yet for them the law lives again in Christ's commands, wherein its principles are confirmed and their scope widened, so that "not one tittle falls to the ground".[29]

[25]John 15 : 13 ; [26]Matt. 22 : 40 ; [27]1 Cor. 9 : 21 ; [28]Rom. 7 : 4 ; Gal. 2 : 19 ; [29]Luke 16 : 17.

The believers will only pass beyond law when their
" mortality is swallowed up of life ", and they are
incorporated into the new Millennial " heavens " as
" kings and priests ". There will be no more need then
for regulation from outside themselves, applied for the
control of their own nature—for that is the sense in
which the term " law " has been used here.

So long, however, as Adamic nature remains on
earth, law in some form must remain to control it. In
every age the political " heavens and earth " have been
a setting for human nature. In most, they have evolved
out of that nature itself by man's attempts at self-rule.
In the Mosaic age, they were divinely designed and
given to bring human nature under control to God ;
and that will be even more true of the Age to come.
But only when the last enemy is destroyed with the
elimination of sin and the abolition of death does the
race pass into the " new heaven and earth " in which
God can tabernacle with men, with all barriers to
intercourse removed.[30] Salvation is the aim of Divine
law : and when the last human beings have been brought
through law into obedience to God, and so to union with
Him, the law will have reached its completion and its
object will be accomplished. As law—as a mode of
control—it will vanish away with the constitution which
belongs to an unredeemed world ; for when law passes,
the social cosmos of which it is a part passes too. But
as the principle of love it will shine for ever in the perfect
harmony between those who are made " equal to the
angels " and God who makes them the vehicles of His
manifestation. Then the words of Christ concerning the
Law will attain that perfect fulfilment for which the
earlier stages of fulfilment are preparatory.

[30] I Cor. 15 : 26 ; Rev. 21 : 3 ;

2

THE ABOUNDING RIGHTEOUSNESS
(Matt. 5 : 20)

For I say unto you that
> *Except your righteousness shall exceed that of the scribes
>   and Pharisees,*
> *Ye shall in no wise enter into the kingdom of heaven.*

That righteousness must be a fulfilling of the law
and not an annulling of it is indicated by the preposition
" for " which connects verse 20 with what precedes.
This fundamental declaration, of which all that follows
in the Sermon is an exposition, arises out of what Jesus
has said concerning the law, and its importance is
marked by the use again of the phrase, " I say unto
you ".

The prophet says of the day of the Kingdom :
" Thy people shall be all righteous : they shall inherit
the land for ever ".[1] Righteousness is, therefore, the
condition of inheritance, and the question what constitutes righteousness is the fundamental problem of
life.   That problem was the special concern of two
classes of people who were intermingled. First were the
professional jurists, who were also teachers. Governed
by Rabbinic precedent, their task was to work out the
application of the law to every conceivable and incon-
ceivable case, not only which arose in practice, but
which might be invented by legal ingenuity. The
avowed object was that the law might not be over-
stepped at any point.

The other class included a number of brother-
hoods bound by vows to the observance of the law as
interpreted by the scribes. The principle they strove

[1] Isa. 60 : 21.

to maintain was the sanctity of the whole people as the " holy nation ", and on this ground they extended into the life of the laity practices such as ceremonial ablution before meals which originally pertained to the priesthood in the Temple. It was on the ground of ceremonial purity that they avoided contact with " the people of the land "—so that their self-righteous separatism from some of the nation actually arose out of their belief in the priesthood of all the nation. To the Pharisees the Jews were mainly indebted for the synagogue system and the schools associated with them. In the Temple itself they were in continual conflict with the haughty Sadducean priesthood ; and they had been successful in instituting daily prayers, and securing the presence of representatives of the people while the sacrifices were offered. It was the Sadducees, in spite of their worldly Hellenic culture, who adhered rigidly to the letter of the law. The priesthood had become an exclusive professional caste with little concern for popular religion ; the Pharisees, for all their ritualistic austerities, were in history, in theory, and in practice, far more closely identified with the people.

To the scribes and Pharisees, then, the people looked for guidance in righteousness : yet Jesus says that without righteousness which " abounds more " than theirs, entry into the Kingdom is impossible. He cannot mean a more abundant righteousness of the same kind—more washings and purifyings, more legal hair-splitting. Does he speak of their " righteousness " ironically, because it was hypocrisy? The Jews themselves satirized the play-acting of some of the Pharisees, such as the " bruised Pharisee ", who in avoiding looking at a woman bruises himself against a wall ; or the " pestle Pharisee ", who walks with head down like a pestle in a mortar. They were, therefore, not without self-criticism : nor were there lacking rabbis who urged spiritual religion and denounced formality.

The service of the law was voluntary, and Rabbis normally maintained themselves by the practice of a craft. Hillel was a wood cutter ; Shammai a builder ; and others were shoemakers, blacksmiths, and so on. Gamaliel III said : " All study of the Torah without work must in the end be futile, and become the cause of sin ". Yet it is evident from the denunciations of Jesus that some were " covetous ", and knew how to profit by their reputation for sanctity even to the extent of " devouring widows' houses ".[2] Among the Pharisees were noble characters ; but as a class they had by no means escaped the peculiar spiritual dangers of those who are " righteous overmuch " ; their faults were those which beset the Puritans of every age. And yet it is surely not their unrighteousness, but their righteousness, which has to be exceeded. It is not those who were blameworthy by any standard, but those who " as touching the righteousness which is in the law " were " found blameless ", who would come to reckon the very righteousness which they had pursued so eagerly a dead weight on the wrong side of the scale.[3]

Two incidents in the Gospels may help to an understanding of righteousness as Jesus taught it. The first, which in Matthew follows close on the Sermon, deals directly with the ground of admission to the Kingdom. When Jesus " marvelled " at the centurion who had sent the message, " Speak only the word, and my

[2]Luke 16 : 14 ; Matt. 23 : 14 ; [3]Phil. 3 : 6-7.

servant shall be healed ", he said : " Verily I say unto you, I have not found so great faith, no, not in Israel. And I say unto you that many shall come from the east and the west, and shall sit down with Abraham and Isaac, and Jacob, in the kingdom of heaven : but the sons of the kingdom shall be cast forth into the outer darkness ".[4] This was a clear pronouncement that Gentiles would share in the promises to the fathers and enter with them into the Kingdom, when descendants of Abraham by right of birth would be excluded. On what ground will these from the east and the west enter ? The faith shown by the centurion supplies the answer.

The other incident is in the house of Simon the Pharisee. Jesus says of the woman who anointed his feet with ointment, " Her sins, which are many, are forgiven : for she loved much ". And to the woman he says : " Thy faith hath saved thee : go in peace ".[5] Without faith there could have been no love : she could not have loved the Saviour had she not believed that he could save. Where others questioned inwardly, " Who is this that forgiveth sins also ? " she knew : and she had no doubt that the sins were in fact forgiven.

Three terms are therefore brought into close relation—righteousness : faith : love. It becomes evident that the righteousness without which the Kingdom cannot be entered is an expression of the love which has its root in faith ; and the object of what follows in the Sermon is to show the form which that expression must take. In this righteousness, says Jesus, the law has its fulfilment.

This conception of righteousness is in conflict not only with the worst but with the best in contemporary

4Matt. 8 : 10-12 ; 5Luke 7 : 47-50.

Judaism ; for the worst was the corruption of the best. However deep its roots in the law, the righteousness Jesus preaches differs radically from the very aim of religious life as then understood ; and it is this conflict which Jesus declares so uncompromisingly in Matt. 5 : 20.

It is from Paul, the one-time Pharisee, that we can best learn the essence of Pharisaism. To the " zeal for God " of men of the type of his teacher, Gamaliel I, he bears hearty witness ;[6] yet it is the zeal of ignorance, not of knowledge, for in " going about to establish their own righteousness " they are " not submitting themselves to the righteousness of God ". The ideal they set themselves is the perfect observance of the law as a legislative and ritual code. The man who can avoid transgressing any of its clauses has established a claim to righteousness, and earned a title to future blessing. It is this conception of a legal righteousness which a man attains for himself that Paul is opposing when he repudiates " works of the law " as a means of gaining eternal life. The object for which the law is given as a legislative code is not to provide a ladder by which men may climb up to life—for that is impossible to human nature : its object is to bring home the knowledge of how far short human nature falls from the Divine standard, and hence to bring the desire for the salvation which God alone can give. Reliance on works of the law is part of the fallacy that man has within himself the power of effecting his own salvation. Men cannot build up a bank balance of merit in the Divine account ; they cannot place God in their debt. But that is just what legal righteousness is trying to do.[7] The principles

[6]Rom. 10 : 2 ; [7]cf. Rom. 4 : 4 ; Eph. 2 : 8 ; Rom. 11 : 6-8, etc.

of spiritual economy are those of the " householder "
in the parable of the labourers ;[8] and in this is to be
found the germ of Paul's teaching. It is the doctrine of
Jesus that before God all men are slaves.[9] They cannot
work overtime because all their time is His : and
therefore there is no increment that they can claim :
no merit has been accumulated, and no gratitude is
due to them. Turning to Paul again as the Lord's
interpreter, the master from whom men may earn
wages is not God, but Sin, and he pays only the coinage
of death ; " the gift of God is eternal life ". The only
profit which arises is that which the Lord may demand
on the " talents " with which the bondslave has been
entrusted, and if he has failed to trade with these, then
he will be doubly " unprofitable ", and will be " cast
into the outer darkness".[10]

This fundamental teaching on the righteousness of
faith which Paul develops is, therefore, inherent in the
words of Jesus. But not only is the ideal of legal righteousness mistaken theology ; it actually leads to results the
reverse of righteous. It necessarily approaches the law
from the outside ; its concern is with the visible performance of the clauses of a code of works, rather
than the moulding of life by the principles which the
code is designed to express. Such is human nature
that as the legal mind becomes more and more concerned
with externals and minutiae, the principles themselves
are lost sight of, and eventually are nullified. When
legalism defeats the law, a false sense of values comes
into play : ritual demands become more important
than " justice, mercy and truth " : and the way is
opened for evasion and hypocrisy.

[8]Matt. 20 : 1-16 ;   [9]" unprofitable servants ", Luke 17 : 10 ;
[10]Matt. 25 : 30.

A striking example of the corruption of Pharisaism is provided by the practice referred to in Matt. 15 : 1-9 and Mark 7 : 6-13. The Rabbis insisted that once a man had vowed away his goods by saying " Korban is everything whereby thou mightest be profited ", the vow must be observed to the most preposterous degree. The father could not receive from the son so much as a shirt, a piece of bread or a drink of water. This instance of the scribal interpretation of righteousness is peculiarly significant, because the Hebrew word represented by Korban is used for the offering in about 70 passages in the Old Testament, and is derived from a verb meaning " to approach or draw near ". The idea of a means of approach to God is prominent ; and is carried over into Heb. 7 : 19 ; 10 : 22, etc. The law which should be a means of approach the scribes were converting into a barrier between God and the Israelite. While nullifying the Fifth Commandment by a rigid application of the law of vows, they provided for the evasion of this law also by distinctions between oaths which were binding and those which were not.[11] The more firmly the yoke is fixed, the greater the temptation to find some way of easing the strain. But this tendency to make the law void by tradition is the result of a misconception of the nature of law and righteousness. The Pharisee, beginning from the outside, fails to reach the core. Jesus, beginning from the innermost principle, works outwards to externals, so that the whole law is complete.

Bound up with this is another aspect of the problem with which Jesus is greatly concerned in his controversy with the Pharisees. The Biblical idea of righteousness

[11]Num. 30 : 2 ; Matt. 23 : 16-22.

stands apart from all others in that it is only possible to those who know their need of mercy. The fundamental sense of the word seems to be straightness : and the Greeks could define it as " the virtue whose effect is that each and all have what belongs to them, in accordance with the law " ; while the effect of unrighteousness is that " they have what belongs to others, not in accordance with the law ". For this idea of " straightness " between man and man in accordance with customary standards, justice is an adequate translation. For the Hebrews alone in the ancient world, God Himself was the standard, and righteousness was conformity to His character : " Ye shall be holy, for I am holy ".[12] In this connection the word itself must take on an infinitely loftier meaning. It is the antithesis of the Biblical idea of sin—and where God is unknown there can be no genuine and profound idea of sin ; nor consequently of its opposite. Knowledge of Jehovah brings not only a sense of the enormity of sinful acts but also of the inherent tendency to sin in human nature.[13] The first essential for righteousness is the recognition of the righteousness of God. Righteousness —like wisdom—must begin with " the fear of the Lord "—the sense of awe at His holiness ; and therefore the man who is most righteous will be most conscious of his own need of forgiveness. This is a dilemma which can only be finally resolved through atonement : and while Jesus—for good reasons—says nothing of atonement in the Sermon, it is required by his conception of righteousness as opposed to that of the Pharisees. Though the Pharisees included all the ritual of atonement in their " works of the law " they deprived it of

[12]Lev. 19 : 2, etc. ; [13]Psa. 143 : 2 ; 130 : 3-4.

true meaning, because the " righteousness of their own " which they were seeking through the law was self-sufficient.[14] Logically it left no room for mercy and forgiveness. These were so inwrought in the Old Testament revelation that they could not be eliminated—any more than believers in the immortality of the soul could eliminate the doctrine of resurrection so long as regard for scripture was retained. Yet these gifts of grace really became extraneous to the theological scheme. This was the significance of Jesus' saying, " I am not come to call the righteous, but sinners to repentance ".[15] Forgiveness and righteousness alike are impossible without humility ; and the demand for a righteousness exceeding that of the Pharisees cannot be understood unless it is related to the blessing on the merciful, " for they shall obtain mercy ".

Is the law as Jesus gives it a new and better code? How utterly inappropriate such a description would be will be seen as it is examined in detail. The sayings in which Jesus applies his law to life are not judicial enactments, and cannot be so applied, and are not so applied even in his own practice. They are, none the less, commands ;[16] they have the force of law without the form. The fact that the law of Moses had to be framed to provide an administrative machinery for a nation imposed a limitation from which the law of Christ is free ; and so he could burst the bonds of the Law's terms in order to fulfil its principles.

There is a two-foldness in the believers' relation to law. For them the law is dead, and the law lives : similar language can be used in opposite ways according to which aspect is in view at the moment. This two-

[14]Phil. 3 : 9 ; [15]Matt. 9 : 13 ; [16]John 14 : 21 ; 15 : 14.

foldness arises from a duality in themselves. In so far as being " in Christ " they are " made to sit together with Christ in heavenly places ", they are beyond law, but in so far as they are in the flesh they are under law. They have a law in their members which wars against the law of their mind ; and so those " members " must be brought in subjection by a law outside themselves. To meet the needs of their nature in this dual relationship, Jesus gives to believers a law in which the old law lives again in a form so new that the very meaning of the term has to be expanded in order to include it. For it is a law to be implanted within them, " written in their hearts ", and so remaking them from within outwards, moulding them in thought and character, as no formal legislation could.

3

THE LAW OF THE HEART (Matt. 5 : 21-24)

Ye have heard that it was said to them of old time—
Thou shalt not kill ;
And, Whosoever shall kill shall be in danger of the judgment ;

But I say unto you that—
Whosoever is angry with his brother without cause,
Shall be in danger of the judgment ;
And whosoever shall say to his brother, Raca,
Shall be in danger of the Council ;
And whosoever shall say, Thou fool,
Shall be in danger of the Gehenna of fire.

If therefore thou bring thy gift to the altar,
And there rememberest that thy brother hath ought against thee
Leave there thy gift before the altar,
And go thy way ;
First be reconciled to thy brother,
And then come and offer thy gift.

Jesus does not interpret the law in general or abstract terms ; he quotes excerpts from the law as commonly understood, and against these he puts in contrast the true righteousness, illustrated by examples from daily life. Penetrating as these are, they are illustrations only ; at no point do they define the limit of what is required of a disciple. They are not always stated in a strictly literal form, and they are given with the entire absence of qualification which is the mark of oriental speech. They are designed to work through the imagination so as to create a certain disposition of mind and mould of character.

The formula " Ye have heard " is " a traditional scribal phrase with the sense of ' you have understood this to mean ' ". " It was said " is a customary form which reverently avoids naming God as the speaker ; " to them of old time " is a reference to the contemporaries of the giving of the law on Sinai. But the effect of the whole formula is to contrast what he says with scribal tradition, rather than with the written law. Filtered through the mouths of scribes, the law had been made burdensome and remote ; but when he said, " I say unto you ", the word was brought " very nigh unto them ", so that it might be in their mouths and in their hearts, that they might do it.[1]

[1]Deut. 30 : 14.

Because every saying of Jesus leads back to the springs of action in the heart, it is his principle that the disposition to do wrong is equivalent to the act. A deed which a man would do if he dared, is a deed done but for the chance to do it; and so it is reckoned in the judgment of God as though it had been committed. Elementary as this may seem to us, it did not seem so to the Pharisee Josephus, who says, " The purposing to do a thing, but not actually doing it, is not worthy of punishment ". His context precludes the possibility that he was thinking merely of human judgment, and the remark is a sidelight on the Pharasaic mind. But Jesus takes us still further back. Murder begins not with the thought of murder, but with the thought of uncharitableness; from that germ it may grow through contempt to anger, and from anger to hatred, until desire to be rid of the enemy burns like a red flame in the mind.

The law said, " Thou shalt not kill "[2]; and by way of summary Jesus adds, " whosoever killeth shall be in danger of the judgment " : for the law said, " He that smiteth a man so that he die, shall surely be put to death ".[3] Three forms of offence are paralleled with three degrees of judgment : anger unexpressed renders a man liable to the local court; the contemptuous word, " Empty head ", makes him liable to the Sanhedrin; and abuse of a man's moral character makes him liable to the most disgraceful form of capital punishment, when the body is thrown out to be burned— a parable of divine rejection. The margin of the R.V. makes " Thou fool " stand for the Hebrew *moreh*, which is used of the " rebellious " son in Deut. 21 : 18, 20; it means the folly of stubbornness in rebellion

[2]Exod. 20 : 13; Deut. 5 : 17; [3]Exod. 21 : 12.

against God's law. Many commentators concur; and in this case the Greek *mōre* would be a transliteration as with *raca*. It might, however, be a translation for *nabal*, the word which only too aptly gave a name to the churlish husband of Abigail.[4] It seems in any case to carry a suggestion of moral perversity.

No tribunal can judge unspoken anger, and no judiciary could enforce the death penalty for a word. The language belongs to the realm of parable. But how impressive is the picture of the city elders in conclave to determine whether a black look had the germ of murder in it; or the whole Sanhedrin weighing whether a word of contempt was meant to stab like a sword! How solemn the portrayal of the utter rejection of a man who had used defamatory language! Here in the first of Jesus' applications of his law to life we are confronted with his habit of speaking in pictures; a single phrase can, on his lips, have the vividness and compactness of a cartoon. The lesson on his method which the example gives is to be borne in mind as the rest of the Sermon is studied. Even if " without cause " is an interpolation, it is not the use of the words in themselves which is condemned: for Jesus uses the very same term of the Pharisees in their blindness.[5] It even occurs in the Sermon, applied to the man who builds on sand.[6] It is the angry mind which comes under judgment; and Jesus assumes that the anger is of a kind which betrays the absence of love, and therefore (however incipiently) the presence of hate. There may be a righteous anger consistent with love; but whether it is so may be determined by one test: however stern its expression, it will aim at restoring the sinner instead of repelling him

[4]Psa. 14 : 1; 1 Sam. 25 : 25; [5]Matt. 23 : 17, 19; [6]Matt. 7 : 26.

by one's own self-righteousness. But for Jesus there is no neutral state : the absence of love is hate, and hate is murder in embryo. He goes beyond the law, " Thou shalt not hate thy brother in thine heart ", and lays bare the sources from which the bitter spring can flow. To treat such sayings as these with prosaic literalism is to limit their scope, and thus defeat their aim. What Jesus is doing is by a series of verbal pictures to give a portrait of that invisible heart of man which is betrayed by the bitter and hasty word. " Death and life are in the power of the tongue : and they that love it shall eat the fruit thereof. "[7]

Perhaps Jesus' extension of the meaning of the verb " to kill " is in the mind of James in a singular passage where it can scarcely be taken literally, for it would mean that murder was a not infrequent practice in the early Church ! " Ye lust, and have not : ye kill, and desire to have,[8] and cannot obtain ; ye fight and war, yet ye have not, because ye ask not. "[9] All the way through the third chapter James's mind is leavened with the words of Jesus, though he reproduces the thought without direct quotation. The association with Matt. 5 : 22 is evident when he says of the tongue, " Therewith bless we God, even the Father ; and therewith curse we men, which are made after the image of God. Out of the same mouth proceedeth blessing and cursing ".[10] It is from his conclusion that " the fruit of righteousness is sown in peace of them that make peace " that James turns at once to its opposite : " From whence come wars and fightings among you? Come they not hence, even of your lusts (literally, pleasures) that war in your members? "[11] And so to verse 2 : " Ye kill, and desire

[7]Prov. 18 : 21 ; [8]R.V. m., are jealous ; [9]James 4 : 2 ; [10]3 : 9-10 ; [11]4 : 1.

to have. " It is murder in the heart, the product of the bitter stream from the poisoned spring.

One section of the law which has a particular bearing on the Lord's teaching is that which concerns malicious perjury.[12] A man who has given false witness with the object of getting an innocent man convicted is himself to suffer the penalty which he might have brought on the other : " Then shall ye do unto him as he had thought to have done unto his brother . . . life for life, eye for eye, tooth for tooth, hand for hand." As at least two witnesses would be needed to establish a charge, such a case would involve a conspiracy to commit perjury. If their testimony was accepted in a case for which the penalty was death, and the sentence was carried out, then they would be guilty of what might be called " constructive murder " ; if the perjury was discovered, then the intention to bring about a death is treated as murder, and the perjurer loses his own life. The case is not quite parallel with the words of Jesus, because perjury is an overt act on which a court could judge the issue of fact ; but it is the one case in the law in which the penalty is imposed for "what he had thought to do "—for the intention rather than for the deed ; and it establishes the principle that even under the law a man could be held culpable before God for what was in his heart.

To enter into the Kingdom will be to come into the presence of God[13] ; and this will only be possible for those who " draw near " before God in the days of mortality. In verse 23 Jesus accepts without question the means of approach appointed for that age—the coming to the altar, and the ritual of sacrifice. But from

[12]Deut. 19 : 15-21 ; [13]Matt. 5 : 8.

the days of Cain and Abel, whether sacrifice was acceptable depended on the frame of mind in which it was brought. Sacrifice is worthless unless it is an act of faith, hence the demand for obedience in observing the form of offering God prescribes. To offer to God a gift of one's own choice, in a way of one's own devising, is a failure to acknowledge God's majesty; it is therefore not faith but presumption, not submission to God, but the assertion of self. It is to make God secondary to our own feelings about Him, and therefore less real than ourselves. Without faith, it is morally impossible to obey the command to worship the Lord our God and serve Him alone.

This principle Jesus carries into a new field. Faith in God is faith in the character of God, who is love; and this faith, unless it animates the worshipper's own life, is dead. Worship " in spirit and in truth " means that the worshipper is becoming progressively more like the object of his devotion, and without reflection of God's mind the worship is neither true nor spiritual. The condition which makes worship acceptable is to be found in a man's attitude not only to God but to men. Only the " pure in heart " shall " see God "; and there can be no " drawing near " with murder in the heart. " The sacrifice of the wicked is abomination : how much more when he bringeth it with a wicked mind? "[14] For this reason, verses 23-24 arise as a conclusion from the preceding verse, linked by " if therefore . . . ".

A man has come to the Temple with his offering, has passed through the court of the Gentiles and the court of the women, up the steps and through the splendid Nicanor gate into the court of the Israelites.

[14]Prov. 21 : 27.

117

The lamb has been found without blemish, and accepted ; it is slain, and is about to be cut up to be laid on the altar of burnt offering when there is a surprising interruption : the worshipper asks that it may be left until he has gone on an errand and returns.

We can imagine the astonished looks of the priests. Only religious duty, and that of the most pressing kind, could justify such an unconventional course. Has the offerer omitted some ritual requirement? The Talmud says, " If a man is on the point of offering the Passover, and remembers that there is any leaven left in his house, let him return to the house and remove it, and then come to finish his Passover." But Jesus applies this principle to "the leaven of malice and wickedness". The man has at the last moment remembered a grievance, not which he has against some one else, but which some one else has against him. It must be removed before he can be in communion with God. Far better, of course, to remember sooner, and not to disturb the orderly service of the Temple ; but Jesus, in his vivid way, has pictured the extreme example so as to impress the lesson. " Let a man examine himself, and so let him eat . . . " that he does not eat and drink " judgment unto himself ".[15]

One more example, which follows under this general heading of the law of murder, opens up a wide view of man's standing before God.

[15] 1 Cor. 11 : 28.

4

JUDGMENT AND MERCY (Matt. 5 : 25-26)

Agree with thine adversary quickly,
Whiles thou art in the way with him ;
Lest at any time the adversary deliver thee to the judge,
And the judge deliver thee to the officer,
And thou be cast into prison.

Verily I say unto thee—
Thou shalt by no means come out thence,
Till thou hast paid the uttermost farthing.

A man owes a long standing debt. His creditor
decides to sue for recovery, and comes to the house to
demand the debtor's attendance at the court. As they
go together, there is still a chance to compound with
the creditor, who can then have the case withdrawn
from hearing. But pride and self-interest combine to
suggest a more cunning way. There is some past
transaction which can be made the subject of a counterclaim. The debtor thinks, " If you take the law, the
law you shall have ; perhaps it can be made to serve
my ends as well as yours." And so he comes before the
judge acting his part. As the plaintiff's case is unfolded,
the defendant's expression and gestures portray pained
surprise, indignation, and resignation at the perversity
with which the righteous are afflicted. His defence is
presented with fervour and ingenuity, and with pro-
testations of the justice of his cause ; and he waits with
an air of triumph to hear the decision. But it is not the
first time that the judge has heard a counterclaim which
would never have been thought of but for the bringing
of the claim : the counterclaim is dismissed, judgment

is given for the full amount of the claim, and as the defendant cannot pay, he is committed to prison.

Some such picture is called up, with a touch of ironic humour, by the Lord's words. On the obvious level, it was a rebuke to the litigiousness which is almost a part of daily life in the east. How futile is this attempt to assert your own rights and gain your own ends! So Jesus was saying in effect. And how loveless! What a violation of the essence of the law!

But some words in James' letter may lead us to see a deeper meaning: for when James says, " Mercy rejoiceth against judgment ", he is stating the obverse side of the picture of " judgment without mercy " which is the climax of this parable.[1] As one sees more and more reflection of the Lord's words in his epistle, it becomes a growing conviction that James is consciously alluding to this passage. The situation he describes is different, but it must be borne in mind that as Jesus uses the word, mercy is not the prerogative of the plaintiff: the defendant may show the same spirit in his readiness to come to an agreement.

James says that those who show favour to the well-dressed man and despise the poor are become " judges with evil thoughts ";[2] and their fault is not only in being bad judges, but in being judges at all—for he has in mind Matt. 7 : 1. By constituting themselves judges of men they too come under judgment by a law which knows no mercy, for under it transgression in one point is a breach of the whole. Sin being lawlessness, he who stumbles in one command is guilty of all. But there is another law which James calls " the law of liberty ", " the perfect law ", into which a man

[1] James 2 : 13 ; [2] 2 : 4.

120

may gaze so that he continues in it as " a doer of the work ", and is " blessed in his doing ".[3] It is a paradoxical phrase, like speaking of " the restraint of freedom " or the control of uncontrol. James has spoken of it as " the royal law ", and J. F. McFadyen paraphrases : " God's law is an imperial law, meant for freemen, and not for slaves ". This is the law of the merciful man whose love for his neighbour is not limited to the narrow channel of specific commands, but spreads over life with the completeness of the natural love for one's self. The man who, living in this law, reflects the qualities of his Heavenly Father, will be judged with the mercy which he himself gives. " So speak ye, and so do ", says James, " as men that are to be judged by a law of liberty." Under that law alone mercy may " glory " against judgment ; it belongs to those who are merciful because they know their need of mercy.

This carries our vision up to a higher court than any which judges debts between men ; and in making this story of the self-righteous defendant a parable of Divine judgment Jesus was speaking in a way not outside the grasp of contemporary thought. Something of the parabolic framework is contained in one of the *Sayings of the Fathers* : " They that are born are destined to die ; and the dead to be brought to life again : and the living to be judged, to know . . . that He is God . . . He the Discerner, He the Judge, He the Witness, He the Complainant." Moreover the words " whiles thou art with him in the way "[4] contain an echo of the LXX of Isa. 55 : 6 : " Seek ye the Lord, and when ye find him, call upon him ; and when he shall draw nigh to you, let the ungodly leave his ways . . . and let him return

[3] 1 : 25 ; [4] R.V.

unto the Lord, and he shall find mercy ". The word for "adversary" is *antidikos*, which has the meaning of complainant or opponent in legal proceedings.

In the light of these facts we might freely paraphrase the thought of the Lord's parable as follows : " If you think to get the advantage by taking your stand on the law, then by the law you must be judged. But that is a two-edged weapon ; you will find yourself involved in a law suit to which there can be only one issue. You will be indicted by God's Righteousness in the Court of God's Justice, and the arm of God's Law will carry out the sentence. It will mean imprisonment until the debt is discharged, and that will be for ever ; for the prison is the grave, and the debt is your life, and for that no redemption can be paid, nor can any man pay a ransom for his brother."[5] And we might add, as being implied in the parable : " But if yours is the spirit of mercy, then he who was your Adversary becomes your Advocate ". For if " we have an Advocate with the Father ", it is God Himself who has provided " Jesus Christ the righteous " for that purpose.[6]

The object of this parable, then, is to show that the law of murder enshrines a principle which, having first been used to search the inmost motives of man to man, is next extended to cover all the conflicts of life. But in so doing it relates a man's attitude to other men to the fact that he himself stands under judgment ; and if the footing on which he stands before God is purely legal, judgment must be synonymous with condemnation. And so the exposition of the law has kept in view the problem confronting the reader in verse 20 : what is righteousness? With what can a man stand before God,

[5]Psa. 49 : 7-8 ; [6]I John 2 : 1.

and enter into His Kingdom? Not with a legal righteousness, for all are debtors. The theme is the same as that
which is treated from another angle in the Parable of
the Unmerciful Servant.[7]

This implied contrast between legal righteousness
and the righteousness of faith—which, though the terms
are not used, is at the root of the teaching of Jesus—is
maintained by James. He distinguishes between the
" royal law ", " the law of liberty ", on the one hand,
and the law which condemns—which we might by
antithesis call " the law of bondage "—on the other.
The principle of this law is a living faith made manifest
in works of love,[8] and it is this which James is expounding
all through his epistle. The final contrast with the
" law of works " is found in his last word : " He that
converteth a sinner from the error of his way shall
save a soul from death, and cover a multitude of sins ".[9]
Law reveals sins, and brings death : love covers sins
through bringing the sinner to find forgiveness ;[10] and
so—though in perfect consistency with the righteousness
of God—love brings a triumph over judgment. The
" law " which triumphs in saving life is the law of love
and liberty ; and in that we find the essence of that
" grace and truth " which James derived from him
who is " the Glory ".[11]

It is a law of liberty because it has its root in the
" truth " which " makes free ", and so is a law for free
men. It stands in contrast to that " yoke " which (said
Peter in James' presence) " neither we nor our fathers
could bear ".[12] Even apart from the elaborations of
Rabbinical tradition, the Law of Moses is through the

[7]Matt. 18 : 21-35 ; [8]James 2 : 14-26 ; [9]James 5 : 20 ; [10]cf. Prov.
10 : 12 ; 17 : 9 ; [11]James 2 :1 ; [12]John 8 : 32 ; Acts 15 : 10.

weakness of the flesh a "ministration of death", a "bond written in ordinances" which was "contrary to us"; there was not, and could not be, "a law given which could have given life".[13] The law of liberty, on the other hand, is a "ministration of the spirit".

It is Paul who gives one of the most beautiful illustrations of the principle, in which, as a "follower" of Christ, he becomes in some sense a type and figure of the Saviour. Writing on behalf of the converted Onesimus, he makes himself responsible for the money which the slave had stolen from Philemon: "If he hath wronged thee, or oweth thee ought, put that on mine account; I Paul have written it with mine own hand, I will repay it: albeit I do not say to thee how thou owest unto me even thine own self besides."[14] The master of the runaway was not unmerciful; and doubtless he would recognize his greater debt, not only to Paul who had saved him with the word of life, but to the Lord that bought him.

At the roots of the thought of both James and Paul is to be found the same contrast between bondage and freedom, judgment and mercy, law and life; and, however rich the diversity in their development of the thought, fundamentally they are at one. James, as truly as Paul, is opposing legalism with grace. They are at one because they start from the same point in the teaching of the Glory, who is Lord to them both. Their common ground is that the idea of a legal basis for life before God has been demolished for ever by him who came to fulfil the Law.

[13]Rom. 8 : 3 ; 2 Cor. 3 : 7 ; Col. 2 : 14 ; Gal. 3 : 21 ; [14]Philemon, verses, 18, 19.

5

THE THOUGHT AND THE ACT (Matt. 5 : 27-32)

Ye have heard that it was said to them of old time,
Thou shalt not commit adultery :
But I say unto you that—
Whosoever looketh on a woman to lust after her,
Hath committed adultery with her already in his heart.

And if thy right eye cause thee to offend,
Pluck it out, and cast it from thee :
For it is profitable for thee
That one of thy members should perish,
Aud not that thy whole body
Should be cast into Gehenna !

And if thy right hand cause thee to offend,
Cut it off, and cast it from thee :
For it is profitable for thee
That one of thy members should perish,
And not that thy whole body
Should be cast into Gehenna !

The second example in which Jesus contrasts the new with the old is in the law concerning adultery. He quotes the Seventh Commandment,[1] and adds a comment which would, on the face of it, seem to imply that the law was concerned only with externals. But, as Paul shows, the desire as well as the act was forbidden by the law of Moses : " I had not known lust, except the law had said, Thou shalt not covet ".[2] The Law itself penetrates beyond acts to motives, and in so doing, lays down a principle in which God alone can

[1] Exod. 20 : 14 ; Deut. 5 : 18 ;   [2] Rom. 7 : 7 ; cf. Exod. 20 : 17 ; Deut. 5 : 21.

be man's judge. The contrast which Jesus makes is rather with the current understanding of the law.

Proverbs has many passages which foreshadow the Lord's words. Concerning the " strange woman " the Wise Man says : " Lust not after her beauty in thine heart ; neither let her take thee with her eyelids ". No part of scripture is more definite that man is not judged only by his outward acts : " Keep thy heart with all diligence, for out of it are the issues of life ".[3]

The stress Jesus lays on the importance of the heart is therefore not new. What is new is the teaching that the act contemplated comes into the same class in God's judgment as the act committed. Jesus is far too much of a realist not to know that there is a vital difference between them—just as there is a wide difference between hard words and murder.[4] But that difference is in the injury suffered by the other person, and Jesus has in view the effect on the sinner rather than on the one sinned against. Not the man's act, but his state of mind erects a barrier between himself and God, disrupting his covenant relation with God : and this must—unless his mind is changed by repentance—exclude him from the Kingdom : for into that City of God none may enter who is among the " whoremongers, and murderers, and idolators, and whosoever loveth and maketh a lie ".[5] And among these is the man who " looks at a woman and cherishes lustful thoughts ".[6] " The Greek (says a commentator) seems to show that our Lord speaks neither of the involuntary occurrence of evil thoughts, nor of the involuntary awakening of the sexual impulse, but of looks whose deliberate purpose is to awaken the latter." All too easily, none the less, a man may pass

[3]Prov. 6 : 25 ; 4 : 23 ; 16 : 2 ; 21 : 2 ; [4]cf. verses 21-22 ; [5]Rev. 22 : 15 ; [6]R. F. Weymouth.

from involuntary thought to the stage where it begins to find a foothold, unless the thought is rejected and positive truth is put in its place. This being so, what will the judgment of Christ be on a civilization in which immense industries connected with publishing and entertainment are so largely engaged in playing upon the weaknesses of human desire?

Jesus is still dwelling on the condition without which a man may " in no wise enter the Kingdom "[7]; and because desires normal in themselves and in their right place in life may become a snare if they usurp a wrong place, he adds the sayings which show that it is better to sacrifice the part in mortal life than to lose the whole on the threshold of eternal life.

The words are a recollection of the law, " eye for eye . . . hand for hand, foot for foot "; but here the law is in reverse, for it is not another man's members but one's own which are to be cut off. Yet it cannot be a literal mutilation, for with one eye a man can be as guilty of " lust of the eyes " as with two; and even he who had lost both could conjure up mental images of the objects of desire which had been stored in memory. Physical mutilation (as Paul said of the ordinances, " touch not, taste not, handle not ") could only have " a show of wisdom in will-worship ", but would not be " of any value against the indulgence of the flesh, "[8] and certainly not against the fleshly mind. Paul uses a similar figure to Jesus (perhaps with a conscious allusion) when he writes, " Mortify, therefore, your members which are upon earth ", and goes on to name the sins of which the " members " may be the agents: " fornication, uncleanness, passion, evil desire, and covet-

[7]Matt. 5 : 20 ; [8]Col. 2 : 20-23, R.V.

ousness ".[9] The " members " are put by metonymy for the deeds and desires.

Once again, Jesus is talking in pictures : and the picture he draws stands for a radical moral act which Charles Gore describes as " the equivalent of moral self-mutilation ". To give examples : it is easy to recognize that a man with a weakness for alcoholic liquors—or even one who lives in an environment which brings special dangers—will be well advised to abstain altogether (and perhaps in our world that applies to all of us). It may be less easy to apply the principle to other sides of life. Human beauty at its best is one of the highest examples of God's handiwork, and response to it may be natural and pure : but a man who found that even pictures aroused desire would do better to avoid all portrayal of it, rather than it should be a stumbling-block to him. For the time he might lose a great deal in mental and artistic culture—a real loss, far greater than a mere physical abstinence : but if he thereby avoided losing himself in the Day of Judgment, the loss in this life would be gain.

To take another example : ambition—" the pride of life "—is no less a " lust " than the " desire of the flesh ". Rightly directed and controlled it provides a stimulus to effort, just as natural desire affords the means of " replenishing the earth ". But ambition pursued for its own sake is no less corrupting to the individual, and infinitely more ruinous to others—as millions of dead in war may witness. A certain calling may bring a man in contact with people wealthier and of higher social status than he is. If he is ambitious by temperament, a strong desire to be their equal may be aroused, and step by step he may become absorbed in trying to reach his

[9] Col. 3 : 5.

mark. Once there, another level opens up beyond, and the striving may end only with death. To refuse opportunity, to turn to another occupation where he is less tempted, to accept deliberately the lower level in life, may very well be cutting off the hand or plucking out the eye : but it may save the soul.

These are illustrations only ; to multiply examples is needless, for these have been chosen to stand for the threefold human desire which is " not of the Father, but of the world ", and with the world must " pass away ".[10] But there is one outstanding example in the Gospel record itself—that of the Rich Young Ruler,[11] who was not asked merely to disburse his wealth, but to cut off a part of himself, his " trust in riches ". Prosperity was his assurance in his standing before God ; to discard it would be an amputation of his self-esteem. We need not doubt that he was in earnest in seeking the " good thing " which he might do to gain eternal life. He would have been ready for the most exacting " works of righteousness " ; but Jesus showed him that eternal life is not gained by trying to place God in our debt, but by recognizing that we are in His debt. When the young man was asked to sacrifice himself, the cost was too great, and he went away sorrowing—keeping part only to lose the whole.

Only the man or woman can know where danger lies for him or her, and apply the principle. Its application to the stage, screen and novel is obvious ; but avoidance of these will not alone meet Christ's searching demands, which are concerned with the passions themselves rather than with their incidental expression. Whatever may be said today on the dangers of repression,

[10] I John 2 : 16-17 ;   [11] Matt. 19 : 16-30 ;   Mark 10 : 17-30 ; Luke 18 : 18-30.

Christ's teaching is clear : there are things in life which must be " cut off ". Certainly that is not all : Christ's teaching is in harmony with the psychologist's solution to the problem, which is expressed in the term sublimation. While a particular outlet may have to be ruthlessly sacrificed, the psychic energy must not merely be dammed up, or the result is disaster ; it must be turned into a higher channel—and there is no better channel than the Truth of God in its fullness, with all the scope it offers for vision and emotion, intellect and will. " Seek ye first the kingdom of God, and his righteousness ; and all these things shall be added unto you."

In two parallel passages,[12] Jesus mentions the hand, foot and eye together as possible causes of erring—the hand for doing, the foot for going, the eye for seeing, standing respectively for action, way of life, and impressions received. The order leads from the act to perception and the response it evokes ; from the outward to the inward. The deeds a man does will reflect the course in life he pursues, and this in turn will accord with the choice and control which he exercises over impressions.

> Blessed is the man that walketh not in the
>   counsel of the ungodly,
> Nor standeth in the way of sinners,
> Nor sitteth in the seat of the scornful :
> But his delight is in the law of the Lord :
> And in his law doth he meditate day and night.[13]

In both these parallel passages the context lays stress on the danger not only of stumbling oneself, but of causing others to stumble. The disciples had been disputing who should be greatest in the Kingdom of

[12]Matt. 18 : 8-9 ; Mark 9 : 43-48 ; [13]Psa. 1 : 1-2.

Heaven, and Jesus had set a child in their midst, saying, "Except ye be converted, and become as little children, ye shall in no wise enter the kingdom of heaven". Rather than be a source of stumbling to one of the " little ones " who believe in him, he said, it were better for a man to be thrown into the sea weighted down by a " great mill stone "—a stone turned by an ass in contrast to the small domestic mill which women turned by hand. The connexion of thought is pointed in Matt. 18 : 7-8 : " Woe to that man by whom the offence cometh ; and (A.V. wherefore) if thy hand or thy foot offend thee, cut it off . . . ". The danger to others was the result of danger to themselves, and to help others they must first watch themselves.

The thought has widened out to include all forms of unregulated desire ; but the starting point in the Seventh Commandment has none the less been kept in view, and to this Jesus returns in a comment on an aspect of the law which is subordinate to the main commands dealing with the relations between man and woman :

> It hath been said,
>> Whosoever shall put away his wife, let him give her a writing of divorcement :

> But I say unto you
>> That whosoever shall put away his wife, saving for the cause of fornication,
>> Causeth her to commit adultery ;
>> And whosoever shall marry her that is divorced
>> Committeth adultery.

The general purport is unmistakable : as in the creation God made them male and female, forming the

woman from the man, so in marriage they are again made
" one flesh ". In the eyes of God, there could be no
divorce save where the marriage bond was broken by
adultery. The law in Deut. 24 : 1 regulated morals by
requiring a legal process of divorce, but even this was a
concession to the standards of the time which fell below
the standard implied in the account of the creation.[14]
In practice,[15] divorce had become so easy that it offered
a legal licence for illicit desire. Jesus strips the practice
bare of pretence : those who remarry during the former
partner's life time are morally adulterers. Two points
must be made clear : first, the comparison with the law
of Deut. 24 : 1 leaves no doubt that what is under
discussion is not separation, but a process conferring
legal freedom to remarry ; and, secondly, to the law as
Christ enunciates it there is one exception. For the
suggestion that the " exceptive clause " here and in
Matt. 19 : 9 is not original, there is no textual evidence
whatever ; it rests entirely on grounds of " higher
criticism ". But the exception does not enjoin divorce
in such cases : it only mentions in an aside that they
come in a different category from divorce on other
grounds. Whether the injured partner should seek
freedom must be determined by the general principles
which Christ gives in the Sermon : and who can doubt
that the law of love would call for an erring one to be
treated as Hosea treated Gomer-bath-Diblaim? And,
indeed—since the Father is the example for the sons—as
God treated Israel in the history of which the prophet's
domestic life was a parable?

The method of Jesus is to give principles by which
a man can judge himself, not a code by which he can

[14]Matt. 19 : 3-9 ; Mark 10 : 2-12 ; [15]Especially as interpreted by
the school of Hillel.

judge others. If, however, there be one passage in the Sermon which has the more precise (and therefore more limited) character of an ordinance, it is this. Elsewhere the principle governing marriage is stated in absolute terms free from any qualifying clause ; the fact that a qualification is introduced here implies that the passage is to be regarded more literally. But for that reason it cannot escape the danger which belongs to all legislation : those who want to do so may keep within the letter while nullifying the aim. The " exceptive clause " exists : but it is only too easy for a man to plead the exception when the real motive for divorce is that he has found another woman whom he likes. Who is to judge his motive? Only the man himself (or, indeed, the woman, if the case is reversed). But is not the second marriage in such a case morally adultery, even though the letter of the Scripture would seem to sanction it? Far better would it be if the offended one would remain celibate (supposing—a large supposition—that there was no alternative to ending the marriage completely). A sacrifice? Undoubtedly ; but are not sacrifices often called for from the children of God? Many remain unmarried altogether through loyalty to the commands of Christ.

This is not the place for a detailed examination of a complex subject : the present aim is only to think of some of the wider spiritual principles when the problem is seen in relation to the Sermon as a whole. By its very nature, it is involved in a tangle of human passions, any one of which violates the law of Christ. Apart from the motive of human desire which has been referred to above, an injured partner in marriage may obtain a divorce out of harshness, or refuse to obtain a divorce out of vindictiveness. An unforgiving spirit can often clothe itself in a garment of righteousness ; no ecclesial constitution might be able to deal with it on the letter of the Scripture, but it stands condemned by the law of Christ.

The word rendered "fornication" in A.V. has a wide meaning, but in the context of these two passages in Matthew the reference to illicit sexual intercourse while in the married state can only be questioned by those with a case to make for what is essentially Roman Catholic doctrine.

6

GEHENNA (Matt. 5 : 30)

The utter loss of a man's self in the future which may result from self-indulgence now is described by Jesus as " the whole body " (in contrast to the single member) being " cast into Gehenna ". With one exception, this term is used by Jesus alone in the New Testament. In the Gospels it is found only on his lips ; never in the evangelists' own words. Elsewhere it occurs only in James 3 : 6, where by a bold figure which puts the effect for the cause James says the tongue is " set on fire of Gehenna ". The unruly tongue is a fire ; and by its means the whole life may be brought to the destroying fires of God's judgment. So much is it a foreshadowing of judgment that James describes the tongue as being set alight from the Gehenna flames in which it will end.

Of such kings as Ahaz and Manasseh[1], Jeremiah said : " They have built the high places of Topheth,

[1] 2 Chron. 28 : 3 ; 2 Kings 16 : 3 ; 2 Chron. 33 : 6 ; 2 Kings 21 : 6.

which is in the valley of the son of Hinnom, to burn
their sons and their daughters in the fire ".[2] Josiah, in
his effort to sweep away heathen practices, broke down
every structure and defiled every spot associated with
them, and it is recorded that he " defiled Topheth,
which is in the valley of the children of Hinnom ".[3]
In this Josiah was following a precedent set by Asa,
who, when he deposed the Queen-Mother Maachah,
burnt her " image " " at the brook Kidron ".[4]   In
Hezekiah's reign also the " brook (or *wady*) Kidron "
received the broken remains of the idolatrous altars ;[5]
while Josiah himself burned the vessels of Baal and the
Asherah from the Temple in " the fields " and the
wady of Kidron.[6] If Topheth is correctly placed at the
junction of the two valleys, then probably the lower
parts of both were defiled ; and this is perhaps implied
by Jeremiah's prophecy of the day when they will be
cleansed : " And the whole valley of the dead bodies,
and of the ashes, and all the fields unto the brook of
Kidron, unto the corner of the horse gate towards the
east, shall be holy unto the Lord ; it shall not be plucked
up, nor thrown down any more for ever ".[7]

The object in rendering the place unfit for any
ritual use was not wholly achieved, for human sacrifice
was revived in the reign of Jehoiakim ;[8] but from then
on Hinnom was thought of as a place of Divine retribution for the defilement of God's name.[9] His prophecy
against it is repeated[10] when Jeremiah takes " a potter's
earthen bottle " and goes forth " unto the valley of the
son of Hinnom, which is by the entry of the gate
Harsith ",[11] and there breaks the earthenware as a

[2]Jer. 7 : 31 ; [3]2 Kings 23 : 10-14 ; [4]1 Kings 15 : 13 ; [5]2 Chron.
29 : 16 ; 30 : 14 ; [6]2 Kings 23 : 4, 6, 12 ; [7]Jer. 31 : 40 ; [8]Jer. 11 :
10 ; Ezek. 20 : 30-31 ; [9]Jer. 7 : 32 ; [10]Jer. 19 : 11 ; [11]verse 2.

symbol of the utter destruction of the people and the city. Hinnom therefore becomes a type of that which is broken so that it " cannot be made whole again ",[12] whether applied to an individual or to civic life.

The literary evidence for the Jewish tradition that the valley of Hinnom received the refuse of Jerusalem in continually burning fires is unfortunately no earlier than about 1200 A.D., when Rabbi David Kimchi writes : " Gehenna was a place set apart into which they threw refuse and dead bodies, and there was a continuous fire there for burning the refuse and bones ; because of which it is spoken of metaphorically as Gehenna the place of judgment ". The tradition is reasonable, and Sir Charles Warren says " this may be accepted as the most probable method of disposing of the immense masses of refuse which required to be destroyed for the sake of the health of the city ".[13] It receives some support from Jer. 31 : 40 (quoted above), where the word rendered " dead bodies " may be used of the carcases of men or animals. Perhaps there is a hint of it also in the fate foretold of Jehoiakim : " He shall be buried with the burial of an ass, drawn and cast forth beyond the gates of Jerusalem".[14]

By Talmudic times—from the third to the fifth centuries—the valley of Hinnom had given its name to a mythological region which was credited with fantastic features later borrowed to adorn the Hell of mediaeval Christendom. It would be foolish to dogmatize as to how early these characteristics were acquired ; much depends on the doubtful dating and uncertain text of the so-called " pseudepigrapha "—the Book of Enoch

[12]verse 11 ; [13]*Hastings' Dictionary of the Bible* ; [14]Jer. 22 : 19.

and the rest. Legend would grow more easily away from Palestine, especially where Judaism was corrupted by Hellenic influences.

For the hearers of Jesus—Palestinian Jews of the first century—it is likely, if not certain, that Gehenna already stood for " the final retributive scene and condition ". But (to quote again) " What the common belief of the Jews was on the subject of the nature and duration of the final retribution at the time to which the N.T. writings belong, is a disputed question, and one by no means easy to answer."[15] Perhaps it is enough to say they would have no doubt that Jesus was talking about the issue of final judgment, and the nature of that issue must be discovered from Jesus' own teaching.

Besides the references to destruction in the Sermon itself, that teaching is placed beyond doubt by the comparison between death which cannot prevent resurrection and death irretrievable and eternal which is made in Matt. 10 : 28 : " Fear not them which kill the body, but are not able to kill the soul : but rather fear him which is able to destroy both soul and body in Gehenna". To destroy is more than to kill : it is to bring to an utter end : and so in Matt. 7 : 13-14 " the destruction " (with the definite article) is placed in antithesis to " the life " as the two possible ends for man. Fire is the constant figure of the means by which destruction is to be carried out—a " furnace of fire " like that into which the tares were cast in the parable ;[16] " eternal " fire because it determines the entire future of those who are its subjects ;[17] " fire that shall never be quenched " because (like the fire which consumed Jerusalem)[18] it

[15]D. S. F. SALMOND in *Hastings' Dictionary of the Bible* ; [16]Matt. 13 : 42 ; [17]Matt. 18 : 8, 9 ; [18]Jer. 7 : 20 ; 17 : 27.

would burn till there was no more to consume.[19] The
condemnation and the punishment are always pictured
as bringing " wailing and gnashing of teeth ".[20]

What is the source of this language? The refuse-
burning fires of the valley no doubt make some con-
tribution to it, but to a much larger extent it would seem
to be drawn from those historic fires which destroyed
the emblems of idolatry, these having special significance as a retribution for the fires of human sacrifice.
But a still more important element in the Lord's thought
may be the place which fire holds in the symbolism
of the Old Testament. In the literal sense of the destruction of war to come on Jerusalem it enters largely
into the prophecies of Jeremiah, Ezekiel, and the
Minor Prophets ; but much earlier it has a remarkable
place in the poetry of the Psalms and Isaiah. Fire
accompanies the Divine presence, especially when God
is manifested among men as when he " descended in
fire " upon Mount Sinai.[21] It is the agent of judgment
and the means by which the wicked are extinguished.[22]
Moses had shown the manifestation on Sinai to be a
revelation of the character of God : " The Lord thy
God is a consuming fire " ;[23] and all this imagery
with a literal basis is gathered up in the symbolism
of Daniel's vision of the beasts : the Ancient of days is
enthroned in " fiery flames ", " the wheels thereof
burning fire ". " A fiery stream issued and came forth
from before him " : and when the fourth beast was
slain, and his body destroyed, he was " given to be

[19]Mark. 9 : 43-49 ; [20]Matt. 8 : 12 ; 13 : 42 ; 25 : 30, etc. ; [21]Psa.
18 : 8, 12, 13 ; 50 : 3 ; Exod. 19 : 18 ; [22]Psa. 97 : 3 ; Isa. 30 : 27 ;
Psa. 11 : 6 ; 21 : 9 ; 37 : 20 ; 83 : 13-14 ; 118 : 12 ; Isa. 5 : 24 ;
33 : 14 ; 66 : 15 ; [23]Deut. 4 : 24.

burned with fire ".[24] But the passage on which the
Lord's references to Gehenna are directly based is
Isa. 66 : 24 : "And they shall go forth, and look upon
the carcases of the men that have transgressed against
me : for their worm shall not die, neither shall their
fire be quenched ; and they shall be an abhorring unto
all flesh. "

Literal fire as an instrument for carrying out the
Divine condemnation need not be excluded in the
future any more than it was in the past : but, as in the
visions of the Apocalypse, the literal aspect is subordinate. Gehenna stands as a type of the decisiveness
of God's judgment, the energy and completeness with
which the sentence will be carried into effect, and the
total loss for the individual which it involves.

[24]Dan. 7 : 9 ; 7 : 11 (R.V. m., " to the burning of fire ").

7

THE THOUGHT AND THE WORD
(Matt. 5 : 33-37)

Again, ye have heard that it was said to them of old time :
Thou shalt not forswear thyself, but shalt perform unto the
Lord thine oaths.

But I say unto you—

Swear not at all :
Neither by heaven :
For it is the throne of God ;

Nor by the earth :
For it is the footstool of his feet :

Nor by Jerusalem :
For it is the city of the Great King.

Neither shalt thou swear by thine head :
For thou canst not make one hair white or black.

But let your speech be Yea, yea ; Nay, nay,
For whatsoever is more than these cometh of the evil.

" Thou shalt worship the Lord thy God " : on the
sanctity of God and the fear and reverence due to Him
are based both the Mosaic law which sanctions oaths
and the law of Christ which forbids them. The saying
in which the Lord summarizes the words of " them of
old time " includes both oaths in the stricter sense,
and vows ; and in order to appreciate it we must examine
the position under the Law. There were three forms of
oath or charge in the course of judicial proceedings :

(1) There is the " voice of adjuration "[1] to a man
who has " seen or known " the committing of a sin.

[1]Lev. 5 : 1, R.V.

This was a charge by the priest to testify what he knew. That he should testify truthfully was implied, but this differs materially from the administration of an oath in a modern court of law. (a) It is not an asseveration of truth by the witness, but an obligation to testify, imposed upon him by a judge who is also a priest acting on behalf of God in His kingdom. (b) No magistrate today can speak with the authority of a priest of Divine appointment. (c) There is no evidence that it was universally administered, but rather that it was a power in the hands of the priest for use where needed. The outstanding example of its use in Scripture is by the High Priest Caiaphas to the Lord Jesus himself;[2] and although it was then administered illegally—in that there was no " standing testimony " on which to base a charge against him and that the accused should not be required to testify against himself—Jesus signified his respect for the law and his reverence for the Divine name by responding to the adjuration without reserve.

(2) In cases where property held in trust has been lost or damaged, it was said that " the oath of the Lord " shall be between the owner and the person to whom it was entrusted.[3] That is, the trustee's oath should be accepted, and he should be freed from the obligation to restore the property.

(3) The only clear case of a compulsory oath is that of a woman suspected of marital infidelity, and this was part of the ordeal imposed upon her by the priest.[4] This is an oath in the full sense, uttered by the accused, and it is exacted from her with or without her consent.

In practice these judicial procedures were hedged

[2]Matt. 26 : 63 ; [3]Exod. 22 : 11 ; [4]Num. 5 : 19, 21.

with restrictions. In the light of these enactments, the Rabbis understood that an oath was to be employed " in civil cases only, never in criminal cases, and only in litigations concerning private property, never in those over sacerdotal property ; and over movable but not immovable property . . . Moreover, the oath was administered only in case no evidence, or only insufficient evidence, was forthcoming on either side." It was administered only to the defendant, and was not administered if he was suspected of a disposition to swear falsely.[5] Later, there was a form known as the Mishnaic oath, given in certain other circumstances, but with this we are not concerned.

Apart from judicial proceedings, the Law regulates the custom of men making solemn asseverations by imposing a two-fold restriction : " Ye shall not . . . lie one to another, and ye shall not swear by my name falsely, so that thou profane the name of thy God ".[6] They must be truthful, for a false oath profanes the name called to witness it ; and they must swear in no name but the Lord's. For the command " Thou shalt fear the Lord thy God, and serve him, and swear by his name ",[7] does not impose an obligation to swear, but forbids appeal to any other name on the ground that there is no God but One.

Further, there were under the Law voluntary vows by which a man incurred certain obligations to God, either by dedicating to Him gifts or offerings, or by undertaking some abstinence, and calling on God to witness the undertaking. And in these the man must not deal lightly with God : " If a man vow a vow unto the Lord, or swear an oath to bind his soul with a bond,

[5]*Jewish Encyclopaedia* ; [6]Lev. 19 : 11-12 ; [7]Deut. 6 : 13 ; 10 : 20

he shall not break his word; he shall do according to all that proceedeth out of his mouth ".[8] The Preacher has the perfect comment on the Law : " Be not rash with thy mouth, and let not thine heart be hasty to utter any thing before God : for God is in heaven, and thou upon earth : therefore let thy words be few. For a dream cometh with a multitude of business ; and a fool's voice with a multitude of words. When thou vowest a vow unto God, defer not to pay it ; for he hath no pleasure in fools. "[9] The fool who babbles vows as meaninglessly as a man talking in a dream will find he has spoken to his own destruction. He is free not to vow, but he is not free not to perform.[10]

All the restrictions surrounding oaths and vows are expansions of the command of the Decalogue : " Thou shalt not take the name of the Lord thy God in vain ",[11] where " in vain " may mean either emptily or falsely, and doubtless includes both. The emphasis laid on the exaltation of God brings home the fact that the Third Commandment is a logical development from those which have gone before : " I am the Lord thy God . . . Thou shalt have no other gods before me ". The command concerning His name is a consequence of His Godhead, His unity and His universality : man's speech must be governed by the fact that God is God, whether he names the Lord or speaks only a word of promise. It was in the light of this that one of the rabbis said : " Let thy yea be yea, and thy nay be nay. He who changes his word commits as heavy a sin as he who worships idols : and he who utters an untruth is excluded from the Divine presence."

Such a saying shows vision of a truth which was

[8]Num. 30 : 2 ; [9]Eccl. 5 : 2-4 ; [10]Deut. 5 : 11 ; [11]Exod. 20 : 7 ; Deut. 5 : 11.

nullified in the traditions of less discerning elders : there is no point at which a line can be drawn between what is God's and what is not. To make distinctions between oaths by the Creator and oaths by that which He has created is a futile self-deception. It is, moreover, to violate the command, " Thou shalt not lie ", and so it is in a twofold way to deny the holiness and universality of God " in whom we live and move and have our being ".

The Talmud and Jewish writings even down to Maimonides in the twelfth century give evidence for evasions of the force of an oath, and show that here and in Matt. 23 : 16-22 the Lord is quoting phrases which were in use. There is ample evidence for the way in which this law was " made void " : and Jesus showed easily enough that the very words of Scripture condemned the popular language of asseveration. Through Isaiah the Lord had said : " Heaven is my throne, and earth is my footstool . . . for all those things hath mine hand made. "[12] The Psalmist had sung of Zion : " Great is the Lord, and greatly to be praised, in the city of our God . . . the city of the great King. "[13] If, therefore, the words " thou shalt perform unto the Lord thine oaths " were interpreted to mean that only oaths to the Lord need be performed, Jesus shows that even on that low level these oaths stood condemned, for every one of them contained an implied reference to God. If oaths involved a sacred object, its sole value was that it was sacred to God ; if they named a created thing, its significance was that God had created it.[14]

Most foolish of all was the oath " By my head " or " By my beard ", in which a man neither appealed to a

[12]Isa. 66 : 1-2 ;   [13]Psa. 48 : 1-2 ;   [14]Matt. 23 : 17-22.

greater than himself nor pledged that which was within his own power. He could not change the colour of a single hair : of what value was the oath unless it was an implied appeal to the Creator of the hairs who could turn them white in a night? Men did not own themselves ; how could they swear by themselves? Whether they would or no, those who uttered such things had bound themselves, and stood under judgment even by the law they professed. To set up a double standard in oaths was to trifle with God.

So much was evident from the Law itself, and the distinctions between forms of swearing were examples of the Pharisaic " straining out a gnat and swallowing a camel ". They could only arise where the aim of the Law was buried under the dust of a formal legal interpretation. But even in going beyond this to a wider condemnation of swearing Jesus was not introducing a wholly novel teaching. It was one of the marks of difference between the Pharisees and the Essenes that the latter said " he is already condemned who cannot be believed without calling upon God ". The word that cannot be relied on without an oath is not so much more dependable with it ; in such things a double standard means a divided foundation, and " A double minded man is unstable in all his ways." The Law which demanded that reverence for God should permeate the whole of life therefore contained a principle which must bring swearing to an end, even while it was given formal and restricted sanction because of the " hardness of their hearts ".

Jesus, then, is firstly condemning an interpretation which undermined the Law ; but he also by his own authority transcends the terms of the Law itself ; yet in so doing he is unfolding the Law's true aim. " Let your speech ", he says, " be, 'Yea, yea ; Nay, nay. " If we ask what is the exact force of the repeated words, we have James's exposition : " Let your Yea be yea . . . ". When the substance is " Yes " let your word be " Yes " : that and nothing more : and let it mean what it says.

One of the most striking modern illustrations of what this might mean in practice is to be found— alas !—not among " Christian " peoples ; a soldier whose duties had brought him into business dealings with Chinese merchants in Singapore told the writer that they considered it an affront to their honour to be asked to sign a written contract, but they were scrupulous in fulfilling their spoken word. There have been brethren of Christ whose conduct and repute reached an equally high standard in the framework of a different social custom ; but such integrity is not always synonymous with professed discipleship.

" Whatsoever is more than these cometh of the evil . . . ". With the definite article, English idiom calls for a noun to complete the phrase, making " evil " an adjective. As it stands in the text " the evil . . . " may be either masculine or neuter, and the tendency among scholars has been to treat it as masculine and render it " the Evil One ", on the ground that it is " more in accord with Jewish modes of thought to interpret the originating influence here of the author of evil than of an abstract principle ". But, quite apart from the truth that there is no personal " author of evil " independent of man, this ignores an important Jewish conception which is far more in harmony with the general teaching of Scripture. This is the *Yezer ha-Ra*, the evil impulse, the expression being traced to

Gen. 8 : 21 : " The imagination (*yezer*, that which is framed) of man's heart is evil from his youth ".[15] So also in Deut. 31 : 21, " I know their imagination which they go about ".   From the evil impulse, according to the rabbis, came anger, revenge, avarice, vanity, and unchastity, so that it affords a close parallel with the defilements denounced by the Lord as proceeding " out of the heart ".[16] " Imagination " in Scripture, however, is not necessarily an evil quality, for Isaiah says, " Thou wilt keep him in perfect peace whose mind (*yezer*) is stayed on thee ".[17] The Rabbis also recognized a good impulse (*Yezer Tob*) ; but while the evil is described as born with a man, the good is thirteen years younger : an allusion to the custom that at thirteen a Jewish boy becomes Barmitzveh, a " son of the Commandment ". The good is therefore conceived as entering into a man through the word of God, while the evil is innate. If the *Yezer ha-Ra* tends to become personified, and sometimes to be identified with a mythological Satan, this is the kind of development which might be expected : but it is evident that in origin the *Yezer ha-Ra* is an attempt to explain the psychology of man in rational and Scriptural terms. While these Rabbinical writings belong to a later age than Jesus, they rest on earlier traditions, and may be taken as evidence that Jesus would by no means be unintelligible to his hearers if by " the evil " he meant the impulse of human nature. That which cometh out of a man defileth him, he taught ; for out of the heart proceed evil thoughts and the resulting acts. And how well this background of Jewish thought illustrates Paul's description of the war within him between the " law

[15]cf. Gen. 6 : 5 ; [16]Mark 7 : 20-22 ; [17]Isa. 26 : 3.

in his members " and the " law of his mind " ! The sin that dwells in his flesh, he says, works death even by " that which is good ", because the Law reveals the sinfulness of sin and therefore brings condemnation.[18] How perfectly his reasoning grows out of the Lord's words when " the evil " is understood as human nature's indwelling tendency ! Both Jesus and Paul in different ways are concerned to show that contemporary Judaism could not resolve the conflict of evil and good in man.

In the righteousness which belongs to the Kingdom, no room is left for words or deeds which have their source in the " wisdom which is not from above ", but is " earthly, sensual, and devilish ".[19] When His Reign is fully established and all enemies subdued, God will be " all and in all " ; and the men and women who will then be found in that perfect order will be those in whose minds God is already recognized as " all " —for out of Him all things came and for Him all exist. It is this knowledge of God and of the response due to Him from man which permeates the words of Jesus : and while we may trace parallels in Jewish thought, no one else so clearly saw Him who is invisible, or so penetratingly judged every act and thought by the light of that vision. It is this vision which gives to his sayings about oaths unity and depth. Jesus may use bricks which other men have moulded, but the house he builds is his own, and it is after a heavenly pattern.

For those who have this vision worship will be not an occasional act but a constant attitude ; life will be orientated towards God. Christ alone is the perfect example of that orientation, but he has said that they

[18]Rom. 7 ; [19]James 3 : 15.

who worship God " must worship him in spirit and in truth ".[20]   God is Spirit, and He calls for worship from the spirit—the whole inward consciousness—of man, and in the Divine education of man this lesson was to be enforced by the ending of the ritual of the law—God-ordained though it was—and the desolation of the Temple in the place where God had chosen to place His name.   When the very centre of their worship was destroyed Israel was to be made to know that true worship is the remembrance of God in daily life.   That remembrance must both restrain their words and sanctify their promises.

With this understanding of the mind of Jesus, we are better able to approach two questions : (1) Did Jesus intend to forbid judicial oaths to his immediate disciples? and (2) Are judicial oaths excluded for those who profess his name today?   The words " Swear not at all " may in themselves be not unreasonably regarded as one of his brief, epigrammatic sayings, stripped in eastern style of all qualification.   When they are quoted by James, it is in a context which defines the application James has in mind.   Having spoken of the oppressions to which they may be subject, he has exhorted the brethren to " be patient until the coming of the Lord ", and has instanced the prophets as " an example of suffering and of patience ".[21]   Believers, like the prophets, may be subjected to persecution and reproach. Endurance may be strained to the point where they are tempted to express themselves with profuse oriental emphasis ; and so James says : " But above all things, my brethren, swear not, neither by heaven, neither by the earth, neither by any other oath : but let your

[20]John 4 : 24 ; [21]James 5 : 7, 10, 12.

yea by yea ; and your nay, nay ; lest ye fall into condemnation ".

What are the two things which Jesus places in
contrast by his " But I say unto you " ? His own teaching
is contrasted with the law which forbids (*a*) false swearing,
and (*b*) vows unfulfilled. Against this he says, " Do not
swear at all ", and (by implication, at any rate) " Do
not make vows ". Now, the vows were voluntary, and
this suggests that he has in mind—at any rate primarily
—oaths of a voluntary character also ; a presumption
which is supported by the fact that all these examples
he quotes are taken from the language of the market
place and of everyday life, rather than from that of
judicial proceedings. When to this we add the evidence
of his own conduct when on trial, we can answer the
first question, " No, he did not forbid to his disciples
judicial oaths when conformity to the law of Moses
required it, and while the law stood."

This, however, does not wholly dispose of the
question what our practice should be today—a question
to be decided rather in the light of underlying principles than of the letter of an ordinance. There is no
strict comparison between judicial oaths under the law
of Moses, and judicial oaths in the current practice of
secular courts, either in the authority with which they
are administered or the manner in which they are
employed. As has been shown, under the law they
had a more restricted use, and there is something
repellent in the glibness with which they may now be
administered. What we do must finally be a matter
of private judgment. We know that we are enjoined
to give all due honour to magistrates in the kingdoms
of men and to the courts over which they lawfully

preside; but we may well feel—as the present writer does—that it is more in accord with the spirit of worship for us to adopt a permitted form of affirmation which avoids mention of that Divine Name which is daily profaned. For the disciples there is only one standard of truth, and invocation of the Name can add nothing to it, while true reverence makes us deeply reluctant to call that Name to attest our human asseverations. The one thing certain is that followers of Christ must " do all to the glory of God."[22]

[22] 1 Cor. 10 : 31.

8

THE WAY OF NON-RESISTANCE
(Matt. 5 : 38-42)

Ye have heard that it was said,
 An eye for an eye, and a tooth for a tooth :

But I say unto you,
 Resist not evil :

  But whosoever smiteth thee on thy right cheek,
  Turn to him the other also ;

  And if any man would go to law with thee, and take
   away thy coat,
  Let him have thy cloak also :

  And whosoever shall compel thee to go one mile,
  Go with him twain.

  Give to him that asketh thee,
  And from him that would borrow of thee, turn not
   away!

151

When Jesus turns from the sanctity of God to the disciples' relation to other men, it is immediately clear that he is picturing them as sojourners in an alien world. They will be subject to oppression, injustice, contumely. These are not principles of God's law, or of the Kingdom which the meek are to inherit; they belong to the time of subjection before the inheritance is entered. But that is the time when men show whether they are in God's covenant, and therefore whether the Kingdom is theirs.

If they are, then the principle which governs all their actions is, " Resist not evil ". Again it is literally " the evil—— ", and it cannot mean the Devil either of tradition or of truth, for whatever he is, he is to be resisted.[1] The R.V. renders, " him that is evil "—the violent and oppressive man : but one commentator says : " We need not ask as to the gender of *tō pōnerō*. Just as in 5 : 37 it meant the evil and sinful element in life, regarded from the abstract point of view, so here it is the same element contemplated as in action through an individual ".[2] The question is what we are to do, not with the evil in ourselves, but with the evil shown by others towards us. " Say not, I will do so to him as he hath done to me : I will render to the man according to his work. "[3]

The law did not justify personal vengeance. Retribution was judicial. The Pharisees interpreted " eye for eye, tooth for tooth ", not as literally requiring mutilation for injury, but as technical legal terms which enjoined that compensation should be strictly commensurate with the injury done. So far as the time of Christ is concerned, we may say that the *lex talionis* was not in practice applied literally, and was not inter-

[1]James 4 : 7 ; [2]ALLEN, *International Critical Commentary* ; [3]Prov. 24 : 29 ; 20 : 22.

preted literally in the prevailing view. What exactly was the original intention of the law is a more difficult question. In the code of Hammurabi the law " eye for eye " was applied with a rigidity which led to remarkable consequences. If a builder erected a house so badly that it fell down, causing the death of the owner in the ruins, the builder's own life was forfeit; but if it was the owner's son or daughter who perished, not the builder but his own son or daughter must pay the penalty. Such a perversion of justice could only be based on an entirely different conception of human life from that in the Law of Moses: the son or daughter is viewed not so much as an individual each with a life which is inviolable by man's hand, but rather as part of the property or rights of their father. In the Law of Moses, so far as relations between man and man are concerned, life itself is the supreme value to be safeguarded by law; life with all its attributes as the possession, under God, of each " living soul ". There seems even to be a deliberate allusion to the Babylonian law in Exod. 21 : 31. Here the law lays down that where an ox has been known to gore in time past, the owner's life shall be forfeit if it causes the death of another person; and it is added: " Whether he have gored a son or a daughter, according to this judgment shall it be done unto him. "[4]

So far as killing with intent is concerned, " He that smiteth a man, so that he dies, shall surely be put to death ". No ranson is to be accepted for the life of a manslayer.[5] But Dr. Hertz contended that this specific exception implies that money compensation was not excluded in other cases. The first statement of the law " eye for eye ", in Exod. 21 : 24, actually follows a

[4]cf. Deut. 24 : 16 ; [5]Exod. 21 : 12 ; Num. 35 : 31.

provision for paying compensation to cover loss of time and cost of treatment in the case of a man who is confined to bed by injury (verses 18, 19). Other contexts also present difficulties of a literal interpretation, particularly that of Deut. 19 : 21, where it occurs in the law of Plotting Witnesses.[6]

In whatever way these clauses were to be applied, they established two legal principles. First, all were equal before the law ; the tooth of the poor man was of the same value as the tooth of the princeling ; the law declared his rights as a man of the seed of Abraham, independent of rank or wealth. Secondly, the law established " measure for measure ". Retribution, whatever its form, must be neither more nor less than the offence ; neither exacting double in the spirit of vengeance, nor allowing the powerful to escape with the wrong half-redressed.

This principle of " measure for measure " is the essence of natural justice, and the only equitable basis on which law can be administered in the State. Yet it is precisely this which Jesus says is not open to his disciples. They, of all people, are not to exact their dues or maintain their rights : and there could be no clearer contrast between legislation to be administered by the State and the principles of living for the pilgrims of Jesus. The State must maintain equity between man and man ; Jesus lays down the motive of conduct from a disciple to other men.

What these principles of living are he illustrates by three instances. First comes the personal insult, which is often harder to bear sweetly than material injury. As in Lam. 3 : 31, the blow inflicts indignity rather than injury ; a blow intended to knock a man down

[6]Referred to on page 116.

154

would be struck with the right fist, and therefore would land on the left side. Jesus would in fact seem to have the words of Jeremiah in mind; for the theme of the prophet in the context is the discipline of suffering when it is accepted as a yoke laid on a man's shoulders by the Lord.

> It is good that a man should hope and quietly wait for the salvation of the Lord.
> It is good for a man that he bear the yoke in his youth.
> Let him sit alone and keep silence, because He hath laid it upon him.
> Let him give his cheek to him that smiteth him :
> Let him be filled full with reproach.
> For the Lord will not cast off for ever . . .

So the Servant of the Lord " hid not his face from shame and spitting ".[8]

His own fulfilment of that prophecy is the perfect example of the precept applied. The pain and shame inflicted by the servants of the High Priest or the soldiers of Pilate or Herod—the strain of the trial through a sleepness night and a morning of exhaustion, the scourging, the thorn wreath, the mockery of his royal claims—all these he bore without flinching in the silence of humility. But one incident saves us from too narrow an application of this saying. When in the inquiry before the High Priest one of the officers struck him, Jesus did not literally turn the other cheek ; with perfect calmness he called attention to the irregularity : " If I have spoken evil, bear witness of the evil : but if well, why smitest thou me? "[9] He was not defending

[7]Lam. 3 : 26-31, R.V. ; [8]Isa. 50 : 6 ; [9]John 18 : 23.

his own dignity : it was necessary for the very purpose for which he had surrendered himself to the power of men, that the illegality of the proceedings should be made clear ; he died without fault. The blow had followed his refusal to answer questions before a *prima facie* case had been made out by witnesses, and it was one more evidence of the injustice of the trial. In the same spirit Paul and Silas—not for their own sake, but for the sake of the Gospel—insisted on the Philippian magistrates recognizing the illegality of their conduct.[10]

The next example is a submission to harsh legal exaction. The law mercifully protected the poor : " If thou at all take thy neighbour's raiment to pledge, thou shalt deliver it unto him by that the sun goeth down : for that is his covering only, it is his raiment for his skin : wherein shall he sleep? And it shall come to pass when he crieth unto me, that I will hear : for I am gracious. "[11]

But Jesus forbids his disciples to avail themselves of it. If a creditor demands the less costly under-garment (*chitōn*) in pledge, the more valuable outer garment (*himation*) is to be surrendered too, even if it deprives the debtor of his covering for the night—another example of putting the extreme case so as to enforce the lesson powerfully. The saying is illustrated from the opposite end by a story told of a rabbi who had suffered the loss of a cask of wine through the negligence of the coopers. He took their coats in order to reimburse himself, at which they complained to a distinguished teacher. " Give them back their coats ", was the judgment. " Is that what you call dealing out justice?" asked the rabbi. " Yes ", he said, " walk in the way

[10]Acts 16 : 35-39 ;   [11]Exod. 22 : 26-27 ;   cf. Deut. 24 : 6, 10-13.

of good men, as Solomon commands ".[12]   He gave
them their coats, but they complained, " We are poor
people and have worked all day long and are hungry
and have nothing ". And the judge said, " Come, give
them their wages ". " Is that dealing justice?" asked
the rabbi. " Yes ", said he, " for Solomon continues :
' Keep the paths of righteousness '."[13]

Luke, in his account of the address Jesus gave after
choosing the apostles, gives two similar sayings, but in a
form which relates both of them to acts of violence :
" Unto him that smiteth thee on the cheek offer the
other also ; and from him that taketh away thy cloak
withhold not thy coat also."[14] The omission of " right "
before " cheek " removes the qualification which makes
the smiting a mere flick of contempt ; the mention of the
" cloak " before the " coat " implies the surrender of
the under-garment when the outer has been snatched
away by a robber. These details are two of many which
enforce the belief that Luke is recording a different
address from Matthew : but the variation throws added
light on the sayings and widens their scope.

The third example in Matthew carries non-
resistance into the disciple's relations with authority.
The word for " compel " has an interesting history.
Herodotus applies it to the Persian system of conveying
official despatches by couriers, both horses and men
being relieved at the end of each day's journey. This
is referred to in Esther 8 : 10, which the R.V. renders :
" He . . . sent letters by posts on horseback, riding on
swift steeds that were used in the king's service, bred
of the stud." Royal couriers could impress into state
service the common people and their possessions, and

[12]Prov. 2 : 5 ;   [13]Quoted by FRANZ DELITSCH, *Jewish Artisan Life* ;
[14]Luke 6 : 29.

157

so by the third century B.C. the term had come to be used for requisitioning of services or property—pack animals, or boats, for instance—especially for the transport of military baggage. The best illustration is an inscription of A.D. 49 in the gateway of the temple in the Great Oasis, in which Capeto, prefect of Egypt, refers to exactions which had been made, and decrees that soldiers passing through the several districts are not to make any requisitions or to employ forced transport without the prefect's written authority.[15] This indicates the abuse of authority from which subject peoples in the Roman Empire might suffer. In the gospel record Simon the Cyrenian is impressed into service by the Roman soldiers to carry the cross, and these are the only other New Testament occurrences of the word.[16]

Impressment was a mark of the humiliation of the people of God's Kingdom at the hands of an alien power whom they called " the lawless ".[17] The country was seething with unrest, and there were recurring outbreaks. The day was not far off when the Jews themselves would choose Barabbas, a bandit implicated in murders committed in the course of insurrection, rather than Jesus.[18] It is in this atmosphere that Jesus commands submission to " the powers that be " even when that means accepting a hated foreign rule ; response to official demands, even when power is being abused by some minor representative of the State ; a willing and generous response which does more than is asked. While the command's main aim is to purge strife and bitterness from the heart of the disciple, it shows by implication the attitude of Jesus to worldly

[15]Quoted by HATCH, *Essays in Biblical Greek* ; see also JOSEPHUS, *Antiquities*, 13 : 2, 3 ; [16]Matt. 27 : 32 ; Mark 15 : 21 ; [17]Acts 2 : 23 ; [18]Mark 15 : 7.

authority. The wider lesson was drawn by Peter : " Submit yourselves to every ordinance of man for the Lord's sake : whether it be to the king, as supreme, or unto governors . . . that with well doing you may put to silence the ignorance of foolish men . . . Honour all men. Love the brotherhood. Fear God. Honour the King. "[19] So also Paul : " Let every soul be subject unto the higher powers . . . Render to all their dues : tribute to whom tribute is due : custom to whom custom : fear to whom fear : honour to whom honour. "[20]

The object which the Lord has in view in all these injunctions is to develop the character of the disciple into that of a citizen of the Kingdom. But this presents a peculiar difficulty. If the disciple fulfils the command with the same object—his own self-development—then the motive becomes self-regarding and defeats its own end. The man who receives a blow in silence in order that he may be the more a saint is in grave danger of becoming a prig, and prigs certainly do not belong to the class the Lord calls " blessed ". The Christ-like man suffers the blow so that perchance he may win the giver of the blow, and it may be " save a soul from death " : it is then that " love covers a multitude of sins ".[21] From the application Jesus moves on to the principle, and in the next section[22] he shows the place of love as the active power of the disciple's life—love which must of its very nature look outwards from itself.

This difficulty confronts the disciple particularly in carrying out the saying which forms a climax to the present section. In Luke, as in previous instances, a rather different saying enjoins submission to high-handed action : " Give to every man that asketh of

[19] I Peter 2 : 13-17 ; [20] Rom. 13 : 1, 7 ; [21] James 5 : 20 ; I Peter 4 : 8 ; [22] verses 43-48.

thee : and of him that taketh away thy goods ask them not again. " But in Matthew the thought has moved through (*a*) the response to insult, (*b*) legal exaction and (*c*) official compulsion, to (*d*) the point where a man is free to comply with or to refuse a simple request. The words are in no way new. The law had commanded : " Thou shalt open thine hand wide unto thy brother, to thy poor and to thy needy, in the land. "[23] Proverbs provides the germ of the parable of the importunate neighbour : " Say not unto thy neighbour, Go, and come again, and tomorrow I will give : when thou hast it by thee. "[24] One of the essential qualities of righteousness in the Old Testament is that a man shall be " good of eye ",[25] which means that he shall be generous in his outlook, in contrast to the " evil eye "[26] which is the sign of the niggardly, grudging heart. But Jesus is surely no less concerned than the sages of old with the disposition which is manifested rather than with the act of giving, and the generous spirit can rest content with nothing less than the well-being of the recipient. For this reason, while the request for help cannot be refused, the gift may not always take the form which the giver asks. The question has often been asked : " Am I to give money to a man who will probably spend it on drink at the nearest public house ? " The present writer's answer would be unhesitatingly, " No : to give that which corrupts the recipient is not to give but to get." The return for it may be in self-righteousness at having literally fulfilled a command, or self-satisfaction at the emotional gluttony of giving ; or it may be merely the taking of the easy way out of a

[23]Deut. 15 : 8, 11 ; cf. Psa. 37 : 21, 26; R.V. ; 112 : 5 ; [24]Prov. 3 : 27-28 ; cf. Luke 11 : 5 ; see also Prov. 21 : 26 ; 22 : 9 ; [25]Prov. 22 : 9, A.V. margin ; [26]Deut. 15 : 9.

difficulty : but it is not an act of love which moves outward to the one in need. Yet if the Christ-spirit is there, the appeal will not fall on deaf ears. There are other ways of giving than in money—in food, for instance, or in time or service. They demand more of the giver, are more troublesome and inconvenient—so much so that they may not be practicable in every case at any moment. It may not always be possible to take a man who asks you for money in the street, and pay for a meal for him at a suitable eating-house : but it is at least an instance of what is meant by giving for the recipient's sake, rather than for one's own.

In each of these sayings the Lord is painting in a phrase a mental picture which shows the principle in action. In the parallelism of this one saying there are two scenes. In the first a man turns towards the petitioner at his elbow ; he listens in an attitude of attention which reflects a ready heart. He puts himself in the other man's place. In the other picture the man " turns away " : his head is averted with chilling disinterest. And Jesus says in effect : " Which of those men are you ?" Yet Jesus himself balanced the claims made on him. Though " all men sought him " at Capernaum, he said, " Let us go into the next towns, that I may preach there also : for therefore came I forth ".[27] He did not respond immediately when his mother and his brethren tried to speak to him.[28] He refused a sign to the Pharisees when they asked for it ;[29] and he declined outright a request for aid which was made in a wrong spirit.[30]

Paul in this, as in so many things, faithfully interpreted the Lord in word and deed, and it is to him that we owe an otherwise unrecorded saying which further

[27]Mark 1 : 38 ; [28]Mark 3 : 31 ; [29]Mark 8 : 12 ; [30]Luke 12 : 13.

illumines the Lord's teaching : " Ye yourselves know that these hands have ministered unto my necessities, and to them that were with me. In all things I gave you an example, how that so labouring ye ought to help the weak, and to remember the words of the Lord Jesus, how he himself said, It is more blessed to give than to receive. "[31]   In writing to the Ephesians he gives the example of the replacing of self-seeking by self-giving : " Let him that stole steal no more, but rather let him labour, working with his hands the thing that is good, that he may have whereof to give to him that hath need. "[32]   So the believer will " do good (R.V. : work that which is good) to all men, especially unto them who are of the household of faith. "[33] " To do good and to communicate forget not (Wey-mouth : Do not forget to be kind and liberal) ; for with such sacrifice God is well pleased. "[34]

The self can only grow through forgetting self : the Kingdom can only be attained through seeking the salvation of others.   And while love as the motive of non-resistance to others is not lacking in the Old Testament—see for instance Prov. 25 : 21-22—in the words of Jesus the principle is expressed fully and finally.

[31]Acts 20 : 34-35 ; [32]Eph. 4 : 28 ; [33]Gal. 6 : 10 ; [34]Heb. 13 : 16.

9

THE STANDARD OF PERFECTNESS
(Matt. 5 : 43-48)

Ye have heard that it was said,
  Thou shalt love thy neighbour, and hate thine enemy :

But I say unto you,
  Love your enemies,
    Bless them that curse you,
    Do good to them that hate you,
    And pray for them which despitefully use you,
    And persecute you ;
    That ye may become the sons of your Father
      which is in heaven :

For he maketh his sun to rise on the evil and the good,
And sendeth rain on the just and on the unjust.
    For if ye love them which love you,
      What reward have ye?
    Do not even the publicans the same?
    And if ye salute your brethren only,
      What do ye more?
    Do not even the Gentiles the same?
  Be ye therefore perfect,
  As your Father in heaven is perfect.[1]

By whom was it said, " Thou shalt love thy neighbour, and hate thine enemy " ? The first clause, so
often on the lips of Jesus, is quoted from Lev. 19 : 18 :
" Thou shalt not avenge, nor bear any grudge against
the children of thy people, but thou shalt love thy

[1] The *Bible Society* text (1958) and modern versions omit the words
" Bless them . . . hate you " and " despitefully use you " : what is
left gives a good rhythmic structure, and the words omitted occur
without question in Luke 6 : 27.

163

neighbour as thyself : I am the Lord. " A finer description of true neighbourliness than this chapter would be hard to find, for it includes generosity, truthfulness, integrity and justice, consideration for the afflicted, equity in judgment, freedom from malice or vindictiveness, and sincere effort for mutual understanding.[2] There has already been more than one occasion for referring to it in this study.[3]

The second clause quoted by Jesus is not to be found anywhere in the law ; and while the term " neighbour " in the verse quoted is limited to Israelites, the same chapter states : " And if a stranger sojourn with thee in your land, ye shall not vex him.[4] But the stranger that dwelleth with you shall be unto you as one born among you,[5] and thou shalt love him as thyself ; for ye were strangers in the land of Egypt : I am the Lord your God. "[6] The same law of love therefore applies to aliens as to kinsmen.

Moreover, one of the most impressive provisions of the law precludes hate against the people from whom Israel had suffered most : " Thou shalt not abhor an Egyptian ; because thou wast a stranger in the land of Egypt. "[7] If the Israelites were commanded to " consume " and " utterly destroy " peoples whom they conquered, the object is declared to be to save themselves from corruption by pagan immorality.[8] The one case where this motive does not seem to enter is in the command to " blot out the remembrance of Amalek from under heaven "[9] ; but this was a commission to

[2]See verses 9-10, 11-13, 14, 15, 16-18 ; [3]cf. also Exod. 23 : 4-5 ; [4]R.V. : Do him wrong ; [5]R.V. : As the homeborn ; [6]Lev. 19 : 33-34 ; cf. Exod. 22 : 21 ; Deut. 24 : 17 ; [7]Deut. 23 : 7 ; [8]Deut. 7 : 16 ; 20 : 17 ; 23 : 3-7 ; Num. 31 : 16 ; [9]Deut. 25 : 17-19.

execute a Divine judgment.   No justification can be found here for a spirit of human vengeance.

The Lord's words therefore must interpret the current or traditional attitude rather than the intention of the Law. The Jews had an unenviable reputation as " men-haters ".   Diodorus Siculus speaks of Moses as " having enacted for the Jews their misanthropic and lawless customs " ; and Josephus has to meet similar charges from a number of writers in his reply to Apion. The linking of such sentiments with the name of Moses is an obvious perversion, and is of a piece with the scurrilous legends about Jewish origins which these authors retailed : but they show the general opinion of the Jewish attitude to the Gentiles.   Schürer says : " An exhaustive enumeration of all the Greek and Roman authors who from the beginning of the second century after Christ expressed themselves in a hostile manner against the Jews would furnish a list of distinguished names.   Almost all the authors who have to speak of the Jews at all, do so in a hostile manner."[10]

How far are these charges justified? The distinctiveness of Jewish law would arouse resentment, and afforded Haman his chance to play on prejudices against them[11] ; men also " spoke against " the early Christians as " evildoers " because their faith demanded separateness from the life of a pagan society.[12] Did the Jews likewise suffer an unjust imputation because of their faithfulness to God's law? No doubt they did : but this does not wholly account for their bad name.   To a separatism which under a misinterpretation of the law had become arrogantly self-righteous, they added a

[10]E. Schürer, *Jewish People in the Time of Christ* ; [11]Esther 3 : 8 ; [12]1 Peter 2 : 12.

165

bitter resentment of foreign control; and Paul could rightly describe them as being " contrary to all men "— at cross purposes with all mankind.[13]

Jewish thought committed two errors. It first sought to limit the definition of the neighbour to whom love was due. An example is the lawyer who, " willing to justify himself ", asked, " Who is my neighbour? " His question is answered by another : " Who was neighbour unto him that fell among the thieves? . . . Go, and do thou likewise." [14] Secondly, they presumed themselves free to hate those whom they supposed they were not commanded to love.

Jesus does not inculcate a sentimental attachment to enemies rather than friends, but a quality of living which embraces both. Much difficulty in understanding the command arises from the emotional associations of the word which confuses loving with liking. The emotion by which we are drawn towards those who show beauty of character is sound : without it life would be drab and gross. But there is a love which is a constant attitude of mind knowing no limits, a response to human need which is unfailing. Is a man poor? He may need our help materially. Is he rich? He may need our help spiritually. Is he perverse and oppressive? Will he go to any length to do us injury even to his own hurt? (For " despitefully use " implies as much.) Is he an opponent of the Truth who will inflict suffering on those who profess it? (There are always some who will, and do.) Then he is all the more in need of our example in returning good for evil, and our prayers that his eyes may be opened to his own peril. It is not for us to judge him unworthy of salvation and to act on that judgment.

[13] 1 Thess. 2 : 15 ; [14] Luke 10 : 25-37.

God is judge : and vengeance is His. But what does God Himself do?

Light and water are the prime needs of physical life. But Jesus, as a poet, does not name them in those general terms ; he uses the concrete images of sun and rain. It is the quality of poetry to mean more than it says : and the meaning of Jesus is that men depend for their existence not on the indifference or even the tolerance of God, but on His active love. The words are so beautifully simple that we read them without a quiver of an eyelid ; but their implications are all the more profound because they occur in this context. For it is the very purpose of the Sermon on the Mount to show that God is bringing " many sons unto glory ", and that they cannot be His sons unless they are like the Father : they cannot receive that full and final adoption which is the redemption of the Body unless they have come to reflect God as He has revealed Himself in His Son, the Beloved, the Only-Begotten.

The Divine love which is revealed in the Sermon is therefore essentially discriminating and selective, like the love drawn from us by good qualities in our friends. If it is said of the " poor in spirit ", " *theirs* is the Kingdom of Heaven ", it is because the Father's " good pleasure " is to give them (and not others) the Kingdom prepared for them. The statement, " The meek shall inherit the earth " has a threefold implication : (1) Judgment must be exercised to select those who are meek ; (2) there is a decision that they (and no others) are the fit ones to inherit the earth ; and (3) there must be a Divine intervention to throw out the proud and bring the meek into possession. Judgment, both to make a choice and to give effect to it is, therefore, an essential

167

concomitant of the love of God ; and the love between the Father and His sons is essentially mutual and responsive.

But while " the righteous Lord loveth righteousness ", the fact is that men cannot begin to be lovable until God has loved them. And Jesus shows that it is an act of God's love to give them the conditions of life without which they cannot know Him. This act of love not only comes to men without regard to what they are, but it is not even limited by what they may become. It is free and unrestrained, and not evoked by the quality of those to whom it is given ; so much Christ's words declare. For this we can see a reason : no man can be predetermined to love or made to become a son of God ; the very ideas are self-contradictory. The only love from men which can be of value to God is that which they give of themselves : it must be the self-surrender of individual personalities and independent wills. But, being frail flesh dependent for life on " His spirit and His breath ", they cannot even surrender themselves without His help ; they cannot love freely unless they are freely loved. The love which gives them life must give them also freedom—freedom to respond to or to spurn the love which comes to them.

It is no solution of this problem to say that God gives the gift of His love to those whom He foreknows will love Him, and that other men benefit only incidentally. Undoubtedly sun and rain are among " all things " which " work together for good to them that love God ", and " all things " are for their sakes. Undoubtedly He " foreknows " them and " worketh all things after the counsel of his own will, that they should be to the praise of his glory ". But to say that this truth—glorious as it is—

controls or conditions God's initial gift of love to man as man is to rob Christ's words of meaning. Jesus says that God *maketh* the sun to rise, and *sendeth* the rain, on the evil and good, just and unjust ; it is *His* deliberate action to include both in the scope of these gifts. And this action of God is the type and pattern of love towards enemies. But if God gives sun and rain to Smith, who is now evil, because He knows that Smith will repent, then His action towards Smith is different in kind and quality from His action towards Jones, whom He knows will not repent. Any such distinction in the motive and quality of God's universal gifts is excluded by the words of Jesus : nor could it be otherwise if man's love for God is to be a personal response to God's love to him. To confine this love, as love, to those whom God foresees will respond to it would be a denial of its very nature and a stultification of its very aim.

This conclusion may lead a step further. It is sometimes argued that when John writes, " God so loved the world that he gave his only-begotten son . . . ", the world which is meant is the future order and not that which now exists. A sufficient reply is that *cosmos* has no such meaning in John's gospel ; it refers always to the existing order, and usually contrasts the darkness of the world with the light shining from Christ. But a further answer is that God gave His son " that whosoever believeth on him should not perish, but have everlasting life " : the world which God loves is therefore the world of the perishing—the world which is His enemy because of sin ; and therefore Dr. Thomas was profoundly right when in *Elpis Israel* he combined John 3 : 16 and Matt. 5 : 44 in one pregnant sentence.

The two passages in which Dr. Thomas refers to this

redeeming love are fundamental to his thought, and lay the ground for a true doctrine of the atonement. The first is in Part 1, ch. iv, where the author describes the Adamic " world " which was constituted by the sentences passed and the new law given on the expulsion from Eden. He writes that though transgression upon transgression marked man's career, " ' God so loved the world ' that He determined that it should not perish, but should be rescued from evil in spite of itself ". In the other passage, in Part 1, ch. v, Dr. Thomas is showing that the movement for reconciliation must necessarily come from God. He writes : " God needs not to be appeased by man ; and every system, therefore, which is predicated upon the notion that it is necessary, is not only unscriptural, but *essentially* false. He is already reconciled to the world, which he has always loved ; although it acts the part of, and therefore is, the enemy of God . . ."

In those passages, which need to be studied in their full context to grasp the depth of Dr. Thomas's thought, the truth is shown unmistakably. God loves His enemy : His will towards all men is for their salvation.[15] Therefore neither individually nor collectively are they predetermined to death ; and the love of God is turned towards the world in its need. This love of God, displayed in the impartial gift of the needs of physical life, finds its full expression in the gift of the means of eternal life. " God commendeth his love toward us in that, while we were yet sinners, Christ died for us."[16] Paul once again seems to have the words of Jesus in mind, for he says " *when we were enemies* we were reconciled to God through the death of his Son ".[17] And in his death

[15]2 Peter 3 : 9 ; Ezek. 18 : 23, 32 ; 33 : 11 ; 1 Tim. 2 : 4 ; [16]Rom. 5 : 8 ; [17]verse 10.

Christ consciously identifies himself with his Father's love, giving his life a ransom for many.

Within the simplicity of this saying in Matt. 5 : 45, therefore, are enshrined the two profound and related ideas of the love of God and the freedom of man. Because of this quality of love, says Jesus, the Father in heaven is " perfect ". And as He is, so must they be. Their love, like the sun, must shine on good and evil, just and unjust, and must continue unchanged, uncorrupted, unmitigated. " For such true love to others is to be the expression of an inward nature which instinctively issues in such a noble life, catching the very spirit of the generous God in the fellowship of Jesus, and seeking to act in its own small sphere as the Father acts towards all."[18]

Those who will give love only where they can get a return are the traders in love, the usurers of love. Those whose love is confined to the circle of human kinship have not risen above the level of the animals : for these too can passionately love their own flesh. To represent these two types of the love possible to unredeemed human nature Jesus takes two classes of people. First, the tax-gatherers and toll collectors ; men who as a class valued money so much more than religion or patriotism that they were willing to become the minions of the alien rule. Even they could love where they were loved back ; but what reward could anyone expect if they spent only to get a return? They got what they bought ; was not the account closed?

For the second example the R.V. and others adopt the textual variant " Gentiles " and it gives good sense. To " salute " even in classical Greek could be used

[18]JAMES MOFFATT, *Love in the N.T.*

alongside of " to love " ; James Moffatt quotes an example from Plato's *Republic* : " You seem to have no great love for money. Those who have made money esteem it (literally, ' salute ' it) twice as much as those who have inherited money." " The term (says Moffatt) obviously denotes here and elsewhere more than ' to welcome ' ; it approximates to the meaning ' to be keen upon ', and this eager, desiring affection links it to *agapan*." But Jesus uses the concrete term which calls up a picture of the demonstrative formal salutations between Oriental friends—implying none the less that the wishes for each others' welfare are genuine. He does not condemn this love, so far as it goes ; it is one of the best things in natural life. But it is shown daily by those who are " aliens from the commonwealth of Israel, and strangers from the covenants of promise ". If this is all that disciples give, they bear no mark to distinguish them as the people of the covenant ; they reflect no particular likeness to prove their sonship of the Heavenly Father ; their righteousness does not " exceed " or overflow. How can they stand related to the Kingdom of God ?

Let them love their enemies in the practical ways indicated, so that they may *become* (more correctly than " be ") the sons of their Father. In so doing they will be " perfect " as He is perfect—an obvious recollection of the oft-repeated injunction to Israel, " Be ye holy, for I am holy ".[19] What is meant by being perfect ? Applied to men, it recalls the frequent expression, " His heart was perfect (or " not perfect ") with the Lord his God ".[20] The perfect heart is undivided, whole, entire, complete in its integrity ; and such is God—He is alike all through, if the expression may be allowed. As there

[19]Lev. 19 : 2, etc. ; [20] I Kings 8 : 61 ; 11 : 4 ; 15 : 3, 4, etc.

is no incompleteness in God, so there is no schism in Him—no self-division, and hence no inconsistency. He is the same yesterday, today, and for ever ; the same to all men.

The Hebrew word for perfect (*shalom*) in the references above is the same as for peace ; perfection is unity within oneself; peace is unity with others. James comes nearest to this sense in 3 : 2 : " If any man offend not in word, the same is a perfect man, and able to bridle the whole body." The Greek term in the later New Testament usually has the sense of mature, fully developed, as in Eph. 4 : 13 ; Phil. 3 : 15 ; Col. 1 : 28. But James seems to follow more closely the shade of meaning with which Jesus uses the word : " Let patience have her perfect (full) work, that ye may be perfect (complete) and entire, wanting nothing. "[21] And Jesus says to the young man, " If thou wilt be perfect, go, sell that thou hast . . .".[22] This is the only other occasion that the term comes from his lips (although he uses the verb " perfected " in Luke 13 : 32 and John 17 : 23) ; and, strangely enough, the only time in the synoptic Gospels that Jesus is said in so many words to love anyone is in Mark's account of the same incident : " Jesus looking upon him loved him. "[23]

To a remarkable degree this teaching, regarded as the high watermark of the Christian ethic, is foreshadowed in the Old Testament, and especially in Proverbs. Here we find the equality of men before God :

The poor man and the oppressor meet together ; The Lord giveth light to the eyes of them both.[24]

[21]James 1 : 4 ; [22]Matt. 19 : 21 ; [23]Mark 10 : 21 ; [24]Prov. 29 : 13, R.V. ; for " light " as equivalent to " life ", see Psa. 13 : 3 ; 36 : 9 ; 56 : 13.

The follower of wisdom is forbidden to rejoice over an enemy's discomfiture :

> Rejoice not when thine enemy falleth,
> And let not thine heart be glad when he stumbleth :
> Lest the Lord see it, and it displease him ;
> And he turn away his wrath from him.[25]

Another passage quoted in the New Testament corresponds closely with the Lord's words :

> If thine enemy be hungry, give him bread to eat,
> And if he be thirsty, give him water to drink ;
> For thou wilt heap coals of fire on his head,
> And the Lord will reward thee.[26]

It can hardly be an accident that there is a double parallel between this last passage and the Lord's words : (a) "giving bread" and loving the enemy; and (b) "The Lord will reward thee" and "What reward have ye?"

To trace the influence of these words of Jesus in the New Testament would need an exhaustive study of its teaching on love, but we may note a few passages which manifestly reflect it. Rom. 12 is interpenetrated with the Lord's sayings, but highlights are in verses 12, 14, 17, 19, 20, 21 : " . . . Patient in tribulation . . . Bless them which persecute you : bless, and curse not . . . Render to no man evil for evil . . . If it be possible, as much as in you lieth, be at peace with all men. Dearly beloved, avenge not yourselves, but give place unto wrath . . . If thine enemy be hungry, feed him . . . Be not overcome of evil, but overcome evil with good ". To " overcome evil with good " is the quintessence of the teaching of the

[25] i.e. from him to thee ; 24 : 17-18 ; [26] Prov. 25 : 21-22 ; quoted Rom. 12 : 20.

Sermon. In this Paul could appeal to his own example as a follower of the Lord : " Being reviled, we bless : being persecuted, we endure ; being defamed, we intreat . . . ".[27] Peter, writing in a time of growing persecution, recalled the great Example, " Who, when he was reviled, reviled not again : when he suffered, threatened not ".[28] The same double allusion to the Lord's teaching and Isaiah's prophecy of him occurs in 3 : 9 : " Not rendering evil for evil, or reviling for reviling ; but contrariwise blessing ; for hereunto were ye called, that ye should inherit a blessing. " " Blessed are they — " says the Lord ; and while the influence of the command to bless (to speak well of) leads Peter to choose the cognate word for blessing rather than the " happy " of the Beatitudes, the association of ideas is none the less clear. The parallel in James's rebuke to " blessing and cursing " proceeding out of the same mouth also should not be missed. Other parallels may be found in 1 Thess. 5 : 15 (particularly interesting because of its early date), Gal. 6 : 10 (" Let us work that which is good toward all men "), and in 2 Peter 1 : 5-11.

True sonship to God is described in Eph. 4 : 31-32 in words which powerfully recall the whole teaching of the Sermon, but especially Matt. 5 : 44-48. The attainment of perfection is the aim in Phil. 3 : 8-13 and Col. 1 : 27-28 ; and the knowledge grounded in love which grows to comprehend the love of Christ, the theme of Eph. 3 : 18-19, can only be based on the Lord's interpretation of the love of God.

Finally there is a passage in Col. 3 : 12-15 which gathers up so many of the thoughts of the Sermon— meekness, mercy, forgiveness, love, perfection, peace—

[27] 1 Cor. 4 : 12-13 ; [28] 1 Peter 2 : 23.

that it must be given in full for the reader to trace the nuances and overtones for himself. But let it be noted that the whole passage rests upon the idea of covenant-relationship with God :—

> Put on therefore, as the elect of God, holy and beloved, bowels of mercies, kindness, humbleness of mind, meekness, longsuffering ; forbearing one another, and forgiving one another, if any man have a quarrel against any : even as Christ forgave you, so also do ye. And above all these things put on love, which is the bond of perfectness. And let the peace of God rule in your hearts, to the which also ye are called in one body ; and be ye thankful.

IV. LIVING WITH GOD

1

THE SECRET AND THE MANIFEST
(Matt. 6 : 1-6, 16-18)

Take heed that ye do not your righteousness before men,
 To be seen of them :
Else ye have no reward with your Father
 Which is in heaven.

When therefore thou doest alms,
Do not sound a trumpet before thee,
As the hypocrites do in the synagogues and in the streets,
That they may have glory of men.
Verily I say unto you,
 They have received their reward.

But when thou doest alms,
Let not thy left hand know what thy right hand doeth :
And thy Father which seeth in secret
Shall reward thee openly.

And when thou prayest,
Thou shalt not be as the hypocrites :
For they love to stand and pray in the synagogues and in
 the corners of the streets,
That they may be seen of men.
Verily I say unto you,
 They have received their reward.

But when thou prayest,
Enter into thy chamber,
And having shut the door,
Pray to thy Father which is in secret.
And thy Father which seeth in secret
Shall reward thee openly . . .

   * * *

Moreover, when ye fast,
Be not, as the hypocrites, downcast in countenance :
For they disfigure their faces
That they may be seen of men to fast.

Verily I say unto you,
They have received their reward.

But thou, when thou fastest,
Anoint thy head and wash thy face :
That thou be not seen by men to fast,
But by the Father which is in secret :
And the Father which seeth in secret
Shall reward thee openly.

The principles of Christian life have been unfolded, and the line of thought has been brought to a climax in which it is shown that all have their motive in love, and love has its source in God. By an orderly progression in thought the next section of the Sermon deals with the disciple's communion with the God from whom alone he can learn the love which he is to show.

If he is a son and servant of the invisible God, what form must his religious service take? Jesus first gives one general proposition which cuts at the root of all pious observance performed for any other object than God Himself; he follows this with three illustrations drawn from the three observances on which the Jews dwelt most—almsgiving, prayer, and fasting—which cover three major aspects of spiritual life : regard for others, approach to God, and self-discipline.

The reading " righteousness " adopted by the R.V. in verse 1 (A.V. : " alms ") connects the thought with Matt. 5 : 20—the righteousness which " abounds more " than that of the Pharisees. Not only almsgiving, but all

Pharisaic acts of piety were a theatrical performance in order that they might " be seen as a spectacle " by men. If, like actors in a play, the performers gained the admiration of their audience, that was all the recompense they would get : there would be none from the Father in heaven, for none was due. Their devotion was in fact offered to no god but themselves ; the admiration they drew was incense only to their own nostrils ; all their service was a ministry of self-worship, and mortal self-content was their sole reward. The saying is given its sharp edge by the fact that the Pharisees strove to gain a title to reward by their strict conformity to the law. Recompense in this life for virtue, and a fuller recompense in the future which should rectify any present inequalities : these were the very ground of their religion : and in one phrase Jesus sweeps it all away.

Adolf Deissmann, a leading scholar on papyri and inscriptions throwing light on the language of the time, says the word used, meaning " I have received ", constantly occurs in receipts, and in the light of this evidence the words in the Sermon " acquire the more pungent ironical meaning, *they can sign the receipt for their reward* : their right to receive the reward is realized, precisely as if they had given a receipt for it."

Almsgiving was rated so high that it tended to become synonymous with righteousness : and in the Apocrypha, at any rate, it is exalted into a means of atonement. Jesus ignores this fallacious doctrine of merit—if indeed it was known in this form to Palestine Jewry : where his teaching is grasped, no room will be found for it. His reference to sounding " a trumpet " may be based on a contemporary custom, such as the blowing of the ram's horn *shofar* at the time of public

179

fasts during autumn droughts. The notes of the horn were heard in public places after each of the six benedictions which ended the prayers for rain, and almsgiving was then expected. But any literal element there may be does no more than provide the seed which flowers into a vivid metaphor for self-advertisement.

Times were laid down with great precision for saying the *Shema* and the daily prayer now known as the " Eighteen Benedictions ", parts of which may be as old as the first century. These were to be observed wherever a man happened to be, and the words of Jesus suggest that it was not always an accident if the Pharisees were overtaken by that hour while in the street, or even at the street corner where they could be seen from two ways at once. Praying in the open was common enough for the rabbis to discuss gravely whether, and at what point in the devotions, one man might salute another, and whom he might legitimately salute.

Fasting was required by the law on the Day of Atonement only, but custom during the Exile established other annual fasts which marked disasters in Israel's history.[1] Of these it is believed that only the fast of " the fifth month ", commemorating the demolition of the Temple, was observed in the Lord's time. But public fasts were also called for in time of drought or general calamity. These were kept only on the second and fifth days of the week : a three days' fast, for instance, would be observed on the Monday, Thursday and the following Monday. As these were market days when the cities would be crowded with people from the surrounding countryside, there was an added

[1]Zech. 7 : 3-5 ; 8 : 19.

temptation to sanctimonious display. Fasting on these
two days throughout the year was not a general rule,
but is mentioned in the appropriate tractate of the
Mishna, and is referred to in Christian literature of the
second century as a common practice of the " hypocrites ". The Pharisee of the parable, therefore, who
" fasted twice a week ", would be very likely to think
himself " not as other men ".[2] Refraining from washing,
and sprinkling the head with ashes, earth or dust, were
traditional expressions of mourning, sorrow or humiliation. The Pharisee, his wrinkles lined with ashes
carried down by the runlets of sweat over his unwashed
face, must have looked a sorry figure.

Against all this Jesus sets teaching which, arising
out of the customs of the time, has every whit as much
meaning for our day as for his. In charity " let not
your left hand know what your right hand does "—a
figurative saying obviously proverbial in form, and
perhaps a current proverb. In prayer, go into your own
room and shut the door—a saying which in two phrases
draws a living picture. Jesus does not mean that there
must never be joining with others in prayer, whether
in the assembly or in the home : but just as he has given
a portrait of the hypocrite seeking publicity, so he gives
on the other side a portrait of the disciple seeking
privacy ; and each picture tells its story of the man's
mind. Finally, in fasting, Jesus says in effect, go about
normally without any outward evidence of what you
do. Whether or not he abstains from food, there are
many things in which the world sees " no harm " from
which the disciple will " fast " continually for Christ's
sake : but does he do it with the gloomy self-righteous-

[2]Luke 18 : 11.

ness of the Puritan, or with the joy of life in Christ? It is right to abstain—to cut off the hand or pluck out the eye rather than indulge in those things which may be a snare to ourselves or to others. But there are always some who seem to think that righteousness consists in finding fresh things which must not be done. This dwelling on the negative conflicts with the message of Jesus at several points—first and foremost because the very heart of his teaching is the positive power of love. He blesses the " poor in spirit ", not the poor-spirited. But it is also psychologically unsound (whereas the teaching of Jesus is as fundamentally sane as it is spiritual) : concentration on prohibition strengthens the force of desire ; the true method of casting out the evil is by implanting the good. And finally, where such an attitude of mind does not fail in one direction, it incurs a greater peril in another : it leads to the tendency to draw attention to one's own righteousness. Would not some in modern times whose road of life is sign-posted with " Don'ts " suffer the irony of Jesus as much as the disfigured Pharisees?

As, however, there are many ways in which we may fast, there are even more ways in which we may display our fasting. Sanctimoniousness may be rarer today than when there was a more general standard of profession : it is a disease that battens on religious vitality. Yet every age has its own affectations and insincerities. Wherever there is zeal in spiritual life there is a tendency to want not to be outdone by others, and hence to seek new ways of showing our earnestness : but to whom are we showing it? Just as from him that hath much shall much be required, so the times of greatest gain are those of greatest danger. It may be required of us that we shall do more than others, but not that we shall be seen to do more. And there is yet another danger which has an even closer connexion with fasting. Perhaps we are unduly reticent in " confessing our faults one to another ", but some religious movements have shown only too strongly the opposite danger of parading our past and indulging in emotional orgies of confession which are really self-centred. On all these perversions of the religious life the Lord's command has a direct bearing.

The clue to the mind and practice of the saint is to be found in the repeated phrase, " the Father which is in secret ". He is " the King eternal, incorruptible, invisible, the only God ",[3] and those who love Him will live " as seeing Him who is invisible ".[4] Withdrawing from distraction, they will come from time to time into a realm where the measure and standards of men no longer exist. Even with beloved friends there is a bound which cannot be passed. Even between man and wife in the highest of human unions, where mutual understanding may be most intimate, there is in the last analysis a limit imposed by the very fact that they are two " living souls", two conscious entities whose self-hood is bound up with their animate bodies. " Who among men knoweth the things of a man, save the spirit of the man, which is in him? "[5] But there is One to whom all hearts are " naked and laid open ".[6] Darkness is as light to Him, the thought unspoken is heard by His ears, because He is beyond " things seen "—beyond the visible phenomena of the universe which He has created : and therefore because the Father is in secret, He seeth in secret ; and to the

[3] 1 Tim. 1 : 17, R.V. ; [4] Heb. 11 : 27 ; [5] 1 Cor. 2 : 11, R.V. ; [6] Heb. 4 : 13.

invisible One the invisible things are known. Along with awe at that penetrating knowledge, and grief at the frailty which it reveals, there is joy for disciples in the fact that they are truly known. In private prayer they need not fear men's malice or misunderstanding, and they cannot seek men's praise—unless (God forbid !) it be their own. Here if anywhere in the world, they will be true, because they are alone with the God of Truth. And from such communion a fellowship may grow to reach its fullness in the day when they shall " know even as they are known ", being like the Son in whom the Father is made manifest, for they shall " see him even as he is ".[7]

Only to the man of faith can such a communion be possible ; but he who has it will be in touch with reality. Not only so, but he will have a core of reality within himself, a touchstone for the half-truths that come from his own nature, for the shams in the world around him. He will be more than truthful : he will be a man of truth. He is unmoved by the judgment of men, not from pride towards them, but from humility towards God.

The unbeliever walks wholly in the visible world. For him there is neither secret place nor invisible Being. For him the only standard of value is in the wealth of men that can be seen or the praise of men that can be heard. The changing scenes of life, like shadows thrown on a wall, are the only reality he knows, and through the phantasmagoria of living he moves to the unbroken shade of death. If only he knew it, for him all is " emptiness and a striving after wind ".[8] Among these walkers in a vain show is the hypocrite, who pretends to a knowledge of the unseen reality of

[7] i John 3 : 2 ; [8] Eccl. 1 : 14.

which in fact he knows nothing but the name. He claims to be laying up treasure in heaven while his only treasure is on earth.

The Greek of which " hypocrisy " is an Anglicized form meant originally " to distinguish betweenthings ", and so to answer or interpret dreams. By some association of ideas now lost in antiquity, it came to be applied to declamation by an orator, or to taking part in dialogue. From this the transition was easy to acting in a play, and then to the bad sense of feigning or dissembling in a part. Two instances in the LXX of Job, where it stands for the " godless ", " profane " or " impious " of the original, widen the Biblical usage far beyond its earlier meaning. They are 34 : 30 : " That the godless man reign not, lest the people be ensnared " ; and 36 : 13 : " They that are godless in heart lay up anger ". In the one case it is an impiety which lays snares for men, and in the other an impiety which harbours secret bitterness against God : and in both the deceit has its root in unbelief.

All sin, indeed, is practical unbelief ; the fool hath said *in his heart*, " There is no God ", and from that denial all his violence and corruption grow.[9] But there is a very real difference between sins committed when belief is overcome in an unequal contest with passions, and sins due to a deep-rooted denial of God. The former may be gross and foul, and those who commit them may be made social outcasts ; the latter may be covered with a mask of conformity to social canons. But whereas weak belief may be strengthened till it brings forth repentence, in disbelief there is not even the germ of reformation. The man who thinks

[9] Psa. 14 : 1 ; Psa. 10 : 4, 8, R.V.

God will take no notice has no belief in God's righteousness ; the man who acts as though he could deceive God has no belief in His reality. Ananias and Sapphira, who " lied to the Holy Spirit " with the object of obtaining a reputation for a greater generosity than they had shown, provide the classic example ; it was necessary that right at the beginning of the Church's history the reality of that unseen Spirit which they had despised should be shown with awe-inspiring power.

It is this radical unbelief, making it possible to combine a flattering tongue with iniquitous designs, which is so fiercely denounced in the Psalms.[10] Hypocrisy is a major ingredient in all such sin, and Jesus was following an Old Testament tradition when he poured his most dreadful denunciations on the hypocrites.[11] If there be a difference, it is that while the Old Testament condemns sins which were mixed with hypocrisy, Jesus goes deeper ; he condemns hypocrisy as the root of sin. The man who begins by deceiving his fellows goes on to try to deceive God, and ends by deceiving himself. He is a living lie ; the light that is in him is darkness—and how great is that darkness! Truth cannot penetrate it, because it actively resists truth : and this has two consequences. For the man himself, salvation is all but impossible. He is on the way to the eternal sin—the blasphemy against the Holy Spirit of attributing the work of God to Beelzebub, which by its very nature excludes either forgiveness or restoration. And, secondly, when he finds the light in others he will be compelled to oppose it by every means, including persecution to the death.

Hypocrisy is the most corrupting of vices because it sears the very conscience. The sins of the tax-gatherers

[10]e.g. Psa. 36 : 1-3 ; [11]e.g. Matthew 23.

and harlots were rank ; there was no need in a community where the Law was known for Jesus to explain the loathing in which such trespasses were held in the Divine sight. But by their exclusion from polite society the publicans and harlots were at least saved from hypocrisy, and therefore it was with true spiritual insight that Jesus said he called not the righteous but sinners to repentance ; they at any rate had not deprived themselves of all power to respond. To tear the mask from hypocrisy was the reverse side of the teaching about the Father that " seeth in secret ". The disciple has a secret for which he goes into an inner room : and his secret is God. The hypocrite has a secret for which he stands at the street corner. But it is no secret, for it is only himself—a sounding hollow ; but while the sins of the harlot are manifest, the sins of the hypocrite must be dragged into the light. There is nothing hidden, said Jesus, that shall not be revealed ; and it was as the Revealer and the Judge that with searing words he laid bare the barren heart of the hypocrite.

That Jesus speaks so often of the reward in this Sermon of love may seem strange. There is a measure of deliberate irony in the frequency with which the terms for " wages, hire " occurs in setting forth the contrast between the " righteousness " of the Pharisees and the " righteousness " of the Kingdom. Once only in the Sermon is this particular term applied to the saints,[12] though it is used in the good sense of the reward of the righteous in Matt. 10 : 41-42, Mark 9 : 41, Luke 6 : 23, and in the epistles and Revelation. Everywhere else in the Sermon, however, it has an ironic flavour ; those to whom it is applied are seeking a payment they will not get.[13] A different root supplies

[12]5 : 12 ; [13]5 : 46 ; 6 : 1, 2, 5, 16.

the verb for " your Father . . . shall reward you "—
shall give back, restore, return. The many renderings
which this word receives suggests its wider range of
meaning. The peculiar emphasis on reward in the
Sermon, therefore, is due to the fact that it is set over
against the teaching of the Pharisees, and a distinction
is pointed between their aim and the disciple's. The
Pharisees expect a wage for their works : the disciple is
promised a bounty for his living faith.

That reward has an important place in the teaching
of Jesus is indubitable : did not he himself " for the
joy that was set before him " endure the shame ? Yet
it is morally impossible for the man who reveals the
qualities which Jesus calls blessed to seek the reward for
its own sake alone. The merciful man would not be
merciful if he calculated the advantage of obtaining
mercy : he would be a hypocrite, and when a testing
time came his egotism would be laid bare. The peacemaker would be very unlikely to succeed in making
peace if his real object was to gain the dignity of being
called a " son of God ". And a man would be far
from meek who thought that inheritance of the earth
would be the due return for his meekness. It is a
tragic absurdity to think : " I will be meek because
that is the way to obtain the inheritance ; I will be poor
in spirit in order to be exalted—and then woe betide
those who have trodden on me ! " In that way a man
will attain nothing but an inverted pride : he will be
a play-actor whose performance deceives himself : and
in his unlovely self-righteousness he may not have even
the Pharisee's reward of popular applause.

Stated in this way, all these examples are manifestly absurd : yet by just such incongruities under a

thin disguise the heart deceives itself in every age. "Seek ye first the Kingdom" has too often been read as a call to pursue with a joyless possessiveness the bigger returns which the next life can offer for the surrender of present pleasures ; but meekness and the mercenary spirit cannot exist together.

While this is a truth too often overlooked, it is no less true that God does set before men a prize to be desired and eagerly sought, and to despise the gift would be to despise the Giver : " Come, ye blessed of my Father, inherit the kingdom prepared for you from the foundation of the world. "[14] When He bestows the gift which He has prepared, the Father who knows your secret relation to Him will openly show His love for you. The reward is reward indeed ; but it is above all else the expression of a relationship, the seal of fellowship, the evidence that He has adopted men and women as sons and daughters. Reward is the mark of God's delight in those who are redeemed and reconciled and embraced in His purpose : " Fear not, little flock ; it is your Father's good pleasure to give you the kingdom. "[15] If it is His " good pleasure " to give, is it not our " good pleasure " so to live in fellowship with Him that we may receive the gift? And though the reward is to be gained by striving as athletes—gained as a precious prize by keeping our eyes fixed on the winning-post—does not the very idea of joy in each other between the Father and His sons exclude mere self-seeking, mere grasping at material benefit?

The offer of reward from God to His sons is the final proof of His true personality. To an abstract Supreme Being it would be impossible ; to a Father it is not only possible but natural ; and to those who are

[14]Matt. 25 : 34 ; [15]Luke 12 : 32.

truly His sons the reward is the occasion of responsive delight in that personality. When we are pleased with a gift the choice of which conveys the very personality of a beloved friend, we say, " It is just like him (or her) to send me that ". And it is just like the Heavenly Father to give His children the Kingdom : the gift is as it were a part of Himself ; He has planned it throughout the ages : He has " prepared " it with loving care, And for His children the gift is the bond of love.

2

A DISCIPLINE IN PRAYER (Matt. 6 : 7-9)

And when ye pray, use not vain repetitions, as the Gentiles do :
For they think they shall be heard for their much speaking.
Be ye not therefore like unto them :
For your Father knoweth what things ye have need of, before ye ask him.
After this manner pray ye—

Twice in the Gospels it is recorded that Jesus taught his disciples a prayer ; and each time it is the same prayer, though on the second occasion he gave it in briefer form. The first is here in the Sermon, where, after a warning against Gentile volubility, he sets before them a model with the injunction : " *After this manner pray ye . . .*" The second is in Luke 11 : 2-4, when a disciple who had seen Jesus at prayer asks : " Lord, teach us to pray, as John also taught his disciples " ; and Jesus replies : " When ye pray, *say* . . . ."

Behind both his example and his warning there is a historic background. It was customary for a Rabbi to teach his own disciples a form of prayer which he composed ; and Jesus, though he was not of the Rabbinic schools and therefore was not recognized by the Jewish leaders, accepted the title of Rabbi with which his followers addressed him.

Especially did the Rabbis provide " fountain " prayers, as they were called, containing in summary the substance of the longer petitions which were offered in the Synagogues. The student prevented from attending public services who repeated the " fountain " prayer was regarded as participating with the congregation in their worship, and therefore, like the Lord's Prayer, these were expressed in the plural.

John the Baptist had evidently continued the Rabbinic custom. May we gather from John's teaching what the substance of his petitions might have been? Surely the central theme was the coming of Messiah and his Kingdom ; the manifestation of God's righteousness ; the turning of the hearts of the people towards Him ; and the coming of " the Lamb of God, that taketh away the sin of the world ", so that the nation might be better prepared for the divine judgment which was at hand.

Jesus' disciples were mostly those whose hearts had been prepared by John. The baptism and the descent of the Holy Spirit had revealed Jesus to John as the Messiah for whom he was forerunner ; and the disciples who went with him gained a growing knowledge of the uniqueness of their Master. John's prayers may no longer have been applicable now that the Christ was in their midst ; but more than that, the power of Christ's personality, and the depth of his teaching, would lead them to expect from him a prayer distinct and bearing the impress of his own character. The request in Luke may have been made by a disciple in the larger group outside the Twelve, who had not heard the prayer given on the Mount.

Another side of the nistoric setting is reflected in the warning in Matthew against " vain repetitions ". " Bable not moche ", as Tyndale has it,[1] " . . . for they thincke that they shal be herde for their moche bablynges sake." They " think "—it is their estimate or opinion —but how far from the truth ! The Baal worshippers on Mount Carmel cried from morning till noon, " O Baal, hear us ".[2] The worshippers of Diana at Ephesus shouted for about the space of two hours, "Great Artemis of the Ephesians ! " How far had Jewish prayer been influenced by such heathen examples of battering the gods with reiteration ? Dr. Thirtle[3] quotes examples from prayers for the Day of Atonement in which petitions are heaped up with every variation which ingenuity could devise : " O Lord, do thou it for Thy Name's sake ; do thou it for thy truth's sake : do it for the sake of thy Covenant ; do it for the sake of thy greatness . . ." and so on, forty times over ; " Answer us, O Lord, answer us ; answer us, O our God, answer us . . . answer us, Thou who art perfect . . ." and so on, until " answer us " is repeated seventy times. Confession of sins is likewise spun out into a catalogue of every imaginable fault. These are ancient prayers, conserving habits still older.

Such importunity seems to imply, not a childlike trust in the goodness of God, but a fundamental disbelief either in His love or in His reality. In His love—because a deity who needed to be stormed with petitions must

[1]He is followed by the R.T.S. version of 1938 ; [2]1 Kings 18 : 26 ; [3]J. W. THIRTLE, *The Lord's Prayer : an Interpretation* (1915).

be reluctant and capricious. In His reality—because such wordy elaboration is really directed less to God than to oneself. " How beautifully I am praying! How thoroughly I have left nothing unsaid ! " Such is the unuttered thought ; and its root is the same when it takes the form : " How well *they* will think I am praying ". Let it be added that extempore prayer may be just as hollow if its eloquence and fervour are designed to catch the ears of men.

" Much speaking " translates a well-known word whose meaning is beyond doubt. It is used in the LXX rendering of Prov. 10 : 19 : " In the multitude of words there wanteth not sin." The term rendered " vain repetitions ", however, is never found in Greek (except once in a very late writer) unless it be in reference to this passage ; it has presented one of the linguistic problems which surround the Prayer. The word is *battologeō*, and is now usually regarded as formed from a Greek verb and an Aramaic root meaning " vain, useless ", which the Sinaitic Syriac version uses to render this phrase : " Do not be saying idle things " Thirtle, however, has an ingenious suggestion that it means, " To speak from *Beth* to *Tau*" (that is from the second letter to the last in the Hebrew alphabet), and is used to designate a system of praying alphabetically. The use of the acrostic form as an aid to memory has the sanction of inspiration, for it is found in several of the Psalms, and in Lamentations. Some artificial regularity, such as acrostic, alliteration, or rhyme, affords a means of recalling a composition in proper order ; but in time the use of the device had degenerated into a means of spinning words. Thirtle again gives examples. Long prayers, sometimes in double acrostic two lines for each letter—labour through (as we might say) from A to Z, the clauses being framed to meet the requirements of the alphabet rather than the needs of the spirit. In contrast to all such pretentiousness, the Lord marks the simplicity of the prayer he teaches by beginning with A—" Abba, Father "—and there remaining. It is a prayer in Aleph ; from Beth to Tau is left to those who " for a pretence " or " show " make long prayers.[4] This view (which is quoted here with due reserve) has the attraction that it makes the reference to the Gentiles ironic. Still thinking of Pharisaic custom, Jesus pierces their skin with a subtle shaft : the Gentiles had been before them in their mode of prayer. And whether Gentile or Jewish, such prayers were equally devoid of reality. For the Father knows before He is asked ; and the true disciple, living in the reality of God's presence, knows that He knows and will give that which is good.

By giving a form or model Jesus did much more than accede to a custom : he established the need for discipline in prayer ; and in so doing he gave the perfect example of depth of thought in brevity of words. True prayer is not a mere outpouring of emotion, any more than it is a mere exercise of the intellect. Men must choose the things for which they pray ; choose worthy objects of prayer comprehending all genuine needs, and set in the framework of God's purpose : and then, with those objects in view, they must direct the heart, mind and will to God. If we enter into prayer with a conviction of the reality of Him whom we address, our mood will reflect something of Abraham's, when he said : " Behold now, I—which am but dust and ashes—have taken upon me to speak unto the Lord ".

[4] Mark 12 : 40 ; Luke 20 : 47.

Yet Abraham was praying for his kinsman Lot: and we, who pray not only to a Friend but to a Father, cannot bar from our prayers intimate requests for the well-being of those we love. How often does Paul speak of " making mention " of believers in the various ecclesias in his prayers.[5] If we know how to give good gifts to our children, how much more must it please our Heavenly Father when we ask His good gifts for them? Even love, however, can become narrow and possessive ; memory of the Prayer can ensure that the most personal petitions are kept within the universal framework of creative purpose. Testing our own prayers by the pattern will lead to the breadth of mind which is "never distracted by the particulars, and never lost in the contemplation of the entirety."

Nor does restraint before the awfulness of God empty the prayer of passion. Rather, it raises the level : for prayer demands a discipline of feeling as well as of thought, and in the very conciseness of the Lord's words there is concentration of feeling. Phrases so simple hide their depth from casual eyes : yet " Hallowed be Thy Name " says in four words all that can be said in the amplitude of the noblest of Jewish prayers : " Blessed, and praised, and glorified, and exalted, and extolled, and honoured, and magnified, and lauded be the Name of the Holy One, blessed be He." Only by discipline of thought can we so enter into the Lord's phrases as to see that they have the quality of poetry, of words raised by constriction to the highest power ; and only then can we begin to apprehend the strength of emotion which they both express and control.

The economy and strength of the Prayer's language are very apparent in its use of verbs. This is most

[5] Rom. 1 : 9 ; Eph. 1 : 16 ; 1 Thess. 1 : 2 ; Philem. 4.

notable in the first three petitions, where the order of the words in Greek is : " *Hallowed* be Thy name : *Come* Thy kingdom ; *Done* be Thy will ". The verb, expressing action, naturally tends to be the strongest member of the sentence ; here it is given added vigour by being placed in the strongest position. Moreover, scholars tell us that in the Greek these verbs are not only in the imperative mood but in the tense which describes a state of action independently of time, and therefore they are in the most vigorous form. Prof. James Hope Moulton comments that the language of petition to human superiors is full of periphrases whereby the request may be made palatable. " To God we are bidden by our Lord's precept and example to present the claim of faith in the simplest, directest, most urgent form with which language supplies us."[6]

Did Jesus intend the Prayer to be repeated ? Luke's record, " When ye pray, say . . . " answers the question affirmatively ; yet in the very act Jesus saves us from attaching a superstitious importance to the words by varying them himself. (We need not doubt that the Prayer was in fact given twice.) Jesus does not even despise literary device as an aid to recollection : for in Matthew the prayer has a marked regularity in structure, and the Greek shows assonance in the line endings. The purpose is clearly to provide for the prayer not only to be said but to be taught. In almost entirely eschewing its public use, we have doubtless swung too far in reaction against its abuse. It is " much *speaking* ", not " much *praying* ", that Jesus condemns ; and he himself, in the hour of his agony, " went away and prayed, and spake the same words ".[7]

[6]*Grammar of N.T. Greek, Prolegomena* ; [7]Mark 14 : 39 ; Matt. 26 : 44.

Yet it is far better that the words themselves should never be used than that they should become a mumbled incantation. Meaning is greater than words, however perfect their choice. A Churchwoman with more sympathy with liturgical forms than most of us has written : " It is too often supposed that when our Lord said, ' In this manner pray ye ', he meant not ' these are the right dispositions and longings, the fundamental act of every soul that prays ', but ' this is the form of words, which, above all others, Christians are required to repeat '. As a consequence this is the prayer in which, with an almost incredible stupidity, they have found the material of those vain repetitions which he has specially condemned. Again and again in public and private devotion the Lord's prayer is taken on hurried lips, and recited at a pace which makes impossible any realization of its tremendous claims and profound demands."[8] There is evidence for this perversion as early as the Second Century.

The prayer is the Lord's because it was his gift to the disciples. There are echoes of it in Gethsemane in his use of " Abba, Father ", and his exaltation of God's will.[9] Yet as a whole it is designed for their use, not his own. Allowing to the full his identity with human nature, could he say, " Forgive us our debts ", or, with the Lucan version, " Forgive us our sins " ? It was to the Twelve that he said at the time of their testing and his, " Pray that ye enter not into temptation " ;[10] and for them and those who have followed them the Prayer is, as Hugh Latimer called it, " The sum and abridgement of all prayers ", comprehending all that they can rightly ask, and providing a standard by which they

[8]EVELYN UNDERHILL, *Abba*; [9]Matt. 26 : 39 ; Mark 14 : 36 ; Luke 22 : 42 ; [10]Luke 22 : 40.

can measure the quality of their own utterance. If their prayer conforms in substance to the level and the scope of these thoughts, then, granting that it is sincerely offered, it is good and acceptable in the sight of God.

Finally, this is not a prayer for the use of the unregenerate. Its whole tenor involves not only knowledge of God's purpose but a mind already at peace with Him, and renewed after the likeness of Christ. Who else can say that they forgive all debtors?

3

THE HEAVENLY FATHER (Matt. 6 : 9)

Our Father, which art in heaven . . .

In the Old Testament " Father " describes the relation of God to the people whom He redeemed. As with so much of the most significant language of the prophets, the word has its roots in Moses : " Is not he thy Father that hath bought thee? Hath he not made thee, and established thee?"[1] Nor is it a mere coincidence that the idea of fatherhood is found in the context of the verse in Deut. 8 which Jesus quoted in the temptation : he treasured the passage in all its meaning. Through the knowledge that man lives by the word of the Lord, Israel were to come to know God Himself, and to know Him as a Father who chastens His children in love. The theme is carried on in the prophets. When in Jeremiah the Lord says " I am a father to Israel, and Ephraim is my firstborn ", the context offers a striking example of what this fatherhood

[1]Deut. 32 : 6.

198

means. It shows that in the end of their history not only will Israel be physically regathered but they will be spiritually restored; for " They shall come with weeping, and with supplications will I lead them : I will cause them to walk by the rivers of water in a straight way, wherein they shall not stumble ".[2] God's parental love is expressed throughout their history in a divine education which leads Israel through sorrow and repentance to a new spiritual life in His Kingdom. A remarkable verse in Isaiah seems to foreshadow the Prayer by linking together " father ", " redeemer " and " name " : " Doubtless thou art our father, though Abraham be ignorant of us, and Israel acknowledge us not : thou, O Lord, art our father, our redeemer ; thy name is everlasting. "[3]

All these speak of fatherhood in a national sense ; for it was as a people Israel were redeemed, as a nation they were constituted in covenant with God, and as a people and nation they shall be restored. Only Psa. 103 : 13 anticipates a more personal use of the relationship and that only in a simile : " Like as a father pitieth his children, so the Lord pitieth them that fear him ". But here also redemption is in view, for the Lord whom the psalm praises is He " who forgiveth all thine iniquities ; who healeth all thy diseases ; who redeemeth thy life from destruction ".[4] The Psalmist's theme is the restoration of men and women to God.

With the coming of the Lord the term takes on a new character. Only in John is it used more often of God than in Matthew. In the Sermon on the Mount the expression " your Father " points the contrast between the children of God and the world, and in the

[2]Jer. 31 : 9 ; [2]Isa. 63 : 16 ; [4]Psa. 103 : 3-4.

very act calls on the children to bear witness of the Father to the world by their lives.[5] The term marks also their entire dependence for all their needs on Him who knows the fall of a sparrow. As their Father, he holds them in His hand ; and whatever may in His providence happen to their bodies, He will not suffer one hair of their heads to perish.[6] All this is carried forward in the invocation, " Our Father ", which at the same time declares their bond with one another : " One is your Father "—" all ye are brethren. "[7]

Yet it is a remarkable fact that Jesus never joins himself with the disciples in the expression, " Our Father ". All through the Gospels he maintains a clear distinction between " my Father " and " your Father ". The kingdom of heaven is the kingdom of " my Father ", and only those who are in a state of correspondence with His will can enter into it.[8] The same " doing of my Father's will " is the nexus of relationship to Christ himself.[9] The truth of his Messiahship is revealed to Peter by " my heavenly Father ".[10] Christ alone is the way of approach to his Father, who has delivered all things unto him.[11] Men's destiny will be determined by whether Christ confesses or denies them before " my Father "[12] ; for every plant which " my Father " hath not planted shall be rooted up.[13] He will come in the glory of his Father.[14] Even when he speaks of joining with them in fellowship in drinking the fruit of the vine, it is " in my Father's kingdom ".[15] And to those who, having shown their love for the least of his brethren, have shown it for him, he says : " Come, ye blessed "

[5]Matt. 5 : 9, 16 ; [6]Matt. 6 : 26, 32 ; 7 : 11 ; 10 : 29-31 ; 18 : 14 ; [7]Matt. 23 : 8-9 ; [8]Matt. 7 : 21 ; [9]Matt. 12 : 50 ; [10]Matt. 16 : 17 ; [11]Matt. 11 : 27 ; [12]Matt. 10 : 32-33 ; [13]Matt. 15 : 13 ; [14]Matt. 16 : 27 ; [15]Matt. 26 : 29.

—not of your Father, but—" of my Father ".[16] In all this we have a foundation for the doctrine of the Father and the Son as it is unfolded in John's Gospel : " Believe me that I am in the Father, and the Father in me " ; " I came forth from the Father, and am come into the world : again, I leave the world, and go to the Father ".[17] Even in the place where, after his resurrection, Jesus calls the disciples his " brethren " and speaks of God as their Father and his, he maintains a distinction which is more apparent in the original than in the English : " Go unto my brethren, and say unto them, I ascend unto my Father and your Father, and my God and your God ".[18] The definite article used before " father " in the first instance is reproduced in the *Interlinear* version : " I ascend to the Father of me and Father of you, and God of me and God of you. "[19]

Jesus gives the term " Father " a new value not through some spiritual genius of his own, but because he alone can fully reveal God as Father. " As many as received him, to them gave he the right to become children of God, even to them that believe on his name."[20] "Neither knoweth any man the Father, save the Son, and he to whomsoever the Son will reveal him. "[21]

It is because he himself is Son that he can give the right to others to become sons, for he alone can show the full meaning of sonship, and therefore of the father-hood. And just as Christ shows the fulness of sonship by obedience even to the death of the Cross, so God shows the fulness of fatherhood by bringing His only-begotten to the Cross, and beyond it to resurrection.

[16]Matt. 25 : 34 ; [17]John 14 : 11 ; 16 : 28 ; see also 16 :27, R.V. ; 17 : 11, 21, etc. ; [18]John 20 : 17 ; [19]Interlinear Gr.-English N.T. (1958) ; [20]John 1 : 12, R.V. ; [21]Matt. 11 : 27 ; John 14 : 9.

The Father indeed "chastens" His Son with the discipline of Divine love : it is because God is the Father of our Lord that He made him perfect through suffering ;[22] and therefore the fatherhood of God is revealed precisely at the point where it seems most hidden— where Jesus cries : " My God, my God, why hast thou forsaken me? " But Christ was " made perfect through sufferings " not only for his own sake, but in order that through him many sons might be brought unto glory ; and therefore the Cross reveals the fatherhood of God not only for him but for those who believe on him. For them God is Father because He is Redeemer ; He is " the father that bought them " through the gift of His own Son, that they might become sons by adoption. Whether for the literal or the spiritual seed of Jacob, the essence of His fatherhood is to be found in the divine act for them which is described in the metaphor of purchase or redemption.

The death and resurrection of Christ is therefore seen as the climax of the two-fold revelation of God as Father indicated in the words of Jesus : "My Father and your Father ". At the same time the Cross reveals the demand which God's fatherhood makes on all who will be sons—the demand of the love which perfects them—the demand which is ritually represented by burial in water into Christ's death.

It can hardly be doubted that Paul refers directly to the use of the Prayer, naming it in Hebrew fashion by its first word, when he writes : " God sent forth his Son . . . that we might receive the adoption of sons. And because ye are sons, God hath sent forth the spirit of his Son into your hearts, crying Abba, Father. "[23]

[22]Heb. 2 : 10 ; [23]Gal. 4 : 6.

A similar allusion in Romans is connected with the same thought of sonship by adoption.[24]

"Our Father" is therefore a memorial of God's redemptive act; and it stands at the same time for His reaching forth towards men through the Holy Spirit, so that He may dwell with the humble in heart. That reaching forth is accomplished through the word which is the Spirit made manifest, and through Christ who is its embodiment. "Father" therefore signifies the indwelling of God in human lives through Christ; as the Master said: "I in them, and thou in me, that they may be made perfect in one".[25] Yet the very phrase which declares the most precious intimacy of God with man declares also that He is hidden from man: He is "Our Father, which art in heaven". For these words imply very much more than the bald fact that God's Spirit-being is focalized somewhere in that fathomless space which in relation to earth-bound creatures is "the heavens": they bring home to us that He whom we can call Father is "the high and lofty One that inhabiteth eternity".

Height, loftiness, exaltation, are physical terms, but they are the only language in which we can speak of a spiritual reality. That He is "in the heavens" is a fact, but it is also far more a symbol of the truth that "as the heavens are higher than the earth, so are his ways higher than our ways, and his thoughts than our thoughts".[26] That "no man has seen God at any time" is not only historically true: that He dwells in light unapproachable is not merely (if we may so express it) physical fact. These are facts implying profound spiritual truth—the truth that God is hidden from man

[24]Rom. 8 : 14-15 ; [25]John 17 : 23 ; [26]Isa. 55 : 9.

by His own light—hidden by the very nature of His inviolable purity. While "our Father" reveals the Lord who is Redeemer, "which art in the heavens" declares His separateness : and both aspects of God's relation to men are portrayed in the Cross. For here is one who is the gift of God's love that men may not perish ; while Christ's death is his own act of obedience, it is none the less God's redemptive act which declares His fatherhood for those who will receive it. God has provided the Lamb. But because Christ hangs on the Cross as the representative of sin-stricken humanity, there has to be in that hour, a withdrawing from him which brings the cry, " My God, my God, why hast thou forsaken me? " This withdrawing is an essential part of his sacrifice, for it testifies to the separateness of God who is so exalted above man that He must remain hidden from the eyes of sinful flesh. The antithesis which underlies the simple words of the prayer is brought into the fullest light by the dreadful realities of the Cross, and is reconciled in the resurrection.

Yet there is still another side to this thought : for it is this very exaltation of God above man which makes possible what we may call the spiritual miracle of divine forgiveness. It is not in human nature to forgive ; nor can we supply any merely logical grounds why God should forgive. But it is precisely because His thoughts are as high as the heavens above human thoughts that the call comes to seek the Lord, who will abundantly pardon the penitent.[27] " For as high as the heaven is above the earth, so great is his mercy towards them that fear him. As far as the east is from the west, so far hath he removed our transgressions from us."[28]

[27]Isa. 55 : 6-8 ; [28]Psa. 103 : 11-12.

And so the words in which the prayer are addressed to God declare how close He is to us, and how infinitely far off. They show that He who makes His dwelling with the humble is the very same as the One who inhabiteth eternity; and He who is exalted above all height has a Father's compassion upon his children whom He draws to Himself.

4

THE HOLY NAME (Matt. 6 : 9)

Hallowed be thy Name.

It is said of this " high and lofty One " that " His name is Holy ".[1] That name is not merely a verbal description which can be thought of as a kind of property or appendage of Him who bears it; the Name is God declared, and God is the nature which the Name reveals. When, for instance, it is said that " His name is everlasting ", the meaning is not that because He is undying, a name must always exist as an appellation for Him; it is that the Name is eternal because it is the expression of the eternal God. And holiness is the essential quality of that eternal name.

The radical meaning of the term " holy " is " separate ", and its prime use in Scripture is to gather up into a single world all those qualities of God in which He is other than man : " I ", He says, " am holy." Other usage is subordinate to this : a place, a mount, a tent, an altar, a bowl or a firepan, is holy not for any quality of its own, but because God has made it His.

[1] Isa. 57 : 15.

So also with a nation or people, but with one vital distinction; those who have minds of their own are called to show that they are His by their acts: they are summoned imperatively, " Be ye holy, for I am holy ".

Isaiah uses a parallelism which shows that " God, the Holy " is as distinctively a Divine Name as " the Lord of Hosts " : " The Lord of hosts shall be exalted in judgment, and God that is holy shall be sanctified in righteousness ".[2] That is to say, the nature embodied in the Name shall be made manifest—the Holy shall be made known as holy—through His acts of righteousness. The adjective " holy " sometimes stands alone as a synonym for the Divine Name in such a way that English translators feel compelled to supply the noun " one ". An example is in Isa. 40 : 25, where it is chosen with marked appropriateness to emphasize how incomparable and unique is God : " To whom will ye liken me, or shall I be equal? saith the Holy One ".[3] Some thirty times in Isaiah He is so described—usually " the Holy One of Israel ". Closely associated with the holiness of God is His " glory "—that awe-inspiring effulgence by which He says that the place where He meets Israel shall be " sanctified ".[4] The two ideas are paralleled in Lev. 10 : 3, where Moses acknowledges that the holiness of God demands that He shall be honoured by service of His own appointment and not of man's devising : " This is it that the Lord spake, saying, I will be sanctified in them that come nigh me, and before all the people I will be glorified. "

The same twofoldness which was found in thinking of the Father in the heavens is apparent also in His holiness : He is at one and the same time separate from

[2]Isa. 5 : 16; [3]cf. Job. 6 : 10; Hosea 11 : 9; Hab. 1 : 12; [4]Exod. 29 : 43.

man and very near, a devouring fire and yet the God who forgives sin; and these are not antithetic qualities but are included within the one quality of holiness. This is brought out in a remarkable passage in Hosea, where God declares that because He is holy He will not destroy the people and the city whom He has loved : " I will not execute the fierceness of mine anger, I will not return to destroy Ephraim : for I am God, and not man ; the Holy One in the midst of thee : and I will not enter into the city ".[5] He is " not man ", and yet He is " in the midst " ; He is entirely other and exalted, and yet He is among them : and for that reason, because of His very holiness, He refrains from doing what His very holiness might seem to demand ; He withholds from destroying them not only because He is merciful, but because He is holy. His thoughts indeed are not men's thoughts.

God will sanctify His Name when He fulfils His purpose in the restoration and salvation of His people. Because for their sins they have been captive and scattered by His judgment, His Name has been profaned ; the nations have said in scorn, " These are the people of the Lord, and are gone forth out of his land ". And so " for His holy Name's sake " the nations shall know that He is the Lord when (He says) " I will be sanctified in you before their eyes."[6] This demonstrates one aspect of the term to sanctify or to hallow : it is to make Him known as holy, to exhibit before men the quality of holiness by which He is unique and unchangeable, and utterly other than unredeemed man.

In the other aspect of the word's meaning, God is acknowledged by men as holy. This acknowledgment

[5] Hosea 11 : 9 ; [6] Ezek. 36 : 20, 23.

is never a matter of words only, but the recognition in their lives of the demand which His holiness makes. It was in this sense that He said to Israel : " Therefore shall ye keep my commandments, and do them : I am the Lord. Neither shall ye profane my holy name ; but I will be hallowed among the children of Israel : I am the Lord which hallow you ".[7] In the day of Israel's restoration, He will be hallowed in both senses of the term : " Therefore thus saith the Lord, who redeemed Abraham, concerning the house of Jacob, When he seeth his children, the work of mine hands, in the midst of him, they shall sanctify my name ; yea, they shall sanctify the Holy One of Jacob, and shall stand in awe of the God of Israel ".[8] The verbs are the same as in Isa. 8 : 13, that for to " dread " or to " stand in awe " being used in this particular form only in these two places. Those who rely on God's word sanctify Him by their belief in His abiding holiness ; and in the day to come, that holiness will be so made manifest that it will be known and acknowledged by all the world.

The experiences of Jewish history had given a particular content to the idea of " hallowing the Name ". In Maccabaean times many suffered death rather than violate God's law by offering or partaking in profane sacrifices. Such martyrdom was a " sanctification of the Name ". In a far deeper sense Christ " sanctified " himself throughout life, and in the end " glorified " the Father by his final declaration of God's righteousness, when he obediently submitted to death on the Cross.[9] His sacrificial death was the supreme " sanctification of the Name ".

[7]Lev. 22 : 31-32 ; [8]Isa. 29 : 22-23 ; [9]John 17 : 1, 19 ; Rom. 3 : 21-25.

With these considerations in mind we may turn to the first petition of the prayer. Granted that we really believe God to be all that the invocation " Our Father which art in heaven " declares Him, what more fitting, what more inevitable, than that we should first of all pray for the day when He will be known as Holy and as Father by every living creature? Does not love with all the heart, soul and mind generate above everything else an intense desire for this universal recognition of God? This would be the natural result if we mean wholly what we say. But we are bound to admit that here at the threshold the prayer imposes a great test upon human nature. For the holiness of God is the supreme expression of His reality, His utter independence and transcendence of man ; and the petition therefore requires us to examine ourselves to determine, not only whether we believe in God as Father, but whether in any real sense we believe in Him at all.

Men may accept the proposition that God exists in the same way that they believe that things equal to the same thing are equal to one another, or that the circumference of a circle is approximately three times its diameter ; but such cold assent will bring no yearning for His name to be hallowed. Worse still, " God " may mean for men no more than a personification of their own ideas of right and good will. In that case " God " is for them the dream of an ideal. They retain the dream because life would be rather more drab if it faded, just as life would be duller without the occasional beauty of a sunset ; yet doubtless they could live well enough if they had to in a climate where no sunset was ever seen. Such a God is really subordinate to themselves. And if God depends on men, they may violate

209

every principle of goodness He is supposed to embody in order to defend their ideal.

This tendency to subjectivity in men's ideas of God has been markedly increased by the modern emphasis on His benevolence at the expense of all other Divine qualities. A God who is conceived merely as personified kindliness serves only to fulfil the needs and desires of men. Such a God is deprived (in men's conception of Him) of the qualities of holiness, majesty, righteousness, justice and judgment—the very qualities which reveal His transcendence. If God is thought of merely as a convenience, it is not men who serve God, but God who serves men ; and a God who thus becomes dependent on men will inevitably fade into a myth. He will become for modern men just what Gilbert Murray described the Olympian deities as being for the Greeks of the first century : " Not gods in whom anyone believes as a hard fact ", but " gods of half-rejected tradition, of unconscious make-believe, of aspiration ".[10] Belief in God in modern England has in large measure declined to this level. The extreme example is a man who, asked if he believed in God, said : " I don't believe there is such a thing, but it's a good thing to have it instilled into people so that there's something there if the man needs it." This evaporation of any belief in God as an objective reality is the inevitable result of thinking of Him, first, as the personification of men's own ideas of goodness, and secondly, as One whose sole function is to give men what they want.

Even professing Christians may profess the name of the Father, Son and Holy Spirit, and yet have so little real belief in God that they are not drawn together

[10] *Five Stages of Greek Religion.*

to think upon His name. If we are slack in attendance at meetings for worship and study, God and His Christ are not sufficiently real to us for their Name to have compelling power. On the other hand, we may attend regularly, we may do the things we are supposed to do, and (more definitely, perhaps) refrain from doing the things we are supposed not to do—and yet not believe. All this may be convention, a respectable habit. We may be active in organizing and in ecclesial business, because such activity suits our temperament—and yet not believe. We may be diligent in research, and keen exponents of doctrine or prophecy—and it may be no more than an intellectual hobby. We may even find outlet for a naturally energetic and kindly disposition in good works—and yet not believe. " And though I have the gift of prophecy, and understand all mysteries, and all knowledge ; and though I have all faith, so that I could remove mountains, and have not love, I am nothing. And though I bestow all my goods to feed the poor, and though I give my body to be burned, and have not love, it profiteth me nothing."[11] And the first element of love is an intense assurance of the reality of the object loved.

We do not love a dream ; that is only a kind of self-love, like the fabled Greek who fell in love with his own reflection in a pool. We cannot love a convention, a respectability ; that is only a refuge for dried-up souls, who by running in a groove can evade the need of loving. We do not love a hobby (however much we may *like* it), because a hobby in itself is only an expression of our own energy, mental or physical. The fact is that we cannot love God unless we know Him to be

[11] I Cor. 13 : 2-3.

211

wholly other than ourselves; and then we can say
with the Psalmist:

O Lord, thou hast searched me, and known me.
Thou knowest my downsitting and mine uprising,
Thou understandest my thought afar off . . .
Search me, O God, and know my heart:
Try me, and know my thoughts:
And see if there be any wicked way in me,
And lead me in the way everlasting.[12]

It is true that " Hallowed be thy name " is a prayer
for the fulfilment in the future of something which only
God can accomplish—an end which He has declared
rests upon the certainty of His own being: " As truly
as I live, all the earth shall be filled with the glory of the
Lord ".[13] We know that He " truly lives "; that He
who is, is also the One who *is coming*; does prayer for
that day imply that its accomplishment depends on our
prayers? Clearly it cannot; what we do when we
pray " Hallowed be thy name " is to identify our
desire with His; to say that the end for which we long
is His purpose, not our own; the ambition which we
cherish is for His glory, not our own. We declare that
we look constantly and passionately for that day, come
how and when it may in the working of His wisdom.

But the hallowing of God's name cannot really
be our desire for the future unless it already moulds our
present. He had made Israel holy by redeeming them
out of the land of Egypt for His own possession; therefore
He required them both to acknowledge His holiness,
and to make Him known as holy. And the means of so
doing was by obedience to Him. The Apostle Paul
says to the converted Gentiles at Corinth: " But ye

[12]Psa. 139 : 1-2, 23-24 ; [13]Num. 14 : 21.

are washed, but ye are sanctified, but ye are justified in the name of the Lord Jesus, and by the Spirit of our God ".[14] They who are sanctified by God must sanctify God by showing forth the character of the Father who has bought them. The Name which they bear is " a glorious and fearful Name ";[15] and that Name is sanctified when those who fear the Lord " think upon his name ",[16] and reveal the fruit of their thoughts in their lives. As Christ sanctified the Name upon the Cross, so disciples will sanctify the Name when they obey his command : " Whosoever will come after me, let him deny himself, and take up his cross, and follow me."

When Christ is perfected by resurrection, the Name of the Father includes also the name of the Son in whom He is manifested—a truth illustrated by a remarkable phrase in Peter's first letter : " Sanctify the Lord Christ in your hearts ".[17] Peter is adapting Isa. 8 : 13, which he has quoted in the last words of the previous verse ; and he boldly applies to the Messiah the words originally used of the Lord of hosts. But his context also recalls the Sermon, and he may, by a double allusion, have the first petition of the prayer in mind as well.

[14]1 Cor. 6 : 11 ; [15]Deut. 28 : 58 ; [16]Mal. 3 : 16 ; [17]1 Peter 3 : 14-15, R.V.

5

THE KINGDOM AND THE WILL (Matt. 6 : 10)

Thy Kingdom come,
Thy will be done,
As in heaven, so also on earth.

The kingship of God is eternal and universal. " The Lord is the true God . . . and an everlasting king. "[1] To the inhabitants of the earth, He is " King of Nations ", a title used in verse 7 of the same chapter, and (according to many MSS.) in Rev. 15 : 3. This conception of God's sovereignty is a pervading thought in Jeremiah, and is reflected in Revelation in the not infrequent use of " almighty " or " omnipotent ". The very fact that God sends judgment upon Gentile nations implies His sovereignty over them.[2] These prophecies witness to the truth declared to Nebuchadnezzar, that " the Most High ruleth—is Governor—in the kingdom of men."

Yet, though "the earth is the Lord's, and the fulness thereof ", it is also true that in a future day the challenge will go forth, " Lift up your heads, O ye gates ; even lift them up, ye everlasting doors ; and the King of Glory shall come in." The possession is His for ever, but a day will come when He will visibly enter into it ; and so in the Psalms the kingship of God is mainly spoken of as future. Psalm 93 and others which follow it in the Fourth Book combine the idea of a definite divine act of entering upon kingship with that of the eternal character of the kingship. " The Lord reigneth " is rendered by J. E. McFadyen and others as, " Jehovah hath taken His seat on the throne " ; and the Psalmist continues :

[1]Jer. 10 : 10 ; [2]Jer. 48 : 15 ; 51 : 57.

" Now the world stands firm ", the emphasis marking a contrast between the " now " and time past. But the next verse shows that the act of entering upon the throne of the world is only one aspect of everlasting kingship : " Thy throne is established of old ; thou art from everlasting ". Yet in Psalms 96-99 the expression " the Lord reigneth " is clearly prophetic.

There are, then, two aspects of the kingship of God ; the eternal, and the future ; and the first includes the second as the universal includes the particular. In the same way, while all the earth and all its inhabitants are God's, He chose Israel to be His own purchased possession, a kingdom of priests, and an holy nation, in order that among them His sovereignty might be open and avowed. He is therefore in a special sense " King of Jacob " ; and He says to them : " I am the Lord, your Holy One, the creator of Israel, your King ". He has chosen them as His witnesses in the earth.[3] But now there is no longer a nation, a land, a system of law and worship, welded into one whole as the Kingdom of God : and its restoration depends upon the return to earth of " the son given " to sit upon David's throne.[4]

As God already reigns unchallenged in Heaven amid the praises of the angelic host, so also He must reign on earth. Therefore, to pray " *Come* Thy Kingdom " is to recognize that God's rule, however real, is not yet manifest in the earth ; but that it shall be manifest in a future day when He will openly enter upon His reign. That reign is not yet public ; but it will then be published and proclaimed and even the outward form of human dominion will be swept away. " The verb (come) is in the point tense, precluding the

[3]Isa. 41 : 21 ; 43 : 15 ; 43 : 10 ; [4]Isa. 9 : 6-7.

notion of gradual progress and development and implying a sudden catastrophe as declared in 2 Thess. 2 : 8."[5]

What is it that we pray for when we use this petition? Later in the Sermon the Lord draws a contrast between the Gentiles with their consuming anxiety for material needs, and the disciples, for whom " these things " take a subordinate place because their main thought is filled with the Kingdom of God and His righteousness. In its context in Luke, this saying forms part of a sustained contrast between light and darkness, reality and appearance. Men with a single eye to the word of God live in reality, and are filled with light. But if the light in men is darkness, how great is that darkness ![6] From Cain onwards the darkness in man has opposed the light and persecuted those like Abel who lived in the light. Yet the saints need not fear even if the men of darkness slay their bodies. The only final reality is the mind of God, and men cannot destroy the future of those who live in His purpose.[7] The kingdom stands for the reality of God : it is light against darkness, the abiding against the transient, reality against appearance. The material world is real enough as an aspect of the purpose of God : but life and its needs in the present order of the world are the shadow ; God, and life in Him, are the substance. The saints of God will not so grasp the shadow as to lose the substance. To desire God's kingdom and righteousness is to desire the day when all nations whom He has made shall come and worship before Him ; when " Truth shall spring out of the earth, and righteousness shall look down from heaven ", for " Righteousness shall go before him, and

[5]W. E. VINE, *Expository Dictionary of N.T. Words* ; [6]Luke 11 : 34-36 ; [7]Luke 12 : 4-5.

shall make his footsteps a way ".[8] It is to desire that His reign and His righteousness, like His holiness, shall be known and acknowledged throughout the earth. This desire, if it is anything more than empty words, is a desire that we may serve His purpose. If we look for His sovereignty to be manifested in the future, then we must acknowledge that sovereignty now : we must live under His reign. It is in this sense alone that we may rightly speak of a present aspect of the kingdom of God ; but it is an aspect reflected back from the future. The future kingdom is the governing reality, and the reign of God on earth can be a fact in our present only because it will be a fact in the world's future.

While, however, to desire the kingdom merely as an end for ourselves would not be to desire God's kingdom but our own, it would at the same time be a sham to think we can desire the kingdom impersonally, caring nothing whether we ourselves attain it. That kind of cold altruism is a hollow self-complacency, and remote from the spirit of the Word. If in any real sense we desire His kingdom we desire also that we may share in it : and God Himself looks forward to the inheritance of the kingdom by individual men and women foreknown to Him. And this thought leads on to the last petition of this first strophe of the Prayer : " Done be Thy will ". To prepare is an act of will : and therefore when the kingdom is inherited by those for whom He has prepared it, the will of God will be fulfilled, will be accomplished, will be " done ". Towards that fulfilment the divine will has been working throughout the ages of the human story.

The wisdom personified in the Book of Proverbs declares :

[8]Psa. 86 : 9 ; 85 : 10,13.

217

The Lord possessed me in the beginning of his way,
Before his works of old.
I was set up from everlasting, from the beginning,
Or ever the earth was . . .
When he gave the sea its bound,
That the waters should not transgress his com-
    mandment :
When he marked out the foundation of the earth :
Then was I by him, as one brought up with him :
And I was daily his delight,
Rejoicing always before him ;
Rejoicing in his habitable earth ;
And my delight was with the sons of men.[9]

The stately language of the English version partly
conceals a bold poetic figure. So intimately is the eternal
wisdom associated with God that it is pictured under
the metaphor of His nursling, or foster-child. The R.V.
adopts an alternative interpretation of a word of many
possible meanings, and renders it " Master-workman ",
but the A.V. accords better with the verb used for
" rejoicing ". This usually describes derisive laughter,[10]
but in the present context it can only mean an aban-
donment of joy, a sportive, child-like exuberance. The
Jewish Version therefore reads :

Then was I by him, as a nursling ;
And I was daily all delight,
Playing always before him,
Playing in his habitable earth,
And my delights are with the sons of men.

It is a poetic parable of divine joy in looking to the
end of His purpose ; and where the wisdom exists to
foresee that end, there is the will to effect it. The

[9]Prov. 8 : 22-31, partly with R.V. ; [10]as in Psa. 2 : 4.

Twenty-Four Elders in Revelation declare that all things were created through the " pleasure " or " will " of God :

> Worthy art thou, O Lord our God,
> To receive glory and honour and power :
> For thou hast created all things,
> And by thy will they have their being, and were created.[11]

The end towards which that will works is to be reached through an instrument—and he is one who delights to do the will :

> Then said I, Lo, I am come ;
> In the roll of the book it is prescribed to me :
> I delight to do Thy will, O my God.[12]

And Paul, quoting this verse in Heb. 10 : 5-10, indicates the purpose on which the will is set when he comments : " By the which will we are sanctified ". Jesus himself declared it in so many words when he also used the Psalmist's term : " For I am come down from heaven not to do my own will, but the will of him that sent me. And this is the will of him that sent me, that of all that which he hath given me I should lose nothing, but should raise it up at the last day. And this is the will of my Father, that every one that beholdeth the Son, and believeth on him, should have eternal life ".[13]

In Ephesians the working of the Divine will is the central thought out of which the whole theme grows. Paul writes as " an apostle of Jesus Christ by the will of God ", to those whom God has foreordained to adoption as sons " according to the good pleasure of his will ". He declares that God has made known unto

[11]Rev. 4 : 11, R.T.S. version ; [12]Psa. 40 : 7-8, R.V.m ; [13]John 6 : 38-40, R.V.

us " the mystery of his will, according to his good pleasure which he hath purposed in himself " : and that in Christ " we were made a heritage, having been foreordained according to the purpose of him who worketh all things after the counsel of his will ". Paul shows the end when he prays that they may know what are the riches of God's heritage in the saints : and he shows the means to that end when he adds : " And what the exceeding greatness of his power to us-ward who believe, according to that working of the strength of his might which he wrought in Christ, when he raised him from the dead, and made him to sit at his right hand in the heavenly places ".[14] This is the power in action.

Here is a remarkable assemblage of terms, almost exhausting the resources of language, to describe, first, the Divine intelligence and desire which conceives the end : *Wisdom and understanding,* [15] *purpose, counsel, good pleasure* ; secondly, the will to pursue the end ; and thirdly, the power to attain it : *power, strength, might,* " *working* ", " *worketh* ".[16]

And the object of this ineffable concentration of the mental and moral and active qualities of God is to " sum up " or " gather together in one all things in Christ ". This is the will of God : to unite the whole creation under the headship of Christ : in other words, to reconcile a world unto himself—a world in which all things will be made new. And it is for this we pray when we say, " Thy will be done ".

These words form the strongest and most active

[14]Eph. 1 : 1, 5, 9, 11 (R.V.), 18-20 ; [15]verse 8 ; [16]The last two terms represent energy in operation, and in fact translate words which are cognate with our word energy, which is merely Greek in English dress.

petition in the prayer. It may be their use by Jesus in Gethsemane which has led many to associate them with mere resignation to misfortune. But when Jesus prayed, " O my Father, if this cup may not pass away from me, except I drink it, thy will be done ", he was not passively suffering the inevitable ; he, who had a will of his own, was submitting his will to the active will of God : " Nevertheless, not as I will, but as thou wilt ".[17] Knowing that this will for the unity of all things could only be accomplished through the Cross, towards the Cross he steadfastly set his face. How often the Cross proves the true interpreter of the Prayer !

The first three petitions are bound together in one framework between two references to heaven : " Our Father which art in the heavens "—" as in heaven, so on earth ". Those last words qualify equally the petitions for the Name, the Kingdom, and the Will. All have a present accomplishment in heaven, and all are referred to a future accomplishment upon earth. In each one the disciple who utters them identifies himself with the purpose of God : and, acknowledging—nay, desiring— that purpose for the future, he claims it as governing his own life now. Simple as the words are, and easy to be said by the humblest saint, there is no height of divine wisdom or depth of divine knowledge which is not comprehended in the thoughts of this first strophe of the Prayer.

[17]Matt. 26 : 42, 39.

THE ESSENTIALS OF LIFE
(Matt. 6: 11-12, 14-15)

Give us this day our daily bread:
And forgive us our debts, as we forgive our debtors . . .
For if ye forgive men their trespasses,
Your heavenly Father will also forgive you.
But if ye forgive not men their trespasses,
Neither will your Father forgive your trespasses.

The first of the group of petitions which are more directly for ourselves recognizes physical need as the basis of spiritual life. In Sheol, where there is no remembrance of God and none can give Him thanks,[1] there can certainly be no fellowship with Him; and where there is no life there can be no growth. Therefore the prayer acknowledges our dependence on God for the very elements of that existence which is the foundation of all our consciousness; and therefore of all our knowledge, faith, love and hope; and therefore of all chance of developing character fit for God's Kingdom.

This simple view is not always accepted: for the greatest linguistic controversy to which the Prayer has given rise has revolved for many centuries round the word rendered "daily".[2] Does the expression mean "bread for today", "for the coming day", "bread of subsistence", "needful bread", or "continual bread"? Or are we to carry it right out of the realm of the material, and understand it as "spiritual food", "the food of eternal life"? That the last named view should find many advocates is not surprising among those who start from the postulate of the immortality of the soul:

[1]Psa. 6: 5, R.V.; [2]*epiousios.*

the fact that man is a dust-formed "living soul" returning to the dust, alone provides true ground for understanding this petition.

The difficulty is that the word occurs only in the two records of the Prayer, and nowhere else in Greek literature. Origen, in the third century, thought it was coined by the Apostles. As Origen was presumed to know his own tongue better than anyone later could do, his statement that it did not exist before was generally accepted ; it did not occur to commentators that Origen might have been too academic to know the Greek of the market place.

In recent years, however, much study has been made of fragments of papyri from Egypt which reveal the use of colloquial Greek near the first century A.D.—a vernacular much modified from the classic Greek of an earlier age, and the common tongue in use among all the varied peoples of the Roman Empire. Adolf Deissmann has been able to record the finding of the words *ta epiousia* in a papyrus from Fayoum which he described as "the remains of a housekeeper's book". This expression, he said, corresponded with the Latin *diaria*, which occurred in a similar list of household requisites in a Latin wall inscription in Pompey. "Both words probably signify the amount of daily food given to slaves, soldiers and labourers, and probably usually allotted a day beforehand." On the ground of this research, Deissmann says : "The strict meaning of the Prayer is : 'Give us today our amount of daily food for tomorrow'."[3] There is a striking parallel to the idea (though not to the term) in Luke 12 : 42 : " Who then is that faithful and wise steward whom his lord shall make

[3]A. DEISSMANN, *The N.T. in the Light of Modern Research*, pages 84-86.

ruler over his household, to give them their portion of meat in due season?" It is precisely for such "supplies in due season" that the member of the Household of God asks in the Prayer. We ask to be saved not only from starvation, but from continual uncertainty where the next meal is coming from; for in that state it is beyond human nature to retain a quiet mind, and we dare not challenge such a strain on the flesh we know to be so weak. Nor, on the other hand, may we beg for a distant security or assured wealth when His grace is sufficient for us. We ask only for the coming day.

Can, then, those who happen to possess this world's goods join equally in this petition with others? Yes: first because all stand equal as brethren before the Lord, praying not only for themselves but for one another. And secondly, woe betide any if they forget that rich and poor alike depend on God for their daily needs! Wealth is largely a social fiction; a turn of the stock market—a collapse of currency—let alone a Marxist revolution—and it may vanish in a day. A shower of bombs, and the most solid possessions can be destroyed. Modern wealth is not less but more vulnerable than ancient forms which suffered the slow attack of "moth and rust". "Ye know not what shall be on the morrow": have not the words of James gained new poignancy for us in two world wars? The rich man, therefore, has as much need to ask as the poor; and he may only ask for his "portion in due season" as a household servant. All he has beyond that is an added trust from God to be used in love to God and his neighbour.

From the first need of all life the prayer passes to the basic need of spiritual life: "And forgive us our debts, as we forgive our debtors". Men cannot live before

God apart from His forgiveness : for without it they cannot be in fellowship with Him ; and without that fellowship they cannot ultimately live at all. And they cannot be given the forgiveness of God, nor can they genuinely accept it, unless in their own contrition of heart they are willing to forgive. For God to forgive the unforgiving would not only be contrary to His righteousness : it would be a moral impossibility. The unforgiving spirit is a sign of the unbroken heart which does not know its need, and, like hard-baked clay, will allow mercy neither to flow out nor to flow in. Once again the Prayer searches human nature to the very core, making demands on those who will repeat it before which they stand abashed. We know that we need not so much exposition to tell us what it means as the power in frail flesh to carry it out.

The term " debts ", however, opens up an illuminating train of thought to which the way has been pointed by Dr. Thirtle. The Law provided for the remission of debt in the Lord's name at the end of every seven years, when " every creditor that lendeth ought unto his neighbour shall release it ; he shall not exact it of his neighbour, or of his brother ; because it is called the Lord's release ".[4] Servitude was also limited by the seven-year period ; and seven such heptades led to the year of jubilee, with its general proclamation of liberty and the restoration to family ownership of land which had been sold. The economic and social life of Israel rested on the principle that all land, the basis of wealth, was vested in the Crown—that is, God—and was held upon a tenure which, by forbidding freehold sale, and limiting the term of leasehold sale, was designed to maintain the distribution of land in family holdings.

[4] Deut. 15 : 2.

Linked with this remarkable system of land tenure was the periodic release from debt. Both were parts of a single economy, which, had the Law been faithfully observed, would have prevented social inequalities by keeping wealth widely distributed ; and this unique solution of a problem which still baffles the wisdom of men was only possible because it rested on a moral principle— that what they had was not their own, but God's. Illuminated by that truth, the economy of Israel was the only one in the world to enshrine among its fundamentals the principle of forgiveness.

This principle Jesus carries over into the realm of spiritual life ; and he illustrates it by the Parable of the Unmerciful Servant, in which the debt the servant refuses to forgive is so paltry, and the debt he has been forgiven is so overwhelming. We turn to the Cross once more for the supreme example of the meaning of the Prayer— that Cross from which the word is uttered, " Father, forgive them, for they know not what they do ". And Peter—fiery Peter—reflects his Lord's thought in saying to the Jews : " Brethren, I wot that through ignorance ye did it, as did also your rulers ".[5]

When we use this petition we ask God to pass by our indebtedness to Him as in the year of release, " in such manner that the account can never again be presented for payment " ; and we ask it, knowing not only the magnitude of the debt but the majesty of the Divine Creditor. For two other terms are used as synonyms with it which show the nature of our indebtedness. The petition is the only one on which Jesus directly comments in the context of the Prayer in Matthew, and there he speaks of " trespasses ". The same word is used repeatedly by Paul in Rom. 5 (" But

[5]Luke 23 : 34 ; Acts 3 : 17.

not as the *offence*, so also is the free gift ", etc.) and also in Eph. 2 : 5 and Col. 2 : 13 in the expression " dead in sins ". In Luke's version of the Prayer the petition reads : " Forgive us our *sins* ; for we also forgive everyone that is *indebted* to us ". Debts, trespasses, sins, are therefore all used to describe the relation in which human nature stands to God, and from which it needs release. And yet those who pray in these terms do not come to God as unregenerate sinners. Granted the one great remission when they take on themselves the name of Christ, they still need—in the frailty of human nature—continual forgiveness for shortcomings : but they can only ask it as the reborn who know and acknowledge God's law— the law of " the Lord's release ".

At the same time God's forgiveness is not simply a wiping clean of the slate. If it were, prayer would be immoral—a mere incantation to bring about a magical result : and we need to be continually wary of the pagan conception which would reduce it to such a level. Repentance is the recognition of the need for change within ourselves, and of the divine love which can effect it. To ask forgiveness is to lay ourselves open to the cleansing fire of God's grace that it may burn up the chaff. The Psalmist probes the nerve of it when, after praying for the blotting out of transgression, he writes : " Create in me a clean heart, O God ; and renew a right spirit within me. Cast me not away from thy presence ; and take not thy holy spirit from me ".[6] God binds us closer to Himself by our very weakness : we must needs depend on His grace not only to bring us into His fellowship but to maintain us in it. By repentance and renewed effort we grow in grace, " rising on stepping stones of our dead selves " ; but His forgiveness is the

[6] Psa. 51 : 10.

227

necessary condition of that growth. The Pharisaic mind that does not know its need of forgiveness does not know its need of God ; it is therefore cut off from the very source of life, and dead while it lives. God cleanses the heart by contrition : and if the Prayer does not directly ask for our hearts to be made pure it is because the thought of the Psalmist is included in the petition, " Forgive . . . "

The act of praying for forgiveness demands an understanding of the mind of Him who forgives. When we throw ourselves on the mercy of God, our pride, our self-sufficiency, our self-assertiveness, are broken down in the knowledge of our need and of His pity towards them that fear him ; do we re-erect those thorny barriers when we turn to our fellow men ? Or do we reflect towards them some gleam of His mercy and compassion ? It has been said that " the Christian doctrine of forgiveness is so drastic and so difficult, where there is a real and deep injury to forgive, that only those living in the Spirit, in union with the Cross, can dare to base their claim on it ".[7]

[7]EVELYN UNDERHILL.

DELIVERANCE FROM EVIL (Matt. 6 : 13)

Lead us not into temptation :
But deliver us from evil.

The words might be those of a timid child—in
faith, if not in years—standing on the brink of the
adventure of spiritual life. At once thrilled and tremu-
lous, even in the grip of the Father the little hand
shrinks as the sense of the vastness and power of the
world into which it is venturing almost overwhelms the
childish heart.

Yet the petition is unerringly placed at the climax :
it is the last stage in the education in prayer which has
been carried forward step by step. The child—spiritually
or physically—will as like as not be confident in its own
self-sufficiency ; will be foolishly venturesome ; the
words are baffling to undeveloped minds. But the last
three petitions imply the breaking down, one by one,
of the defences of the inner self. First prayer for bread
is a confession of dependence on God for physical life,
and a recognition that what is received is only a slave's
allowance, not something possessed in our own right.
Secondly, prayer for forgiveness confesses dependence
on God for the very condition which makes fellowship
with Him possible, and requires us to reflect the sunlight of His goodness upon others. And finally, prayer
that the leading of God may be away from temptation
rather than into it is the overthrow of self-sufficiency's
last refuge ; it is the admission that we are not strong
enough to court trial.

God leads—but where? Sometimes into positions
where we are tested ; and if the testing comes, then, says

James, " count it all joy when ye fall into divers temptations ;[1] knowing that the trying of your faith worketh patience. But let patience have her perfect work, that ye may be perfect and entire, lacking nothing ". We desire to be " made perfect " ; does it not follow that we should desire to be tried? Is it not the logical conclusion that we should pray, " Lead us into temptation "? It might be—but for one fact : such a request would reveal a self-sufficiency more destructive than any temptation from outside. That is precisely the quality which the Prayer calls on us to abandon.

These words form one of the threads running through the account of the Passover meal and Gethsemane : and it is from those dark hours that they receive their fullest light. " Simon, Simon ", says the Lord, " behold, Satan hath desired to have you, that he may sift you as wheat : but I have prayed for thee, that thy strength fail not : and when thou art converted, strengthen thy brethren."[2] But to Simon Peter this solicitude for him seemed needless. Was he not a zealous disciple who had forsaken all to follow the Lord? " Lord, I am ready to go with thee both into prison, and to death." Was there a note of expostulation in his voice as well as assurance? How little Peter knew what humiliation the next few hours would bring him ! " I tell thee, Peter, the cock shall not crow this day, before that thou shalt deny thrice that thou knowest me." Before the next morning came, Peter's self-esteem was in ruins. In his love for his Lord he had dared to follow nearer him than any save John; but in so doing he had run into temptation, and he had failed at the test—not of prison or death, but of a word, a taunt. With the crowing of the cock the knowledge of his failure rushed

[1]trials, R.V. margin ;　[2]Luke 22 : 31-32.

in upon him; and a heartbroken man "went out, and wept bitterly". How deeply ever after Peter would have known the meaning of those words in the Prayer!

Had not the Lord dwelt on them time and again that night? When he was at the Garden, he said, "Pray that ye enter not into temptation". And they —who had joined in Peter's asseveration of valiant loyalty—"all forsook him and fled". How much they too had needed the Lord's intercession in the hour of his own agony! You who declared your own strength fit for any test—"What, could *ye* not watch with me one hour?" "The spirit indeed is willing, but the flesh is weak."[3]

But the highest illumination is given to the words once more by his own example. He, who had taken upon him that which was prescribed in the roll of the book: who knew that it was binding upon the Christ to suffer: who knew that he was "a polished shaft" strengthened by the Spirit for the work of redemption[4] —even he did not say, "Lead me into this trial for which I am come". Far more acceptable to the Father were the words that welled up from his heart: "Father, if thou be willing, remove this cup from me: nevertheless not my will, but thine, be done." That he could desire the cup to pass from him is at once the deepest mark of his humanity and the sublimest height of his spirituality. It was the evidence of his kinship with ourselves that he had a desire of his own which needed to be set aside; an angel could not have prayed in those words, still less a co-eternal "God the Son"; only one "made a little lower than the angels for the suffering of death" could use them. They are at the same time the utterance of perfect humility. He does

[3]Matt. 26 : 40-41 ; [4]Psa. 40 : 7-8 ; Isa. 49 : 2.

231

not say, " Bring me to this shame and suffering : I will face the worst ", but prays even at the last moment that if some less dreadful way of redemption is possible, he may be spared the Cross. How striking the contrast with Peter's bravado ! How far beyond any fancy to invent, or tradition to evolve such spiritual insight !

So this last petition is the final and most searching confession of dependence upon God : let not evil have us in its grip ; maintain us in that fellowship with Thee for which thou didst make us and to which thou hast brought us. Paul has a notable echo of the Prayer which at the same time expounds it when he writes : " The Lord will deliver me from every evil work, and will save me unto his heavenly kingdom ".[5] With this petition we may compare a prayer in the Tractate *Berokot* in the Talmud, which asks to be delivered from " evil man and from evil act, from evil impulse, from evil companion, from evil neighbour, and from Satan ". Here the impulse (*yezer*) is clearly distinguished from " Satan " —who becomes, indeed, a needless appendage to this comprehensive list of evils. Leaving out Satan, therefore, we have a very interesting illustration of what " the evil " might mean to a Jewish audience. Indeed, C. Taylor, in the standard edition of *The Sayings of the Fathers*, conjectures that the expression in the Prayer means the *Yezer ha-Ra* ;[6] this may narrow it too closely, but is undoubtedly nearer the truth than the rendering of the R.V. text, " the evil one ", which was condemned as unjustifiable even by scholars who were themselves believers in the personal Devil. Already in the Sermon " the evil " has been used for the diabolic tendency of human nature (*a*) as experienced in oneself, and (*b*) as manifested in others in their conduct towards us.[7]

[5] 2 Tim. 4 : 18, R.V. ; [6] see pages 146-148 ; [7] 5 : 39.

Here in the prayer the term covers in the widest sense that " evil " having its source in man's corrupted will which is the adversary of God and men.

As the first section of the Prayer turned upon the command, " Thou shalt love the Lord thy God ", so the last section enshrines the principle, " Thou shalt love thy neighbour as thyself ". The petitions for bread and for forgiveness in particular lay stress on our common humanity and the claims of all men upon us ; but the plural in all three petitions declares them to be uttered both with and for the whole body of the saints.

Throughout the Prayer, just as we do not directly ask for purification, so there is no direct request for eternal life. Both are implied : the one, as a corollary of forgiveness ; the other in a two-fold way. We pray, first, for the coming of God's Kingdom ; and secondly, for our continuing fellowship with Him ; that is, we pray to be identified with His purpose, and to abide in His love. Eternal life for ourselves individually will follow as a consequence ; but it is significant that it is in the Prayer only by implication and not by direct statement. " Seek ye first the Kingdom ", says Jesus, truly : but he excludes mere self-seeking in the name of the Kingdom. We are not investing in an endowment insurance payable in the after-life ; we are looking for the perfection of our adoption as sons of God—the fullness of redemption, with all that it involves. Here in the Pattern Prayer, we have the truest education for that end : our Shepherd leads us to still waters that restore our souls, for from these springs we may drink of eternal life.

The doxology, " For thine is the Kingdom, the power, and the glory, for ever : amen ", is omitted by practically all modern editors and versions. The textual evidence, however, is not so conclusive as this would imply, and it is worth quoting the cautious words of Dr. Scrivener : " It is right to say that I can no longer regard this doxology as certainly an integral part of St. Matthew's Gospel but (notwithstanding its rejection by Lachmann, Tischendorf, Tregelles, Westcott and Hort) I am not yet absolutely convinced of its spuriousness . . . It is vain to dissemble the pressure of the adverse case, though it ought not to be looked upon as conclusive."[8] The words have been curiously subject to textual variation, a few cursive MSS. even adding to " glory " the words " to the Father, and the Son, and to the Holy Spirit "—a patent interpolation. But it is unlikely that the Prayer would be given without some closing ascription of praise to the Father, and it is possible that this clause was omitted by some MSS. in an effort at harmonizing the text with Luke's account of the Prayer. The familiar words are fitting and beautiful as an acknowledgment of the universal dominion of God of which the future Kingdom on earth will be a particular expression ; and it is worth noting that they render quite inappropriate the translation " Evil One " in the words immediately preceding. While there can be evil, there can be no Evil One, if God is the universal King.

[8]F. A. SCRIVENER, *Plain Introduction to the Criticism of the N.T.* (edition of 1894).

V. LIVING IN GOD

1

THE MAGNET OF THE HEART (Matt. 6 : 19-23)

Lay not up for yourselves treasures upon the earth,
Where moth and rust doth corrupt,
And where thieves dig through and steal ;
But lay up for yourselves treasures in heaven,
Where neither moth nor rust doth corrupt,
And where thieves do not dig through nor steal :
For where your treasure is, there also will your heart be.

The lamp of the body is the eye :
If therefore thine eye be single,
Thy whole body shall be light :
But if thine eye be evil,
Thy whole body will be dark.
If therefore the light that is in thee be darkness,
The darkness—how great it is !

The underlying theme of 6 : 1-18 has been that the true and eternal reward can only come as the result of a life of communion with God ; and this leads on to a new section in which the reward is contemplated as the true treasure of life. The two sections are joined in thought by several interwoven strands. In contrast with the true worship is hypocrisy ; and in contrast with the true treasure is avarice. The two are so often found together that they may be reckoned as the twin spiritual perils of the pursuit of righteousness ; and if the righteousness which many of the Pharisees showed was hollow, so were the riches in which they trusted.

With a force which tends to be weakened in translation, Jesus says : "Treasure not up for yourselves treasure upon earth . . ." Men think they make lasting provision when they lay by a store of valuable clothes, supplies of corn, or a hoard of money. But moth may destroy the fabrics, insects and rodents corrupt the grain and render it worthless, and thieves may burrow through the mud walls of the houses (" dig through ", the R.V. margin has it) and steal the gold, perhaps killing the owner to escape detection. The saying covers all the forms in which wealth was customarily horded. Rust is literally " eating " and more probably refers to devouring by vermin than to chemical changes in metal. James, however, in a passage obviously based on the Lord's saying, uses a word which specifically means metallic corrosion.[1]

Buried in the Lord's words is a double allusion to Isaiah which calls for a further examination of some passages referred to in an earlier chapter. In a prophecy of the Suffering Servant in 50 : 9, it is said : " Lo, they all shall wax old as a garment ; the moth shall eat them up ". In the following chapter the faith of the Servant is made a pattern for the people of God for whom he suffers, and his words are repeated in calling on them to look at the eternal realities in contrast to the " heavens " and " earth " of a passing world order. And so " the people in whose heart is God's law " are adjured not to fear the reproach of men : " For the moth shall eat them up like a garment, and the worm shall eat them like wool : but my righteousness shall be for ever, and my salvation unto all generations ".[2]

When the allusion to those passages is recognized, the Lord's reference to the everyday facts of decay and loss carries an overtone of meaning. The saying still declares plainly enough that earthly riches may perish,

[1]James 5 : 2-3 ; [2]Isa. 51 : 6, 7, 8.

and only the treasures of the spirit are unfading ; but the spoiled grain and the moth-eaten cloak are also pictorial emblems for something more. They are the symbols of a world in which men set their hearts ; and those whose hearts are in the world are as doomed to perish as the world order to which they belong : they, like it, shall vanish like smoke. Behind the Lord's words is the same profound belief as in the prophet that enduring life can only be found in the eternal and victorious righteousness of God.

Therefore, says Jesus, " Treasure up for yourselves treasures in heaven . . ." " Earth " and " heaven " as simple terms for place give the saying poetic antithesis ; but in Jewish usage heaven is a reverential synonym for God, and " in heaven " is equivalent to " with God ". The Old Testament speaks of God as " laying up " a store for the righteous.[3] If their desire is set on this divine treasure then they indeed have " treasure with God ". But God may store judgment for the future as well as goodness, and a man's own life determines of which kind the store shall be. So men may be said to lay it up by their own action : " Riches profit not in the day of wrath : but righteousness delivereth from death ".[4] For this reason James in the passage quoted above, tells the godless rich : " Ye have laid up your treasure in the last days ".[5] In heaping up earthly treasures by extortion and oppression they have accumulated another store—the wrath that is reserved for them in the day of judgment ; and James, with the proverb about " the day of wrath " in mind, is giving a pungent turn to the figure used by Jesus. It is another example of the rich allusiveness of Scripture, in which streams from two sources can merge in a single phrase.

[3]Psa. 31 : 19 ; [4]Prov. 11 : 4 ; [5]James 5 : 3, R.V.

237

Paul also has his allusion to the Lord's words when he exhorts Timothy to " charge them that are rich in this world " not to " have their hope set on the uncertainty of riches ", but on God, and that " they be rich in good works . . . laying up in store for themselves a good foundation against the time to come, that they may lay hold on the life which is life indeed ".[6]

Not only does God lay up treasure for those who are God-fearing, but they are a treasure to Him. " They shall be mine ", he says, " in the day that I do make, even a peculiar treasure. "[7] This is the kernel of Malachi's message that the true Israel are " they that fear the Lord ", and who alone are written in His book of remembrance ; and it deliberately recalls the use of the same expression at the beginning of Israel's national history.[8] They are chosen as God's prized possession. But it is Abraham's seed by faith who are truly God's treasure ; and so Peter writes to those " sojourners of the Dispersion " who are " elect according to the foreknowledge of God the Father, through sanctification of the Spirit, unto obedience and sprinkling of the blood of Christ ", and in the language of the law and in the spirit of the prophet he says : " But ye are an elect race, a royal priesthood, an holy nation, a people for God's own possession, that ye should show forth the excellencies of him who has called you out of darkness into his marvellous light."[9]

These are the Lord's " inheritance ", a term which is used of Israel of old.[10] And Paul, applying the Old Testament language to the spiritual Israel, can write to the Ephesians of " the riches of the glory of God's

[6] I Tim. 6 : 17, 19, R.V. ; [7] Mal. 3 : 17, R.V. ; [8] Exod. 19 : 5, R.V. ; [9] I Peter 2 : 9, R.V. ; [10] Exod. 34 : 9 ; Psa. 33 : 12 ; cf. Psa. 78 : 71 ; Isa. 63 : 17.

inheritance in the saints ".[11] But if they are the Lord's inheritance He also is theirs. " The Lord is the portion of mine inheritance and of my cup : thou maintainest my lot. The lines are fallen unto me in pleasant places ; yea, I have a goodly heritage. "[12] The words are those of the spirit of Christ in the Psalms, but what is true of him is true also of those who are " in him ". If they are the Lord's treasure, so He is theirs, and they can cry with Asaph : " My flesh and my heart faileth : but God is the rock of my heart, and my portion for ever. "[13]

In the light of these sayings of the Psalmist we can feel the force of the Lord's words, " For where your treasure is, there also will be your heart ". The heart will turn as surely as the needle of the compass towards what we really value. No amount of outward religious perform-ance will change its direction for long if the world provides its pole. But if God is our prized possession, then to Him our hearts will be drawn ; and He is the only possession which can never perish, and can ensure that the possessors will never perish either. We cannot pretend that delight and a sense of wealth in God come easily to human nature ; only a long and constant direction of the mind can bring the consciousness of that precious treasure. " Set your mind ", says Paul— set it like a ship on a course—" on the things that are above, not on the things that are on the earth. For ye are dead, and your life is hid with Christ in God. "[14] Life is our treasure ; and our treasure, like our citizen-ship, is in heaven.[15]

Christ, too, had his treasure, which God had laid up for him from the beginning of the ages, for he could pray to the Father : " Glorify thou me with thine own self

[11]Eph. 1 : 18 ; [12]Psa. 16 : 5-6 ; [13]Psa. 73 : 26 ; cf. 119 : 57 ; 142 : 5 ; [14]Col. 3 : 2-3 ; [15]Phil. 3 : 20, R.V.

with the glory which I had with thee before the world was ".[16] A share in his glory will be the lot of those who are " meet to be partakers of the inheritance of the saints in light ", for whom " the hope " is " laid up in the heavens ", for " Christ in them " is " the hope of glory ".[17]

The eye is the light-giver of the body ; unless light can penetrate it all is dark within, however bright the sunlight around. And so by a kind of metonymy Jesus calls it the lamp. The world is light for a man with a clear eye, and he himself is as it were filled with light. So it is in things of the spirit : the sunlight of God's truth shines around, but can it enter the man? If it cannot nothing irradiates the darkness of his own nature ; and " if that which ought to convey light is darkened, that which is by nature dark must be dark indeed ".

What can darken the eye so that it fails of its function? The clue is in the context : Jesus has been talking of the treasure on which men's heart is set, and in Jewish usage the " single " and " evil " eye have particular meanings which go back to the Old Testament. When a poor Israelite wanted to borrow, " beware " (says Moses to the potential lender) " lest there be a base thought in thine heart, saying, The seventh year, the year of release is at hand ; and thine eye be evil toward thy brother, and thou give him nought ".[18] The evil eye was blind to the other's need, and saw only the chances of gain or loss. But when famine came in the siege as one of the punishments on disobedient Israel, a man might look on his closest kin with an eye even more perverted : he might be driven to a dreadful greed : " His eye shall be evil towards his brother . . . so

[16]John 17 : 5 ;   [17]Col. 1 : 5, 12, 27 ;   [18]Deut. 15 : 9.

that he shall not give any of them of the flesh of his children whom he shall eat ".[19]

Desire for possession is the motive which corrupts the eye. " He that hath an evil eye hasteth after riches ".[20] Greed leads to envy, and envy to treachery : " Eat not the bread of him that hath an evil eye . . . for as he reckoneth within himself, so is he ; Eat and drink, saith he to thee ; but his heart is not with thee ".[21] On the other hand, " He that hath a bountiful (margin, good) eye shall be blessed ; for he giveth of his bread to the poor ".[22]

In the New Testament, an evil eye is one of the defilements coming from " within, out of the heart of man "[23] ; and when the Householder in the parable rebukes the labourers who grudge the latecomers equal pay, he says, " Is thine eye evil, because I am good ? "[24] Are they greedy and envious because he is generous ?

The evil eye results from an attachment to earthly treasure which corrupts the spirit and blinds the heart. The " good " or " single " eye, on the other hand, is that of the liberal man whose vision is unclouded by greed and his mind not divided by envy, and so singleness becomes a New Testament term—and especially a Pauline term—for liberality.

In Luke 11 : 33-36 a similar saying is found in the discourse which follows the Lord's refusal to give a sign other than " the sign of the prophet Jonah ".[25] The generation who sought a sign when they had him in their midst were condemned by the example of the Ninevites and the Queen of Sheba. If they had not been blind they would have no need to make the request ; if they could not see the living sign, it was because they

[19]Deut. 28 : 54 ; [20]Prov. 28 : 22 ; [21]Prov. 23 : 6-7 ; [22]Prov. 22 : 9 ; [23]Mark 7 : 22 ; [24]Matt. 20 : 15 ; [25]Luke 11 : 29.

themselves were full of darkness, and the organ which should let light into them was diseased. In this context " single " and " evil " must have a wider meaning : they were blinded by jealousy rather than by a niggardly spirit. But in Matthew the words form a bridge between the saying about treasure and the warning against Mammon.

2

THE LORD OF THE HEART (Matt. 6 : 24-25)

No one can serve two masters :
For either he will hate the one, and love the other :
Or else he will hold to the one, and despise the other.
Ye cannot serve God and Mammon.

Therefore I say unto you—
Take no thought for your life,
What ye shall eat,
Or what ye shall drink :
Nor yet for your body,
What ye shall put on.
Is not the life more than the food,
And the body than the raiment?

In the first three Gospels the verb " to serve " is applied to the relation between men and God only here and in Luke 16 : 13 ; and in the latter, where a similar saying follows the Parable of the Unrighteous Steward, it takes the form : " No servant—household servant or steward—can serve two masters ". The verb arises naturally from the parabolic figure of two masters, but as applied to the followers of God it has a special fitness, for in oriental life sonship implied service, as in the Parable of the Two Sons in Matt. 21 : 28-30. Where life was mainly agricultural it was natural for the sons to work under the father on the family farm. The more well-to-do, like the father in the parable of the Prodigal Son, would have three forms of service : that of their sons, the " hired servants ", and " bondmen ". So the elder son complains : " Lo these many years do I serve thee, neither transgressed I at any time thy commandment " ; and part of the sin of the Prodigal was that by his departure he had deprived his father of his services.[1]

Strictly, however, the verb means " to be a slave, to serve as a bondman " ; and the stricter meaning has its place in the saying in Matthew. A man might be employed as a hired servant by two masters, but he can be a bond-slave only to one, for only one at a time can own him. What, then, is a man who " treasures up " earthly wealth? Is he not the master of his own resources, to do as he will with them? Does he not control the power which they bring? No, says Jesus ; it is the riches who are master, and he is the slave ; he does not own them so much as they own him. Because they have his heart, they have him altogether. By dominating his desires they corrupt his spiritual vision, and as a blind man he is at their mercy. And so as a climax to the steps in thought in the preceding verses Jesus now personifies riches as Mammon, the master. The term is well known in the Talmud and Targums, and usually occurs with some qualifying expression— " the mammon of wickedness " " the mammon of falsehood ",[2] and so on. In the same way Jesus speaks

[1] Luke 15 : 19, 22, 29; [2] Targum on Hab. 2 : 9 ; Ecclesiasticus 31 : 8, Aramaic text.

of " the mammon of unrighteousness ".[3] Nowhere in Jewish literature, it seems, is " Mammon " anything more than a personification ; and nowhere is the personification so vivid as in the words of Jesus.

In Matt. 6 : 24 Mammon stands unmasked as a false god ; for it is a psychological truth that covetousness is idolatry.[4] It sets up an idol in the heart ; and though, like Molech of old, the idol may be " nothing in the world ", yet like Molech, through its power over the imagination it claims its human sacrifices. In stark opposition, therefore, are God and Mammon, and like the Israelites on Mount Carmel, men must choose whom they will serve. They cannot really halt between two opinions. " Know ye not that to whom ye yield yourselves bondslaves to obey, his bondslaves ye are to whom ye obey, whether of sin unto death, or of obedience unto righteousness ? "[5] Jesus' teaching is uncompromising ; there is no service of God but wholehearted service, and the man who thinks he can serve both God and the world a little deceives himself. " Love " and " hate " may not have here the emotional force which we commonly attach to them ; even in Deut. 22 : 15-17 they mean " to prefer " and " to slight " or " be indifferent to " ; strong preference is described by Hebrew idiom in these sharply antithetic terms. But however we understand them we must not weaken the antithesis. A man is confronted by a moral choice ; he must choose by an act of will ; and as he chooses, so he must live. If he does not choose God, he has by that fact entered the service of God's enemy.

It is one of the remarkable facts about Jesus that he himself demands no less a loyalty from those who would follow him. To the man who wanted to defer a

[3]Luke 16 : 9 ;   [4]Eph. 5 : 5 ;   [5]Rom. 6 : 16.

response indefinitely by pleading home ties, he says :
" Follow me, and leave the dead to bury their dead ".[6]
Warning the disciples of the family divisions his message
would cause, and of the conflict of loyalties which would
result, he says : " He that loveth father or mother more
than me is not worthy of me : and he that loveth son or
daughter more than me is not worthy of me. And he
that doth not take his cross, and follow after me, is not
worthy of me ".[7] He makes on men the same decisive
demands as God : and the apostles (his brothers James
and Jude included) can fittingly call themselves " bondslaves of Christ " for he too is the Master.[8]

It is as the bondslave of Christ, his vision sharpened
by service, that James reflects this irreconcilable
antagonism between God and Mammon when he says
the friendship of the world is enmity with God, and
draws the conclusion from it in concrete terms : " Whosoever therefore will be a friend of the world is the
enemy of God ".[9] The connection is closer than appears
in brief quotation. James has been contrasting " envying
and strife " with " the wisdom which is from above ",
and traces the source of envy to a desire for possession.[10]
The motive of that desire is that men may consume
the possession upon their " pleasures ".[11] The context
shows that by " pleasures " James does not mean only
social pleasure or entertainment (though these are not
excluded) ; his thought includes all the gratification of
human passions which wealth gives the power to
indulge ; and they may be none the less " pleasures "
even if many of them are, like envy, very near to pain.
The " world " with which the men whom he describes
are allied is the sphere of the passions of men whose

[6]Matt. 8 : 22 ; [7]Matt. 10 : 37 ; [8]James 1 : 1 ; Jude verse 1 ; [9]James
4 : 4 ; [10]James 3 : 14-15 ; 4 : 2 ; [11]James 4 : 3, with margin.

minds dwell solely in the material and visible order ; and the Prince of that world is Mammon.

Mammon does not stand only for hoarded wealth. His service includes all anxious striving for material things ; and the poor whose minds are consumed with their poverty may be as much his slaves as the rich who scheme to be richer. Neither can have their hearts in earth and heaven at the same time.

In nothing is human nature more prone to lose the end in the means than in preoccupation with bodily needs. How many people kill themselves with worrying whether they will have enough to live on ! How many more make life a burden for the same cause, and so deprive it of any value ! In moments of detachment we can see this strange self-stultification by which men destroy a thing in the very act of agonizing to preserve it ; and we recognize it as the most poignant example of that " emptiness and striving after wind " which the Preacher found to be characteristic of human life. Yet at some time and in some measure we all fall into the fallacy.

This much is discernible to reasoning which does not rise above the level of the earth : but when Jesus says the life is more than the food which sustains it he carries us to an altogether higher realm. He has implicitly brought God into the comparison. Who gave the life? Who formed the body? If we could not produce these for ourselves, why should we think it depends solely on us to provide the food and clothing which they need? If God has given the greater gift, will He not give the lesser?

" Take no thought ", says the A.V. in the language of the seventeenth century, in which Francis Bacon

246

could say that a man "died with thought and anguish". The sense of anxiety and often of despondency is prominent in the usage of the time and was doubtless present to the mind of the translators. Is this the meaning of the original? Nearly all modern versions give "anxious care" or some equivalent, not because the word used necessarily has this meaning, but because it is the meaning which is deemed to fit the context and to be justified by general Biblical usage. While this removes a possible misunderstanding, we must beware of limiting the idea unduly to mere fret. While the Lord does not forbid honest provision, he certainly forbids all preoccupation with bodily needs, whether the mood be anxious or assertive.

As to Biblical usage, whatever the classical force of the term, both its noun and verb are found in the LXX in contexts which indicate care, anxiety, distress, as the prevailing (though not the exclusive) sense. So too in the New Testament, though the sense of a godly care for one another's welfare is sometimes found. In the Lord's exposition of the Parable of the Sower, where he speaks of cares of this world, and riches and desires, he is thinking of the consuming concern which chokes the germinating word of the Gospel.[12] Particularly interesting is Peter's "casting all your care upon Him",[13] because he is quoting the LXX of Psa. 55 : 22 : "Cast thy burden on the Lord". This act of confident trust is in Peter's mind the sequel to "humbling yourselves under the mighty hand of God"; it is the product of a childlike humility, whereas the effort to carry the burden ourselves is the expression of human pride. In such as association of ideas do we not catch an unmis-

[12]Matt. 13 : 22, Mark 4 : 19; Luke 8 : 14; [13]1 Peter 5 : 7, 6, 4.

takeable echo of the " Chief Shepherd " of whom Peter has been writing? And are we not justified in taking this as a guide to the meaning of the word in the Lord's use? " Take no thought " may then be understood as " Do not burden yourself with care for your life " ; do not try to carry the burden that is not yours, but have peace of mind. The thought is common to Jesus and to Peter that those who are the object of God's guarding care have no need to carry a load of anxiety : " He careth for you ", says Peter (using a different word which means " He makes you the object of His interest "), and in so saying he is drawing out in plain prose the thought which is poetically implied in the Sermon.

While, then, mere human shrewdness can see the folly of ruining life in the effort to maintain it, Jesus sees men under the shadowing arm of God. He speaks with the sublime assurance of one to whom creation is not a remote theory of man's origin but an ever-present fact. God created man, and what He created will be the object of His continuing concern. Moreover, the disciples to whom Jesus is speaking are chosen and called for the fuller life of the Kingdom of God ; they are to be the subjects of a new creation. God, therefore, is not only their source and origin : He surrounds them ; he is their constant environment, they are in Him. And from this Jesus draws one conclusion which for him is self-evident : the daily life that is lived in God is not life without labour or without forethought, but it is emphatically life without care.

THE LORD OF LIFE (Matt. 6 : 26-34)

Behold the birds of the heaven:
>*For they sow not,*
>*Neither do they reap,*
>*Nor gather into barns.*

Yet your heavenly Father feedeth them.
Are ye not much better than they?
Which of you by taking thought
Can add one cubit to his span of life?
And why take ye thought for raiment?
Consider the lilies, how they grow:
>*They toil not,*
>*Neither do they spin:*

And yet I say unto you
>*That even Solomon in all his glory*
>*Was not arrayed like one of these.*

Wherefore if God so clothe the grass,
>*Which today is,*
>*And tomorrow is cast into the oven,*

Shall he not much more clothe you,
>*O ye of little faith?*

Therefore take no thought,
>*Saying, What shall we eat?*
>*Or, What shall we drink?*
>*Or, Wherewithal shall we be clothed?*

For after all these things do the Gentiles seek;
For your heavenly Father knoweth that ye have need
>*of these things.*

But seek ye first the Kingdom of God and his
>*righteousness;*

And all these things shall be added unto you.
Take no thought for the morrow:
For the morrow shall take care for itself:
Sufficient unto the day is the evil thereof.

For his example of freedom from care Jesus called men to look up. There, overhead, free from all visible support, were the birds flying under the arch of heaven. He may have pointed to the rock doves which lived in immense numbers in the valleys around the Sea of Galilee, and literally " fly as a cloud " with a whirr of wings that causes a strong gust of wind. While man by God's ordinance must till the earth, and therefore must look ahead to the fulfilment of nature's cycle of growth, these creatures live for the day: they do not sow and have no harvests. By whom then are they fed? By " your heavenly Father " (he does not say theirs).

> Ask thou the beasts, and they shall teach thee :
> And the fowls of the air, and they shall tell thee :
> Or speak to the earth, and it shall teach thee :
> And the fishes of the sea shall declare unto thee.
> Who knoweth not in all these
> That the hand of the Lord hath wrought this?
> In whose hand is the life of every living thing.
> And the breath of all mankind.[1]

This teaching of the earth and the beasts Jesus interprets. To them God is Creator, and " He giveth to the beast his food, and to the young ravens which cry "; but to the believers He is Father: are not they therefore " of more value than many sparrows "?[2] Man burdens himself with care because he compares day with day and year with year. It is true that he is constituted in the image of God to look before and after, and he is not fully a man unless he uses his faculties diligently. But Jesus has deliberately chosen the example of those who cannot "gather into barns " to show that a

[1]Job. 12 : 7-10 ; [2]Psa. 147 : 9 ; Job. 38 : 41 ; Matt. 10 : 31 ; Luke 12 : 7 ;

250

man's life does not ultimately depend on his storage for the coming year ; if like the birds he depends on God, why should he be consumed with anxiety whether this year will be better or worse than last? He may look to the future by sowing in order to reap, but if he carries the future as a burden on his own back, he will crush the germ of the life of the spirit which holds the promise of the life which is life indeed. Let him " be content with what it is to be a man, be content with what it is to be the dependent, the creature as little capable of sustaining himself as of creating himself. But if Man will forget God—and look after his own sustenance, then material care becomes our lot."[3]

Verse 27 contains a word which may be used of linear measure or (by an extension of meaning) of length of time. Both usages are to be found in the New Testament. Here it is associated with the cubit—a linear measure ; but does not the Psalmist ask to know the " measure " of his days, and say : " Behold, thou hast made my days as an hand-breadth "?[4] " Age " fits the context here and gives the saying a tang of ironic humour : care does not lengthen life, but shortens it. The truest recipe for length of life will be to recognize our powerlessness over it, and therefore to leave it to Him who has the power : " There is no man that hath power over the spirit to retain the spirit. "[5]

While the birds teach the folly of comparing our resources with those of others, the next example shows the folly of comparing our circumstances with others. Care has its roots in just such comparisons, for needs of warmth and decency account for only a small part of the anxiety over clothing. Far more is occasioned by

[3]S. KIERKEGAARD, *Consider the Lilies* ; [4]Psa. 39 : 4-5 ; [5]Eccl. 8 : 8.

social standards, the desire to impress others, or the envy of what others have. Our standards are relative : nearly always we compare ourselves with those one stage above us in rank or means, and so we convince ourselves that we do not ask anything unreasonable in wanting to do as they do in dress, housing, style of living, the distance we travel for holidays or the money we spend on laying out the garden. From a woman's nail varnish to the horse-power of her husband's motor car, there is not one of the outer wrappings of life which may not give us a carking sense of inferiority ; we may reject the idea with scorn, yet, perhaps unknown to ourselves, the worm of envy is gnawing in our rose-bud and cankering the fragrance of living.

Only the very young or the very foolish would wish to ape the luxury of a wholly different class of society from their own. Yet Jesus pricks the bubble of all such comparison by taking as example the extreme of magnificence—Solomon enthroned in regal array. For such comparisons differ only in degree : every step up leads only to emulation of the rank above. We attain with much struggle a level of comfort or standard of appearance which for the moment seems to fulfil our ambition. Ten years later the bloom has rubbed off our prize ; that which gave us a glowing satisfaction is viewed with distaste : we must go on to get something more. Jesus saw that there is no limit to human vanity, and no final standard but the pinnacle of splendour.

So, says Jesus, " Consider the lilies " : the verb is unusual and emphatic—go as disciples and let them be your teacher. To look at the lilies a man must stoop : to " consider " them he must do more—he must humble himself and forget to compare himself with others.

There the blooms grow in unclamorous beauty : they do not strive to be equal to neighbouring flowers, nor by any hint or tacit assumption do they judge themselves superior. " They toil not, neither do they spin." They are what they are, effortlessly and without care— though not without all the incredible activity of root and veins and leaves, of plant physiology and bio-chemistry. The brief beauty of the Galilean spring provides many examples which would serve : iris, ranunculus, a rich purple arum—all have been claimed as the " lilies " of the Lord's allusion : claim can also be made for the native gladiolus, various species of which " grow among the grain, often overtopping it, and illuminating the broad fields with their various shades of pinkish purple to deep violet, purple and blue ".[6] Yet to have seen the intense scarlet hue and silky sheen of the *anemone coronaria* is to be convinced that here is the true comparison with the robes of the most magnificent of Israel's kings. No microscope can reveal flaws, as it will in the finest satins of man's weaving.

Yet what is their end? Still blooming, they will be cut down along with the grass or straw which, dried in the sun for a day, will make quick burning fuel. A few handfuls will be put in the domestic oven— a pit in the ground between three feet and four feet deep and about three feet wide, lined with baked clay. They will blaze up and soon make a good heat. Then the fuel will be removed and the pottery wall wiped as well as may be of the layer of soot and ashes, and wafer-thin cakes of dough will be plastered on the hot sides of the oven with a kind of cushion made to fit. In a few moments they will be baked. And the fuel? Gone in

[6] *Hastings' Dictionary of the Bible.*

smoke and flame, and a few ashes thrown out on the earth : so ends the glory of the lily.

In the prophecy of Isaiah all the " goodliness " of the flower of the field is a type of the man who withers like the grass before the hot wind from the desert :[7] and the lesson conveyed is transience. Jesus draws attention to the lilies thrown into the oven, and the lesson is trust : " shall not your Father much more clothe you? " The way to reconciliation of the difference is already to be found in the prophecy : " . . . But the word of our God shall stand for ever. . . . They that wait upon the Lord shall renew their strength . . .".[8] The children of the Father are " born again, not of corruptible seed, but of incorruptible, by the word of God, which liveth and abideth for ever ".[9] And this is the ground of the comparison which Jesus makes. If God so arrays the lilies which are things of a day, what will He do for the sons of eternity? The conclusion is pointed with the reproachful apostrophe : " O ye little-of-faith ". The one Greek word rendered by a phrase in English is peculiar to Matthew[10] except for the parallel to this passage in Luke 12 : 28.

The use which Jesus makes of the two examples from nature rests on a foundation which was largely common ground for him and the Jews. It assumes first of all that nature is a unity : unless plants, birds and man all belong to one system there would be no point in the illustrations, for there would be no valid ground for reasoning from one to another. The words of Jesus depend upon a doctrine of Creation. For the same reason his thought rests upon the unity of God : it relies upon consistency in His character, constancy in His

[7]Isa. 40 : 6-8 ; [8]verses 8, 31 ; [9]1 Peter 1 : 23-25 ; [10]cf. Matt. 8 : 26 ; 14 : 31 ; 16 : 8.

mode of action, and universality in His power, and these can only be true of the God who is One and who is without rival. God is both at unity with Himself and universal in His supremacy. All depends on Him ; and while Jesus fully recognizes the existence of evil, these passages alone would be enough to show that he did not acknowledge evil as a personal power with a domain of its own. The groundwork of thought under-lying the comparisons is the declaration through Isaiah : " I am the Lord, and there is none else, there is no God beside me. . . . I form the light and create darkness ; I make peace, and create evil : I the Lord do all these things ".[11] From this one God all things have their origin, and in Him they all continue to exist. He alone is absolute Being ; nothing can exist outside of or independently of Him ; all things are His servants.[12]

While, however, all things are maintained as a unity within His universal Spirit, not all are of equal value and significance, for Jesus can reason in com-parative terms—" how much more . . ." Rank and order within the system of creation are determined by purpose, and as the purpose of God is expressed in the terms " righteousness " and " salvation ", the highest place in the order of created things is given to man. The Lord whose name is excellent in all the earth is " mindful " of man and " visits " the son of man, because He made him to be " crowned with glory and honour " and to " have dominion over the works of his hands ".[13] While " all things " are created for His " pleasure " or " will ",[14] man, formed God-like in his potentiality, is made for God's own heart.

It is no mere platitude to bring these ideas into a consideration of the sayings about the birds and the

[11]Isa. 45 : 5-7 ; [12]Psa. 119 : 91 ; [13]Psa. 8 : 4, 5, 6 ; [14]Rev. 4 : 11.

lilies. Human speculations have more often than not run counter to this belief in the unity of creation derived from the unity of its Creator : if for the Jews it was part of the common climate of thought, the reason was to be found in the Scriptures they had received, and not in any genius of their own. And for Jesus, at any rate, we may be assured it was not accepted unconsciously like the air we breathe : it was a reality to be perceived with deep penetration, and with love—of heart, soul and mind—to the Lord who gives all. If in the mind of Jesus flowers, birds and fishes could teach the lesson of God's providence, the reason is that behind all creation is the word of God which brought it into being. So from the lilies we are led back to the great lesson of the first temptation : the word is the reality behind phenomena, and in the Word men find life.

There are people to whom this truth is unknown. Because they have not God in their knowledge they live their lives in the fever and fret of care over externals. They are " aliens from the commonwealth of Israel ", " without God," and " in the world ";[15] having no part in God's covenant, they are ignorant of His power, and without trust in His providence. These are the " Gentiles " : they, naturally enough, " seek " (the verb in this context might mean " hunt for ") to supply their needs of food and clothing and to establish their social standing by the style in which they do it. They have only their own powers to depend on, and only one another's esteem to gain ; and therefore their lives must be a seeking for material things which perpetually vanish away.

But to the disciple comes the assurance : " Your heavenly Father knoweth " your needs. To the Gentiles

[15] Eph. 2 : 12.

these things and all that they represent are a consuming
aim : but the minds and lives of the disciples are turned
to another end. With pointed contrast they are told :
" But seek ye first "—what? They are to seek the
Kingdom and righteousness of God ; they are to seek
His glory and to seek to see His face. That is to say, they
are not so much to strive to get as to give ; and in
giving themselves to God they will have the highest
possession and the richest treasure, and the needs of
this life will be added as the overflow of His bounty.
There will be no need in that case to burden themselves
with tomorrow : for tomorrow is God's. Sorrow and
evil there must be as the discipline of life, but their
measure is in His hand, and each day can bear its own
burden.

VI. LIVING UNDER JUDGMENT

1

JUDGES OR JUDGED? (Matt. 7 : 1-6)

Judge not, that ye be not judged.
> *For with what judgment ye judge, ye shall be judged:*
> *And with what measure ye mete, it shall be measured to you again.*
> *But why beholdest thou the mote that is in thy brother's eye,*
> *But considerest not the beam that is in thine own eye?*
> *Or wilt thou say to thy brother,*
> *" Let me cast out the mote that is in thine eye ",*
> *And, lo, a beam is in thine own eye.*

Hypocrite!
> *Cast out first the beam out of thine own eye:*
> *And then shalt thou see clearly to cast out the mote out of thy brother's eye.*

> *Give not that which is holy to the dogs:*
> *Neither cast ye your pearls before swine,*
> *Lest they trample them under their feet,*
> *And turn again and rend you.*

With Matt. 7 the Sermon enters its final section, which forms a climax. Jesus has portrayed the disciple and his life in the world. He has shown that that life can only be maintained by an intimate and secret communion with God; and this communion carries with it a dependence on God which brings freedom from fear. By contrast he has pictured the anxious and envious mind of those who compare their condition with the condition of others.

Now he goes on to show the result of comparing ourselves with other men, not merely in our outward circumstances but in our character. The perfect example of the man who constitutes himself judge in his own cause is the Pharisee in Luke 18 : 11-12. With fine irony it is said he " stood and prayed thus with himself "— " with himself " because he was his own standard of reference. His words were : " God, I thank thee that I am not as the rest of men . . . or even as this publican ". But both he and the repentant tax-gatherer stood there and then under the scrutiny of God ; and as the outcome one of them " went down to his home justified ", reckoned to be righteous. But it was not the Pharisee who was thus acquitted, but the self-confessed sinner, who had prayed God to " be reconciled " to him.

The parable exactly illustrates the sayings of Matt. 7 : 1-5, which show from yet another angle the contrast between the righteousness of the true covenant-people and the conventional righteousness of contemporary Judaism. The man who lives with God and in God lives under judgment. He is continuously known to the living God, and he either is or is not in a state of peace with God. But beyond that continuous discernment by the all-seeing eyes of God there is a final judgment to come, when sentence will be pronounced and destiny determined. The course of thought which leads to the Parable of the Two Builders leaves no doubt that Jesus has this Day of Judgment in view when he says (as the tense of the verb implies) : " Cease from judging, that ye be not judged ". Judged by whom? Reverent avoidance of the Divine Name by using the passive voice of the verb is part of the idiom of Jesus. What he is saying is that the man who knows God's covenant

259

and keeps it lives his whole life as one who will in that day be judged by God.

Constant awareness of judgment to come may, however, have more than one effect. For a man to know that he is measured by a standard not of his own making, and that in a future day his true and hidden self will be laid bare, must give seriousness and integrity to life. But there is a danger that those who so live will demand that others shall conform to their pattern. In doing this they transfer to themselves that standard by which they have tried to test their own lives ; they make themselves the measuring rule for other men. And so out of their very zeal comes the peril of censoriousness : they make themselves the judges instead of the judged.

They are solicitous for the other man's welfare, and offer help in a way which they think courteous and kindly : " Permit me to cast out the mote out of thine eye ". But in fact their love is self-love. They do not really forget themselves in the other man's need, but their sense of superiority shines the brighter by contrast with his fault. Even if the desire to help is sincere, they will always think, " It was through my strength that he overcame his weakness ". But we may go further : " to judge " in this context cannot escape from its harsher meaning of " to condemn ", and to condemn is potentially to destroy. It is to do violence against a man's soul—an act not of love but of hate, and in the light of Matt. 5 : 21-22, having in it the germ of murder.

Why has a man who was pursuing righteousness fallen into such a slough? Little by little he has come to see the errors to which he was not prone looming large, and his own failings have dwindled. No love is so blind as self-love ; and at last his vision is so blocked that his attempt at aid would be play-acting. He is like a man with the bearing beam of a roof across his eye trying to remove a splinter or a bit of dried stem from someone else's ; for the beam in his eye is his self-esteem. If he them measures out condemnation to others, the same measure awaits him in the day when he thinks he will be justified. The old legal principle of " measure for measure " has returned, not in the material realm but the spiritual ; and the man for whom it was abrogated by the command not to resist evil is himself subject to the penalty of " an eye for an eye ". Forgiveness of others paves the way to God's forgiveness of ourselves ; condemnation of others leads to His condemnation of ourselves. Even in little things the self-sufficient spirit may reveal itself in continual grumbling at others' real or imagined shortcomings, and to this James applies the Lord's words : " Murmur not, brethren, one against another, that ye be not judged : behold, the judge standeth before the door ".[1] The grumblers, like the Pharisees, are more conscious of themselves than of God.

The proverbial saying about the mote and the beam is found in rabbinical writings, and is an example of the caustic Jewish humour. Its picturesque hyperbole gives no difficulty to those who know the speech of the English countryside, where something small may be " about so big as a bee's knee ", or a very thin man " like a rasher of wind ". The salty idiom of unsophisticated men who live close to the soil offers the best parallel to the language of Jesus.

The Lord's words have their reflection in Rom. 2 : 3 : " And reckonest thou, O man, who judgest them that practise such things, that thou shalt escape the

[1] James 5 : 9, R.V.

261

judgment of God?" Rom. 14 is a sustained plea for refraining from judgment in things which can be left to the individual conscience. One man, says the Apostle, may observe dietary restrictions, and do it for the Lord's sake; another, equally sincere, may eat with thankfulness any food which comes. If each acts with the Lord in mind (and his mental state is vital to the argument) then to his Lord he stands or falls. Therefore apostrophizing in turn the representatives of the opposing points of view, Paul says: "But thou, why dost thou judge thy brother? Or thou again, why dost thou set at nought thy brother? For we shall all stand before the judgment seat of God ".[2] We are helped by the parallel which sets "judge" against "set at nought": the judgment which Paul has in mind here is a condemnation which easily passes over into contempt for the brother for whom Christ died.

To Paul himself it is a very small thing that he should be subject to the scrutiny of men; he is not even his own judge, for even if he knows nothing against himself he is not therefore justified. His examiner is the Lord. "Therefore (he says) judge nothing before the time, until the Lord come, who will both bring to light the hidden things of darkness, and will make manifest the counsels of the heart. "[3]

"Judge" is indeed a word of many meanings, and only the context can decide where the balance of the meaning lies in any given case. "Judgment" (in the sense of equitable decision) is cited by the Lord himself along with "mercy and faith" as the "weightier matters of the law" which the Scribes and Pharisees had "left undone ".[4] Lydia could rightly say to Paul and Silas, "If ye have judged me to be faithful to the

[2]Rom. 14 : 10, R.V. ; [3]1 Cor. 4 : 1-5 ; [4]Matt. 23 : 23.

Lord, come unto my house ".[5] If, therefore, judgment in the sense of condemnation of others is excluded, judgment in the sense of discernment is enjoined. The disciple has to be judicious without being judicial—a dilemma which is only fully resolved by a principle given a few verses later. For the remainder of the chapter shows progressive stages of division among men through the action of the word of God. Even in this life the word puts men to a test and reveals something of their true character. And the first division is between those who have reverence for holy things and those who in their sensuality find holy things offensive.

" The holy (thing) " was under the law the term used for food offered sacrificially of which only the priests and their households could partake, and then only if they were ceremonially clean.[6] On the other hand, the flesh of animals torn by beasts was forbidden altogether for food, and was to be " cast to the dogs ".[7] These ritual requirements provide the terms which Jesus applies to things of the spirit. " Dogs " were in Jewish parlance the uncircumcised, and swine were held in special abhorrence from the time that Antiochus Epiphanes ordered them to be profanely sacrificed. But for Jesus the distinction is not a physical one but moral and mental. The contemporary proverb quoted in 2 Peter 2 : 22 (and perhaps partly dependent on Prov. 26 : 11) makes dogs and swine types of the grossness of sensual human nature. Prov. 11 : 22 is the only Old Testament example of swine used in a proverbial simile, and carries a like idea of ignorant sensuality, But (to quote by way of illustration only) the Syriac of Ecclesiasticus 22 : 13 has : " Talk not much with a fool, and consort not with a pig : beware of him, lest

[5]Acts 16 : 15 ; [6]Lev. 22 : 10 ; [7]Exod. 22 : 31.

thou have trouble, and thou becomest defiled when he shaketh himself ". This in turn recalls Prov. 9 : 7-8 : " He that correcteth a scorner getteth to himself shame : and he that reproveth a wicked man getteth himself a blot. Reprove not a scorner, lest he hate thee : reprove a wise man, and he will love thee. "[8]

Pearls of the spirit-word will only evoke blasphemy from the blindly ignorant ; that which is holy is not to be exposed to profanation by sensual men. Are we then to judge them and say, " This one is worthy to have the word, and that one is not "? By no means : it is not for us to condemn—to assess what they are in God's sight ; still less to damn—to deem them outside the pale of God's mercy. (What chance then would there be for a Saul of Tarsus at a time when he was as vicious towards the Church as a thwarted pariah ?) None the less the truth we hold, and the salvation it offers, are God's gifts, and to be handled with reverence for the Giver.

These words do in fact impose on believers one of the most difficult discriminations they are called on to make. On the one hand, no verse is more liable to be used unwarrantably as a veil for moral cowardice or spiritual snobbery ; it cannot mean that preaching is to be withheld for fear that the word should be despised. Yet it does impose a responsibility for judging the time and manner of our witness. Even in spreading broad-cast the Gospel of the Kingdom, we can observe a decent reticence about those things which the natural man cannot receive. God forbid that we should hoard our pearls : but neither should we scatter them like garbage in the pig's trough, where they will be snouted out and trampled in the mire. There is a certain egotism

[8]cf. also Prov. 23 : 9.

in the attempt to force salvation on the unwilling and resentful; it betrays both a lack of regard for the sanctity of God and a lack of respect for the individuality of men. Only God can claim men's hearts, and He " draws " them without forcing them into His mould. We need to remember that while by His grace we may be agents of His word, it is God who works through it, and not we ourselves. When we are most self-forgetful we shall be least self-assertive in our dealings with God and men; and then our work in the saving of souls from death will best stand the test of fire.

2

THE FATHER'S GIFTS AND THE SONS' RESPONSE (Matt. 7 : 7-12)

Ask, and it shall be given you :
Seek, and ye shall find :
Knock, and it shall be opened unto you.

For every asker receiveth :
And the seeker findeth :
And to the knocker it shall be opened.

Or what man is there of you, whom if his son ask bread,
Will he give him a stone?
Or if he ask a fish,
Will he give him a serpent?

If ye, then, being evil
Know how to give good gifts to your children,
How much more shall your Father which is in heaven
Give good things to them that ask him?

Therefore all things whatsoever ye would that men should
Do ye even so to them :   [*do to you,*
For this is the Law and the Prophets.

265

How comes it that the word reveals two classes of men so sharply distinguished? Are men born swine? And if so can they help it? Is not their swinishness predetermined? Are men predestined to be of the one sort or the other? Or is there not in fact a trace of the swine in all of us?

To these problems, which are raised by Matt. 7 : 6, the saying in verses 7-8 provides the answer : and it is vital that we should grasp what that answer is, for our understanding of it will mould our attitude to ourselves and to others. The three emphatic imperatives, " Ask—seek—knock ", imply both that man needs to ask of God and that to ask is in his power. While they have their ground in man's privation, they triumphantly declare his freedom of will. They indicate that a man is not condemned of God because he is by nature sensual, but because he seeks nothing beyond his sensuality. The words are, it is true, spoken to the disciples, who stand related as children to the Father ; but they are disciples as yet very imperfect in understanding and self-control, and the saying really contains a charter of freedom to all who will seek. Seeking, however, is not the casual motion of half-hearted sentiment ; the verbs imply a sustained act, " Be asking—be seeking—be knocking " ; and those who receive are those who are characterized as the " askers, seekers, knockers "—not those who knock once, but those who by reason of their earnest faith continue knocking. Their pattern is the Syro-Phoenician woman ; and in Luke the same saying is introduced by the parable of the friend borrowing loaves at midnight,[1] while the theme is further illustrated by the parable of the widow and the unjust judge. If persistence will

[1] Luke 11 : 5-13.

wear down even human obduracy, what will it do with the loving Heavenly Father who receives it as a mark of earnestness? Therefore, says James, " If any man lack wisdom, let him ask of God . . . but let him ask in faith, nothing wavering ".[2] There must be constancy in his asking.

If the portrait of the asker is thus limned, these verses also and far more fully delineate the Giver. In Matt. 5 : 44-48 God is shown as the Creator who gives sun and rain to all His creatures as an act of uncaused love ; but here He is the Father in a responsive interchange of love with his children. And this is a love of which human fatherhood offers a dim parable. Men may be niggardly in their gifts and dwarfed in their hearts, but when their children ask for food, even human nature revolts from giving them stones without nourishment or reptiles which cause harm. How much more, then, will the heavenly Father, with all His boundless generosity, give good gifts? But what gifts?

In the course of the Sermon's train of thought, bodily needs have now been left behind, and the Lord has dwelt on the disciple's relation to judgment and the holy things. Our contemplation is carried over into the realm of spiritual reality and finality : and it is precisely in these things that even the bounty of God can only be given to those who ask. Only those who hunger and thirst can be satisfied with His righteousness —to others it would seem husks ; and only those who are so " filled " can be sustained with eternal life. A man cannot be " born of water and of the Spirit " without his own desire, and without rebirth in its fullest sense he cannot enter that eternal Kingdom where " flesh and blood " has no place. The spiritual creation

[2]James 1 : 5-6.

is God's no less than the physical, but it is a creation wrought through men's willing, self-surrender. As of old, the operative power is the Word, but the stuff in which the Word works is no longer unorganized dust but the minds of living men. It is for this reason that Jesus here reveals the character of the Divine love from another aspect than in Matt. 5 : 44-48, and while God " giveth to all men liberally, and upbraideth not ", James is unerring in linking " Ask, and it shall be given you " with " wisdom "—that is, with the spiritual endowment needed if faith is to be perfected through endurance, and endurance is to reach its full end in a man grown to his moral stature and complete, lacking no part or member.[3]

Luke's variant of the saying, too, draws out its meaning : " If ye, then, being evil, know how to give good gifts unto your children, how much more shall your heavenly Father give the Holy Spirit to them that ask him? " The Holy Spirit cannot in this context stand for some special gift such as the power to heal or speak with tongues ; whatever is signified here comes as naturally to those who ask as bread. Nor, of course, can it be a supernatural enlightenment which guides without the need of studying the word. It is the Spirit in the Word which works in men as they seek God ; but through the Word God Himself " worketh in you both to will and to do of his good pleasure ",[4] richly giving from His own singleness of heart.

As in Matt. 5 : 44, so here, the character of God is to be reflected in His children. Many of the mis-understandings of the " Golden Rule " of verse 12 arise from overlooking the " therefore " with which it begins. Its antecedent is in verse 8 : " . . . to him that knocketh

[3]James 1 : 3-5 ; [4]Phil. 2 : 13.

it shall be opened . . . Therefore all things whatsoever
ye would . . . ". But while this appears to be the logical
connection, the verses between have richly filled in
the portrayal of the Father, and as a result have en-
hanced the force of the conclusion. This is, in effect :
you ask of God, and He gives ; you would like men
to be as generous in spirit to you as the Father is :
therefore be so to them. God is the pattern for His sons.

But this carries us to a further point : even the
power to conform to that pattern must come from God's
" good gift ", for it does not dwell in human nature. It
is only through His spirit—mediated through His word
—that mortal man can so shine with the reflected light
of God's moral glory. Further than this, the connection
of thought enlarges a principle which has already been
laid down in Matt. 6 : 14-15 : if you forgive, you will
be forgiven ; if not, then not. So in this passage this
condition for acceptable prayer is made to apply not
only to forgiveness but to all the relations of spiritual
life : if you are to receive you must not only ask, but
give ; if God's bounty is to be accorded you, you must
show bounty towards men. The " therefore "—for
this reason—in the Golden Rule has in consequence a
threefold force : it means (1) because God is so to you,
be so to men ; (2) because God gives good gifts, you
will be enabled to be like Him ; and (3) because without
this likeness you cannot be in communion with God,
you must be like Him.

In Luke 6 : 27-36, the context of the saying is the
command, " Love your enemies . . . give to every one
that asketh of thee ; and of him that taketh away thy
goods ask them not again. And as ye would . . . " In
different contexts, therefore, the same command is based

on (*a*) the example of the Divine love which extends to enemies, and (*b*) the love which the Father devotes to His children. And it is in this that Christ's saying is unique. Many moral systems have included the principle, " Do as you would be done by "—usually in the negative form of Hillel's summary of the Law, " That which is hateful to thyself, do not to thy neighbour ". There were ethical thinkers who approached a more positive form, such as the Chinese Mo-tse in the fourth century B.C., who is translated as saying : " If we were to have the same regard for others as we have for ourselves, who would do anyone an injustice? Regard every one else as you would yourself, and look upon the things of others as you would your own ". But even here the kernel of the thought is the avoiding of injustice, and it is from this negative starting point that Mo-tse reasons out to a wider principle of regard for others. Such reasoning reaches one of the highest peaks in civilized thinking on the conduct of man to man. But Jesus stands alone in making conduct to our neighbour depend on our knowledge of God and by this means interlocking the two commands in which the law is summarized : " Thou shalt love the Lord thy God . . . " and " Thou shalt love thy neighbour as thyself ". The positive form in which he casts the injunction follows inevitably from this mode of thought. Love cannot be negative, and will never be confined into a cool restraint from evil ; and therefore the disciples of Jesus are not merely to refrain from doing harm, but to overflow with good ; and where good is the motive of life there is no room for evil. This vital and creative attitude to their neighbours Jesus declared emphatically to be " the law and the prophets ". The essence of law and prophets is to his insight not restraint but love, not the avoidance of malice or injury, but positive goodness; and so, inverting Hillel's summary, Jesus opens up a new vision of the aim of the old revelation.

The language of the command deserves to be examined carefully. " All things whatever " comprises not merely an unlimited number of different things, but the whole of things : the entire attitude of life must be governed by this principle. For it is " even so " that we are to do to men—and " so " means " in this way ", and not merely " that particular thing ". Once the precision of the language is perceived, the command is lifted beyond the reach of any narrow literalism which might frustrate its aim. Circumstances differ so widely that there may be no comparison between particular acts which we might desire to be done to us, and the act which we might conceivably do to this or that other person, but the Lord lays down a principle which transcends all such limitations.

The use of the plurals " men—them " should eliminate misunderstanding in another direction. One of the stock criticisms of the Rule has been : " Suppose two or more men band together to do evil, pledging themselves not to betray one another, is not each doing to the other as he would the other should do to him? " But the Rule is not, " As ye would this man should do to you, do to him " ; it is, " As you would wish all or any men to do to you, so do to any and all of them " : it allows neither of limit nor evasion ; it demands that we shall identify ourselves with any and everyone not ourselves—and with all who are not ourselves—and be to each, to any and to all what we would wish them to be to us. We cannot, therefore, do to anyone what is contrary to the good of mankind. If we cannot do for the peasant in the Gobi desert the same things that we can do for the man who lives next door, we can have the same attitude of life towards both which will find its expression in any way that opportunity affords.

It is this principle which provides the key to the problem referred to in the previous chapter : how are we to distinguish without judging? The answer is, " By placing ourselves in the other man's shoes ". We may know then both his defects and his need. We may recognize all too clearly his unfitness to receive the precious things of spiritual truth, which will only fill him with revulsion, but we shall not judge him by the standard of our self-superiority, and mentally consign him to perdition because he does not come up to our own measurement of ourselves. Christ himself is the supreme example of his own principle. He came " not to be ministered unto, but to minister ", and his service for men culminated in " giving his life a ransom for many ".[5] He " died for the ungodly ", and if " God commendeth his love towards us, in that while we were yet sinners Christ died for us ", we cannot do other than commend our love towards those who are still sinners ; if not, we have not the spirit of Christ, and are none of his. Once again, the Cross of Christ is the perfect demonstration of his teaching. The Golden Rule could never anywhere else have so deep a fulfilment, for here at the same instant by his death Christ repudiated all sin and identified himself with all sinners : he was the representative of humanity in its unfathomable need, for the Lord made the iniquity of us all to meet upon him.

[5]Matt. 10 : 28.

The fact of the Cross, then, must govern our attitude even to the " dogs " and " swine " of degraded humanity. We, too, were sinners ; they, too, are men. What would we that they should do to us if we were as they are? (This does not mean, " What do they want with their present perverted outlook? " It means, " What should I, knowing God's truth, want if I could see myself in their position?") This attitude is not sentimental, because it does not disguise realities. The disciple does not say that after all swinishness is just the swine's way and we must be charitable to it ; he does not tolerate the sinner by minimizing the sin. To do so would not be to proclaim the Cross but to deny it, for the very aim of the Cross was to show sin for what it is. Precisely because sin is sin, it was a binding necessity that the Son of man should suffer if men were to be redeemed from their bondage ; but, sharing their nature which in itself needed redemption, he also morally made himself one with the sons of Adam— not in their sin, but in their need. While his sharing of their nature made such an identification possible, his love made it a reality ; for their sakes he bore the agony of the Garden and the torture of the Cross. And because he has voluntarily done this for us while we were yet sinners, he reveals depth on depth of meaning in these words of the Golden Rule.

For the essence of the rule is such an identification of ourselves with others as he made when he who knew no sin was " made sin " for us, in order that we might " become the righteousness of God in him ". In such an identification with others there is as it were a breaking down of the bounds of personality ; and yet the result is not to empty a man's own personality, but to fill it. Just as Christ becomes not more like those for whom he died but more unlike by the very fact of his surrender on their account, so his disciple, in identifying himself with others, becomes not less a person but more. He does not become a medley of pale reflections of other men, but an individual more distinct because of stronger faith and larger heart. Men take note of him, that he has been with Jesus. He lives : yet not he ; but Christ lives in him ; and the life which he now lives in the flesh he lives by the faith of the Son of God, who loved him, and gave himself for him. It is in this transcending of the bounds of personality whereby personality itself becomes not emptied but enriched, that the Rule as pronounced by Jesus so far surpasses the negative form which merely restrains injustice.

3

THE WAY AND THE GUIDES (Matt. 7 : 13-20)

Enter ye in by the narrow gate :
    For wide is the gate,
        And broad is the way,
    That leadeth to destruction,
        And many there be that go in thereat.

For narrow is the gate,
    And straitened the way,
That leadeth unto life :
    And few there be that find it.

Beware of false prophets,
    Which come to you in sheep's clothing,
    But inwardly are ravening wolves.
By their fruits ye shall know them :
    Do men gather grapes of thorns,
    Or figs of thistles ?

Even so every good tree bringeth forth good fruit;
*   But the corrupt tree bringeth forth evil fruit.*
A good tree cannot bring forth evil fruit,
*   Neither can a corrupt tree bring forth good fruit.*
(Every tree that bringeth not forth good fruit
*   Is hewn down, and cast into the fire.)*
Therefore by their fruits ye shall know them.

The " Golden Rule " is the coping stone of the
Lord's teaching concerning the way of the disciple.
After it, nothing can be added to the exposition of the
true righteousness; all that remains is to show that
life and death rest upon the choice which must be made.
The way Jesus has shown is not an ethic, a philosophy
of conduct, for that would permit of alternative theories,
of a higher or lower level, of more or less; but this
determines eternal destiny. Jesus impresses the magnitude of the choice by three pairs of metaphors—the
Two Ways, the Two Trees, and the Two Builders. All
these reflect the thought of the first Psalm, for this
likens the man who " delights in the law of the Lord "
to a tree by a stream : it declares that the wicked " are
like chaff which the wind driveth away ", and so
suggests the judgment storm which tests the work of
the builders ; and it ends with showing the two ways
and the destiny to which they lead :

For the Lord knoweth the way of the righteous :
But the way of the ungodly shall perish.

With this, however, the Lord has blended imagery
from elsewhere in the Word. The figure of two ways is
frequent in Scripture from the day that Moses set the
choice before Israel.[1] Jeremiah gives it a particular
and graphic application when Jerusalem is condemned

[1] Deut. 30 : 15-20.

275

to conquest and the faithful are exhorted to leave and accept captivity ; for them the road to Babylon is for the time being the way of life : for " thus saith the Lord : Behold, I set before you the way of life, and the way of death ".[2] In general, however, Old Testament usage emphasizes the characteristics of the " way " rather than the idea that it will lead to a destination : it represents the habit or course either of righteousness or wickedness. But to this there are exceptions which many commentators seem to have overlooked. Of the " strange woman " in Proverbs it is said :

> For her house sinketh down unto death,
> And her paths unto the shades ;
> None that go unto her return,
> Neither do they attain unto the paths of life.[3]

For his picture of the " broad way that *leadeth to* destruction " Jesus has evidently drawn on this vivid imagery of Proverbs. But he makes one important change : the end of the road is not merely Sheol, the place of darkness and the powerless dead ;[4] it is Gehenna, the place of those who are condemned and destroyed. The effect is the same—death : but while Proverbs has shown the ultimate result to which a certain course will lead, the Sermon emphasizes that it will be a judicial death, for there is judgment to come. Another distinction must also be kept in view. The passages in Proverbs give prominence to sins of the flesh : but if Jesus is using them as a basis for his figure in the Sermon, then it must be recognized that he enormously widens their scope. For the Sermon has made plain two things : first, that the grosser sins—murder, adultery, false swearing—are ultimately sins of the spirit, and " proceed

[2]Jer. 21 : 8 ; [3]Prov. 2 : 18-19, American Jewish Version ; cf. 7 : 27, R.V. ; 14 : 12 ; [4]as in Prov. 7 : 27.

out of the heart "; and secondly, that the sins of the mind—hypocrisy, avarice, ambition, pride, censoriousness—are as utterly destructive of eternal life as those which put men (or women) beyond the social pale. The self-righteous who judge others are going the broad way to Gehenna as surely as the sinners; the Pharisee and the harlot are treading the same path—but the harlot has the better chance of turning back.

The contrast between the well-trodden way to the city's imposing main gate, and the overgrown track to an obscure entry in the wall, has often been expounded. The narrow gate admits to the Kingdom, for Jesus has already said that " except your righteousness shall exceed that of the Scribes and Pharisees ye shall *in no wise enter* into the kingdom of heaven ", and he is here picking up the same figure. In Luke, this meaning is powerfully enforced by the context of a similar saying which is expanded in a way that recalls the Parable of the Virgins. Here the means of entry is the door of the house, which will one day be shut, and those who then frantically knock for admission will be told by the Master : " Depart from me, all ye workers of iniquity ". And then Jesus expounds the parable : " There (in that place) shall be the weeping and gnashing of teeth, when ye shall see Abraham, and Isaac, and Jacob, and all the prophets, in the Kingdom of God, and yourselves cast forth without ".[5] Life in Matt. 7 : 14 (strictly, " the life ") is synonymous with the Kingdom, as is evident from the parallels in Matthew's account of the young ruler.[6] " The life " is eternal life, and is contrasted with " the destruction " :[7] the passage is a perfect example of antithetic parallelism in every phrase. The

[5]Luke 13 : 24-30 ; [6]cf. Matt. 19 : 16, 17, 23, 24, 29 ; [7]cf. Matt. 18 : 8-9 : "to enter into the life".

teaching of Jesus is firmly based on the doctrine of man's nature and destiny ; in the final issue there is no middle way : men must either " perish " or " receive eternal life ".[8]

Who will guide the seekers for the narrow way? Many may offer their help, and some may be false guides, blind themselves and leading the blind to destruction. How are they to be recognized? Outward signs may all suggest the man guileless as a sheep—bland in manner and fastidious in ways. He may come as though one sent from God, with the appearance of authority and the forms of righteousness. But at heart he may care for none but himself. Self-centred men are always devourers of others, absorbing their energies and dominating their personalities ; but the egoism of these men may destroy for others not only this life but life to come. Such were the " grievous wolves " who Paul warned the Ephesian elders would enter in among them, " not sparing the flock ".[9] By " smooth and fair speech " they might " beguile the hearts of the innocent ", but they were causers of divisions and occasions of stumbling.[10] We can hardly doubt that in these expressions Paul is directly alluding to the Lord's words.

One test is infallible if rightly applied : the tree will be known by its fruits. You do not gather a bunch of grapes from the spiny acacia. It may be flourishing and leafy, but tested by results it is worthless. In the sense of " useless ", " unsatisfactory ", the Gospel record uses " corrupt " almost in the modern sense given colloquially to " rotten " or " mouldy " ; in the Parable of the Dragnet the same word is used of the " bad " fish which were thrown away because they were

[8]John 3 : 16 ; [9]Acts 20 : 29 ; [10]Rom. 16 : 17.

kinds unsuitable for food. So here, each tree yields fruit according to its kind : the " good " gives good fruit ; the worthless sort proves in its fruit to be unpalatable or even poisonous. The contrast would make a ready impression, for not only is Palestine the land of such good fruits as the grape and the fig, but it is said " there is probably no country on earth of the same extent which has so many plants with prickles and thorns ". Not less than 50 genera and 200 species are so furnished.

Like so many of the Lord's figures, this has a history of development in the earlier Scriptures and is carried on in those which follow. Jeremiah borrows the idea and almost the exact language of Psalm 1 (quoted above), but expands it to show both the source of the fruit and the diverse kinds. The man that " trusteth in man ", he says, shall be " like the heath of the desert ", but : " Blessed is the man that trusteth in the Lord, and whose hope the Lord is. For he shall be as a tree planted by the waters . . . and shall not be careful in the year of drought, neither shall cease from yielding fruit. The heart is deceitful above all things, and desperately wicked : who can know it ? I the Lord search the heart, I try the reins, even to give every man according to his ways, according to the fruit of his doings ". As the heart is, so shall be " the fruit of his doings ".[11]

In the New Testament, besides Paul's allusions quoted above, James has one of particular interest because he appeals to the one figure to substantiate another, and both are in fact drawn from the words of Jesus : " Doth a fountain send forth at the same place sweet water and bitter ? Can the fig tree, my brethren,

[11]Jer. 17 : 7-10.

bear olive berries? either a vine, figs? So can no fountain both yield salt water and fresh ".[12] He treats the figure of the trees as a familiar axiom which supports the figure of the fountain—the latter being based on the saying that " out of the overflow of the heart the mouth speaketh " which is closely associated with the reference to the tree and the fruit in Matt. 12 : 32-37.

James may help us in determining what is the fruit which so betrays its origin : is it doctrine or practice? The answer is not as simple as those with a natural predilection for the one or the other would like to believe. John's exhortation to the Jews to " bring forth fruits worthy of repentance " because " the axe is laid to the root of the trees "[13] refers primarily to the conduct of life. But in Matt. 12, where Jesus is speaking to those who " blasphemed against the Holy Spirit " by attributing his works to " Beelzebub ", words enter weightily into his consideration. Though they could not deny the goodness of his works, the Jewish leaders had represented him as an evil tree, and so he (referring to himself) retorts : " Either make the tree good, and his fruit good ; or else make the tree corrupt, and his fruit corrupt : for the tree is known by his fruit " (verse 33). But when in the next verse he turns the same argument against them their words are the fruit by which they are judged, and they, not he, prove to be the corrupt tree : " O generation of vipers, how can ye, being evil, speak good things? For out of the abundance of the heart the mouth speaketh ". And so by their words they would be condemned, for their words were an evil act bubbling out of an evil heart. Luke's " Sermon on the plain "[14] is much nearer to this passage than to Matt. 7 : 20 ; it also links the saying

[12]James 3 : 11-12 ; [13]Matt. 3 : 8-10 ; [14]Luke 6 : 43-45.

directly to the saying about the mote an the beam, but in this context it is the disciple who is called to test himself by examining his own fruit.

Those against whom the Romans were warned were causing schisms " contrary to the teaching " which the Romans had learned—a reference back to Rom. 6 : 17, where they are said to have been delivered from the bond-service of sin by obeying " that form of teaching " which was delivered them (or, " whereunto they were delivered "). Undoubtedly the allusion is to Judaizers such as those who had caused so much " stumbling " in Galatia, where they had preached a substitute Gospel. In Ephesus also Paul had " declared the whole counsel of God ", but the " grievous wolves " who would make havoc in the flock of God were men who would " speak perverse things to draw away disciples after them ". The very metaphor of a wolf implies that, like those mentioned in Romans, they would " serve not our Lord Jesus Christ, but in their own belly ".

The context in James also has to do with words and their effects, for he begins : " Be not many teachers, my brethren ", and continues with warning on responsibility for the misbehaviour of the tongue. " Therewith ", he says, " bless we God, even the Father ; and therewith curse we men, which are made after the likeness of God." But bitterness and conflict have their source in the " earthly " wisdom, while the wisdom which is from above is " full of mercy and good fruits ".

The fact is that no such neat division is possible between doctrine and conduct as we are disposed to make. Words are acts ; teaching is life. What a man believes, that he will become ; conversely what he is reveals what he really believes—and not merely what he professes to believe. As a man " thinketh in his heart, so is he ".[15] If the Gospel of grace is debased, sooner or later the character which it aims to form must be changed ; and if the acts are a denial of the Gospel, the teaching itself will be undermined. The New Testament always suggests that false teaching carries with it a moral responsibility ; perverted doctrine is ultimately traceable to a wrong bent of the emotions and will. The result must be—in the end, if not immediately—to form a different ideal of living and therefore a different standard of conduct. It may be an exacting standard—like that of the Judaizers ; but it is not the standard of Christ.

If we ask, then, " What are the fruits? " the answer is that they are whatever the tree produces in words or deeds. The prophets were to be tested both by what they prophesied and what they did : if either conflicted with the spirit of Christ and the " truth " as that truth is " in Jesus ", then they were false and self-seekers—wolves instead of sheep.

[15]Prov. 23 : 7.

4

THE FINAL TEST (7 : 21-27)

*Not everyone that saith unto me, Lord, Lord, shall
enter into the Kingdom of heaven :*
*But he that doeth the will of my Father that is in
heaven.*

Many will say to me in that day,
    Lord, Lord, did we not prophesy in thy name ?
    And in thy name cast out demons ?
    And in thy name do many mighty works ?
And then I will profess unto them,
    I never knew you :
    Depart from me,
    Ye that work iniquity.

Everyone that heareth these wores of mine,
    And doeth them,
Shall be likened unto a prudent man,
    Who built his house upon a rock :
        And the rain descended,
        And the streams came,
        And the winds blew,
        And beat upon that house :
    And it fell not :
For it was founded upon a rock.

But everyone that heareth these words of mine,
    And doeth them not,
Shall be likened unto a foolish man,
    Who built his house upon the sand :
        And the rain descended,
        And the streams came,
        And the winds blew,
        And smote upon that house :
    And it fell :
And great was the fall of it.

In the act of testing the fruit of the teachers who claim his hearing, the disciple is himself put to the test. Discrimination between the false and the true, the bitter and the good, will be the fruit of his own heart. At the same time that the word is dividing the different classes of men it is searching the individual disciple " even to the dividing asunder of soul and spirit, and of the joints and marrow " ; and the final division will be in the day when the judge will declare who shall " enter into the Kingdom of Heaven " and who shall be " cast forth ". For that time of decision " that day " is in Biblical and Jewish usage a technical term.

The outstanding fact about these verses is that Jesus calmly assumes that he will be the Judge. The destiny of men will be in his hands, and those who come before him will address him with fervent awe as " Lord, Lord ". In such a connection " Lord " passes beyond a mode of courtesy and becomes a divine title : by picturing himself in such a position he claims to be not only Messiah but Son of God. For this climax diligent readers of the Sermon are not unprepared : Jesus has equated suffering for righteousness' sake with suffering for his sake ; he has given a new law as one greater than Moses.[1] The teaching he gave was inseparable from his own person and character. The Sermon could have been preached by no one other than the Christ. But while he himself has shone through the Sermon, he is revealed at this point as though a curtain over the future is drawn aside ; without a word of claim or assertion the hearers are given a glimpse down the vistas of time, and see the Judge enthroned—and he is none other than this Nazarene. The Preacher who could do that was no mere peasant with a genius for morals.

[1]Matt. 5 : 10-11, 28, 34, 39, 44.

Two types are portrayed out of those who come before his judgment seat. The first are wordy and profuse. In their lifetime they have professed his name fervently, for to call him " Lord " in the full sense of the term is a confession of faith.[2] But it is a barren tree that produces only leaves, and a barren soul that yields only words.[3]

In view of this condemnation, others who petition the Judge call their works to witness on their behalf. They have been teachers mighty in the scriptures, powerful in converting men and women and founding churches. (So perhaps we may paraphrase their claims in the terms of today). And if any critic dares to say they would have been better occupied in feeding the hungry and clothing the naked, let him not overlook that they were following the example of Christ himself. In the days of his flesh he was first and foremost a prophet, and his greatest work was in the forgiveness of sins : to preach Christ crucified and bring men and women to be reconciled to God cannot in itself be unpleasing to him. Yet to these also he " professes "— and the term seems an ironic counterpart to their profession of his Name—he " professes " : " I never knew you ". The words are the most dreadful in all Scripture. For all their zeal, these men were unknown to him because they had never known him ; in using his name they had deceived themselves, but he was not deceived. And as the inevitable corollary, he adds in the words of the Psalmist : " Depart from me, ye workers of lawlessness ".[4] In Luke, where they claim, " We have eaten and drunk in thy presence, and thou hast taught in our streets "—they are called " workers

[2]cf. 1 Cor. 12 : 3 ; [3]James 2 : 17 ; John 2 : 4 ; [4]cf. Psa. 6 : 8, LXX.

of unrighteousness ".[5] Neither membership of his church, where he was in their midst at the Breaking of Bread, nor activity in proclaiming his Gospel and establishing ecclesias, ensures his recognition in the day of judgment.

We seem to have reached a deadlock. If neither words nor deeds are accepted, what does this Judge require? And by what law can it be lawless to follow the pattern of his own works? The solution to both problems is found in the criterion for entry into the Kingdom declared in verse 21 : " He that doeth the will of my Father which is in heaven ". To do the will is more than to do the works. For all the appearance of zeal works may be only an external performance, and in the end prove hollow and bitter like Dead Sea fruit. While a man cannot do the will without doing the works—for he is required to do and not merely to know—he may do the works for some other reason than a desire for the fulfilment of God's will. He may do them to gain's men's admiration for his gifts, his zeal, or his self-sacrifice : or his secret motive may be to place God in his debt—that is, he may expect God to fulfil His part of a bargain by granting the zealous one eternal life in return for labours and privations in this life.

Christ's is the law of love : and by that standard what is without love is without law. It therefore follows that " though I bestow all my goods to feed the poor, and though I give my body to be burned, and have not love, it profiteth me nothing".[6] But the man who makes God's will his own, will do the works as though it were by nature : he will not try to keep accounts with God ; he will not count that he has done this and that ; his

[5] Luke 13 : 25-27 ; [6] 1 Cor. 13 : 3.

right hand will scarcely know what his left hand does. He will have become an instrument through which God's will is fulfilled because through love his own will is absorbed in God's. Only a powerful motive could so make a man's personality one whole, uniting his heart to fear the Lord's name.[7] Where it exists, emotion, imagination and desire can be drawn to a focus, and can reinforce the will so as to give a constant direction to the inner life. Then the man's words and works are not disconnected happenings, the effect of self-centred and incoherent motives ; they are parts of a whole, and reflect a greater Personality than his own ; and for such a man Paul's prayer is fulfilled : " The God of peace himself sanctify you wholly ; and may your spirit and soul and body be preserved entire, without blame at the coming of our Lord Jesus Christ. "[8]

We should be hypocrites if we did not admit that such a unity of the mind and will in love seems for every one of us an ideal dimly perceived and unattainably distant ; we cannot maintain our course at all without constant struggle, and the fact is recognized by all the metaphors which liken the way of the disciple to an athletic contest—including the Lord's own words, " Strive to enter in at the strait gate ". Yet this is the ideal to be fulfilled in that future when God is " all in all " ; and where love of God is we shall imperceptibly grow towards it. Without love it cannot be ; and therefore without love there can be no life.

Yet nowhere in the Sermon, and only twice in the Synoptic Gospels, does Jesus use the abstract noun " love ". In the first three Gospels he is sparing even of the verb " to love " and rarely employs it unless he is referring to the language of the Old Testament.[9]

[7]Psa. 86 : 11 ; [8]1 Thess. 5 : 23 ; [9]Deut. 6 : 5 ; Lev. 19 : 18.

Reason for this is not hard to imagine : abstractions can too easily be detached from reality, and become vehicles of cold philosophy or of glib sentiment. The word " love ", in particular, tends to gather an emotional aura which misleads as to its meaning, so that people say " I cannot love that person " when they mean that they cannot feel an emotional attraction towards him. Jesus would rather give a picture of love in its living manifestation ; preference for the concrete over the abstract, so characteristic of Hebrew thought, is nowhere more evident than in his words. Yet if for purposes of thought we are to isolate the quality which is common to all the manifestations Jesus describes in the Sermon—the one quality which is the root from which they all branch— we can find no word for it but love ; but it will be truer to the habit of Jesus and of the older revelation which he embodies if we express it actively in the language of the law : " Thou shalt love the Lord thy God . . . Thou shalt love thy neighbour as thyself ". In the love which the law demanded and which Jesus exemplified by word and act is the secret of the dedicated will. And this principle must be borne in mind when reading the parable with which the Sermon ends.

In one of the narrow valleys leading down to Galilee's lake two men went to build. Summer was young enough for a stream to flow in the rocky bed, but the floods of winter had left behind a stretch of gravel. Here building could begin with little work in levelling, and the water supply was near at hand. One man chose it, and made rapid progress with his house. From time to time he looked up with a satirical smile at the other, who was toiling higher up on a shelf of rock.

This man, however, knew the country. When winter returned, the stream would fill the valley with a raging torrent; the wind, bottled in between hillsides as though poured into a funnel, would blow with a concentrated fury which would raise great billows far out on the lake. Combined with beating rain, these would put any building to the test.

So it came about; and the might of the storm beat in vain upon the house on rock. But the other house it " smote ". The swirling flood sucked away the gravel and rolled stones against the foundations. Rain came as though with hammer blows, and the whole structure rocked and swayed in the gale; until, under-mined beneath and battered above, the timbers gave with a groan, the roof fell in and the walls collapsed. Nothing was left but so much debris in the flood.

In Galilee where the Sermon was delivered all would know that one was a sensible man with foresight, and the other was foolish; just as they would know the necessity in slightly different conditions of digging through the alluvial deposit to the rock below and building on stone arches in order to have a sound foundation. But did they grasp the same principle in the issues of eternal life? Or did they expect that laws of cause and effect would no longer apply in things of the spirit?

The parable has established three things. First, it has declared again the great principle of human freedom; men are able to choose on what foundation they will build. Without that freedom the parable would lose all rational basis; if men were merely automata predestined to life or destruction, the words would mock them. Secondly, it calls for sustained

THE TEACHING OF THE MASTER

effort on the man's part; the foundation is not merely hearing the words of Christ, but the doing of them; and on this foundation he must build. And the third and greatest lesson is that according to the man's doings, so will the result be.

Never was that lesson more needed than in our own time. Things are as they are, and the consequences will be what they will be, and by no attempt to trick Nature can we escape them. Yet people who know that they cannot defy gravitation and the principles of mechanics feel aggrieved that God's ways should be as stable in the spiritual realm as in the physical. They know that the pursuit of perpetual motion is an occupation for the crank who is living in an illusory world of his own making; yet in the intangible things they adopt a sentimentalism which would undermine the moral order of the universe. Why should they think they can or should escape the consequences of ignoring divine principles? To deny that life can only be built to last on God's foundation is to deny order and rationality in His creation: it is to mock God, and " God is not mocked ": for (to borrow another scriptural figure) " whatsoever a man soweth, that shall he also reap: for he that soweth unto his own flesh shall of the flesh reap corruption; and he that soweth unto the Spirit shall of the Spirit reap eternal life ".[10]

The effect of the divine principles was declared of old in the words which form the germ of the Lord's parable: " When the whirlwind passeth, the wicked is no more: but the righteous is an everlasting foundation"; " The wicked are overthrown, and are not: but the house of the righteous shall stand ".[11] Like the wall

[10]Gal. 6 : 7-8; [11]Prov. 10 : 25; 12 : 7; cf. Prov. 1 : 27-31; 14 : 11; Psa. 37 : 10.

" daubed with untempered mortar " the wicked shall be " rent with a stormy wind " in God's fury ;[12] and the wind which will drive them away like chaff is the judgment of God in " that day ".[13]

While this meaning of the parable cannot be stressed too strongly, there is a possible misinterpretation against which we need to be on our guard. It is to derive from the parable a rigid doctrine of salvation by works. Such a misunderstanding would only be possible where the parable was severed from its foundation. The " words " which men are to hear and do comprise the whole body of teaching which has gone before. That teaching has displayed two contrasting ideas of righteousness—on the one hand the righteousness of a code, and on the other the righteousness of the heart.

The defect of a code is that it fails to transform a man's personality. However detailed and exacting it may be there is a limit to its demands ; if every single precept has been carried out, then righteousness has been attained and nothing more can be required. But supposing a man could conform in every particular to such a standard of external conduct, whole areas of his inmost self would remain untouched by it. Something in the core of his own being would remain not merely unchanged by the code but outside its reach.

Practice, however, will fall far short of the highest standard of fulfilment ; and as a result, the man who honestly pursues this legal righteousness will never know true peace of mind—unless, indeed, his code demands no more than the barest social standards of his day. If he aims at anything beyond this inconspicuous level, he will be perpetually dissatisfied as attainment eludes his grasp.

[12]Ezek. 13 : 10-14 ; [13]Psa. 1 : 4 ; Matt. 7 : 22.

Suppose—as may too easily happen—that his mental honesty flags under the strain. One of two results may follow : or perhaps both in succession. At best he will be content with performing the outward acts, whether or not his heart is in what he is doing. Enough that he goes through the motions of righteousness as a ritual performed without flaw. The more precise his code, and the more meticulous he can be in its observance, the more successfully will he hide from himself his inward uneasiness. Once that detached and objective standard has been accepted, the second danger lurks near at hand : he may do the acts in order that men may see how righteous he is ; if they are not done for God, they may be done for men. In either case he is a man acting a part, and in the second case he is a dissembler, deceiving others and perhaps deceiving himself. His action is an outward show which his thoughts and motives may flatly contradict.

Against all this Jesus sets the only righteousness which has any relation to the Kingdom of God : a righteousness which knows no limit, for it treats every act as the expression of a motive, and every motive as a potential act. By that standard the law against murder condemns anger, the law against adultery the lustful look. Its sphere is the whole personality, and under its law there is no point at which we can say, " We have done enough ". The qualities set forth in the Beatitudes are to be reflected in every relation of life ; and only those who so mirror the character of the Heavenly Father are the true Israel of God, the people of His covenant, and His sons.

What, then, is the rock? There is an element of truth in a rabbinic interpretation which applied the second part of Prov. 10 : 25 to the Messiah as the " Just One ", the everlasting foundation on whom the world rested. For Jesus says it is the man who hears and acts upon " these teachings of mine " who builds to last. Christ, then, is the Rock; for from him proceed the words of life which are men's foundation. " Other foundation can no man lay than that which is laid, which is Jesus Christ. "[14] In the light of the fact, however, that Jesus himself has said that " Man shall not live by bread alone, but by every word that proceedeth out of the mouth of God ", he now assumes nothing less than that when he speaks God speaks. If God's word is the substratum of all things, and the words of Jesus are the foundation of life, then the conclusion follows that God speaks in him. No wonder his hearers were astounded, for " he taught them as one having authority, and not as the scribes ". Here is a humble peasant who speaks words of undeniable beauty and profound insight : and he leads up to an implied claim which goes beyond that of any prophet of old, for it is a claim to divinity : his teaching is the basis on which men's destiny will be determined. " Never man spake like this man ! "

Not only is it the foundation, but the word which separates men proves to be his word. Starting with the division between the Church and the world, it has gone on to work within the Household in distinguishing true brethren from false ; and it ends by dividing asunder the hearts in " that day " when the secret things will be made known. Step by step the action of the word has separated men into two classes : the reverent and the sensual ; those who are going towards life and those who

[14] I Cor. 3 : 11.

are journeying to destruction; the true professors of Christ and the false; and finally, those who do the will of the Father, and those who do their own. And in the concluding parable the division is complete: there are those who have built a structure of life and character on his teaching which will stand, while others have built houses which will collapse in total ruin at the coming of the judgment storm. With the Day of Judgment their quality is revealed, for the word which he has spoken judges them at the last day.

A LIST OF QUOTATIONS, ALLUSIONS, ETC.

Roman type: The O.T. in the Sermon—quotations, allusions, parallels.

Italic: The Sermon in the rest of the N.T.—quotations, allusions, parallels. (Parallel passages in Mark and Luke in brackets).

Matt.

5 : 3   Deut. 33 : 29 ; Psa. 1 : 1 ; 18 : 27 ; 68 : 10 ; Prov. 16 : 19 ; Isa. 26 : 6 ; 49 : 13 ; 51 : 5-11 ; 57 : 13 ; 61 : 1 ; 65 : 17-19 ; 66 : 2 ; Zeph. 3 : 11-13.
Jas. 1 : 12, 25 ; 2 : 5 ; 4 : 10 ; 5 : 10-11 ; 1 Pet. 3 : 14 ; 4 : 14 ; Eph. 4 : 1-2 ; (Luke 6 : 20-23).

5 : 4   Isa. 61 : 3 ; 57 : 18 ; 66 : 10, 13 ; Jer. 31 : 13.
1 Cor. 5 : 2 ; 2 Cor. 12 : 21 ; 2 Thess. 2 : 16-17 ; Jas. 4 : 9 ; Rev. 21 : 4.

5 : 5   Psa. 37 : 11 ; 25 : 12-14 ; 52 : 5-8 ; Prov. 10 : 30 ; 3 : 34 ; 16 : 19 (Jewish) ; Isa. 57 : 13-15 ; 65 : 9 ; Zeph. 2 : 9 (R.V.) ; 3 : 12.
1 Cor. 6 : 9-10 ; 2 Cor. 10 : 1 ; Gal. 5 : 21-23 ; Eph. 4 : 1-2 ; 5 : 5 ; Col. 3 : 24 ; 1 Tim. 6 : 11 ; 2 Tim. 2 : 12 ; Titus 3 : 2 ; Jas. 2 : 5 ; 1 Pet. 3 : 9 ; Rev. 21 : 7.

5 : 6   Psa. 16 : 11 ; 17 : 15 ; 22 : 25-26 ; 34 : 8 ; 42 : 1-2 ; 73 : 25 ; 84 : 2 ; 91 : 16 ; 107 : 9 ; 119 : 103 ; Isa. 41 : 17-20 ; 44 : 3-4 ; 49 : 7-10 ; 53 : 11 ; 55 : 1 ; 65 : 13-18.
Matt. 8 : 11-12 ; Luke 13 : 29 ; 14 : 15-24 ; 22 : 30 ; John 4 : 14 ; 6 : 35 ; 7 : 37 ; 2 Tim. 2 : 22 ; 1 Pet. 2 : 2.

5 : 7   Exod. 34 : 6-7 ; Psa. 18 : 24-28 ; Prov. 11 : 17 ; Hos. 6 : 6.
Matt. 9 : 13 ; 12 : 7 ; 2 Tim. 1 : 16-18 ; Jas. 2 : 13.

5 : 8   Psa. 24 : 4 (LXX), 6 ; 11 : 7 ; 17 : 15 ; 18 : 26 ; 73 : 1 (R.V.) ; 140 : 13 ; Isa. 33 : 17 ; 52 : 8 (R.V.) ; Job. 19 : 25-27 ; 33 : 26.
Acts 15 : 9 ; 2 Cor. 3 : 18 ; 4 : 6 ; 1 Tim. 1 : 3-5 ; 2 Tim. 2 : 22 ; Heb. 12 : 14 ; Jas. 4 : 8 ; 1 Pet. 1 : 22 ; 1 John 3 : 2 ; Rev. 22 : 4.

5 : 9   Deut. 14 : 1 ; Prov. 12 : 20 ; 10 : 10 (LXX) ; Isa. 58 : 4-8, 12.
Rom. 12 : 18 ; 14 : 17-19 ; Eph. 4 : 3 ; Col. 1 : 19-20 ; 3 : 15 ; Heb. 12 : 14 ; Jas. 3 : 17, 18.

5 : 10-12   Psa. 31 : 19 ; Isa. 51 : 7-8 ; 66 : 5.
Matt. 10 : 22-24, 41 ; Acts 5 : 41 (R.V.) ; Rom. 5 : 3 ; 8 : 18 ; 2 Cor. 4 : 17 ; 12 : 10 ; Phil. 1 : 29 ; Col. 1 : 24 ; 2 Tim. 2 : 12 ; 3 : 12 ; Heb. 10 : 33-34 ; 12 : 4 ; 13 : 13 ; Jas. 1 : 2, 12 ; 5 : 10-11 ; 1 Pet. 1 : 4-6 ; 2 : 20-25 ; 3 : 14-17 ; 4 : 4, 13-16.

5 : 13   Lev. 2 : 13.
Col. 4 : 6 ; Heb. 6 : 4-6 ; 2 Pet. 3 : 17.

5 : 14-16   Deut. 26 : 19 ; Isa. 43 : 21 ; 60 : 3.
           John 13 : 24-35 ; 2 Cor. 8 : 20-21 ; Eph. 5 : 8-11 ; Phil. 2 : 15-16 ; 1 Pet. 2 : 12 (Luke 11 : 33).

5 : 17   Num. 30 : 8-16 ; Psa. 40 : 7.
           Matt. 3 : 15 ; 26 : 54 ; Rom. 3 : 31 ; 7 : 12, 22 ; 8 : 4.

5 : 19   Deut. 4 : 2.
           Rom. 7 : 3, 8, 10 ; Gal. 5 : 14 ; Rev. 22 : 18-19.

5 : 20   Isa. 60 : 21.
           Matt. 8 : 10-12 ; Rom. 12 : 1 ; 1 Cor. 6 : 9-10 ; Phil. 3 : 6-7 ; 2 Pet. 1 : 11 ; 1 John 3 : 7-10.

5 : 21   Exod. 20 : 13 ; 21 : 12 ; Deut. 5 : 17.
5 : 22   Lev. 19 : 17 ; Deut. 21 : 18-21 (Heb.) ; 1 Sam. 25 : 25 ; Psa. 14 : 1 ; Prov. 18 : 21.
           Jas. 1 : 19-20 ; 3 : 6, 9-10 ; 4 : 2 ; 1 John 3 : 15.

5 : 23-24   Prov. 21 : 27.
5 : 25-26   Isa. 55 : 6 (LXX) ; Prov. 10 : 12 ; 17 : 9.
           Matt. 18 : 21-35 ; Jas. 2 : 13 ; (Luke 12 : 58-59).

5 : 27   Exod. 20 : 14 ; Deut. 5 : 18.
5 : 28   Prov. 4 : 23, 25 ; 6 : 25 ; 16 : 2 ; 21 : 2.
           1 Cor. 4 : 5 ; Eph. 5 : 5 ; Heb. 13 : 4 ; 2 Pet. 2 : 14 ; Rev. 22 : 15.

5 : 29-30   Exod. 21 : 23-24 ; Deut. 19 : 21 ; Psa. 1 : 1 ; Isa. 66 : 24.
           Matt. 10 : 28 ; 18 : 8-9 ; Col. 3 : 5-6 ; (Mark 9 : 43-48).

5 : 31-32   Deut. 24 : 1.
           Matt. 19 : 3-9 ; Mark 10 : 2-12 ; Luke 16 : 18 ; 1 Cor. 7 : 10-11.

5 : 33   Lev. 19 : 11-12 ; Num. 30 : 2 ; Deut. 5 : 11 ; 6 : 13 ; Eccl. 5 : 2-4.
           Matt. 23 : 16-22.

5 : 34-36   Psa. 48 : 1-2 ; Isa. 66 : 1-2.
           Jas. 5 : 12.

5 : 37   Gen. 8 : 21 ; Deut. 31 : 21.
           Mark 7 : 20-22.

5 : 38   Exod. 21 : 24 ; Lev. 24 : 20 ; Deut. 19 : 21.
5 : 39   Prov. 20 : 22 ; 24 : 29 ; 25 : 21-22 ; Isa. 50 : 6 ; Lam. 3 : 26-31.
           John 18 : 23 ; Rom. 12 : 17, 20-21 ; 1 Thess. 5 : 15 ; 1 Pet. 2 : 21-23 ; (Luke 6 : 29-30).

5 : 40   Exod. 22 : 26-27 ; Deut. 24 : 6, 10-13.
           1 Cor. 6 : 7.

5 : 41   *Matt. 27 : 32 ; Mark 15 : 21 ; Rom. 13 : 1-7 ; Titus 3 : 1 ; 1 Pet. 2 : 13-17.*

5 : 42   Deut. 15 : 8, 11 ; Psa. 37 : 21, 26 (R.V.) ; 112 : 5 ; Prov. 3 : 28 ; 21 : 26 ; 22 : 9 (margin).
           Matt. 10 : 8 ; Acts 20 : 34-35 ; 2 Cor. 9 : 6-7 ; Eph. 4 : 28 ; Gal. 6 : 10 ; 1 Tim. 6 : 17-18 ; Heb. 13 : 16 ; 1 John 3 : 17-18.

5 : 43   Lev. 19 : 18 (cf. verses 33-34) ; Deut. 23 : 7.

5 : 44   Prov. 10 : 12 ; 24 : 17-18 ; 25 : 21-22.
         Matt. 22 : 39; Rom. 12 : 9, 10, 17, 19, 20, 21; 13 : 10;
         1 Cor. 4 : 12-13; Gal. 6 : 10; Eph. 4 : 31-32; Col. 3 :
         12-15; 1 Thess. 5 : 15; Jas. 1 : 25; 2 : 8-12; 3 : 9-12;
         5 : 20; 1 Pet. 1 : 22; 2 : 12, 23; 3 : 9; 4 : 8; 2 Pet.
         1 : 5-11; (Luke 6 : 27-28, 35).

5 : 45   Prov. 29 : 13 (R.V.).
         Acts 14 : 17; Rom. 5 : 8, 10; Eph. 5 : 1.

5 : 46-47 *Gal. 6 : 10; 1 Thess. 5 : 15; 2 Pet. 1 : 5-6.*

5 : 48   Lev. 19 : 2, etc.
         Matt. 19 : 21; Eph. 3 : 17-19; Phil. 3 : 8-13; Col. 1 : 27-
         28; Jas. 1 : 4; 3 : 2.

6 : 1   *Matt. 9 : 30; Col. 3 : 23-24; 1 Thess. 2 :4.*

6 : 2   *Luke 6 : 24; 1 Thess. 2 : 5-6.*

6 : 4   *Matt.10:26; 1 Cor. 4:5; 1 Tim. 1 : 17 (R.V.); Heb. 11 : 27.*

6 : 5   *Mark 12 : 40; Luke 20 : 47.*

6 : 7   Prov. 10 : 19; Eccl. 5 : 2-3.

6 : 9   Deut. 8 : 5 ; 32 : 6 ; Psa. 103 : 11-12, 13 ; Isa. 63 : 16 ;
         Jer. 31 : 9 ; Isa. 55 : 6-8 ; 57 : 15 ; Lev. 22 : 31-32 ;
         Isa. 5 : 16 ; 8 : 13 ; Deut. 28 : 58 ; Ezek. 36 : 23 ; Zech.
         14 : 9.
         Matt. 23 : 8-9; Mark 14 : 36; Rom. 8 : 14-15; Gal. 4 : 6;
         Eph. 3 : 14; 4 : 6; 1 Pet. 3 : 15 (R.V.) (Luke 11 : 2-4).

6 : 10   Psa. 93 : 1 ; Jer. 10 : 10 ; Psa. 40 : 7-8.
         2 Thess. 1 : 5; 2 Tim. 4 : 18; 2 Pet. 1 : 11; Rev. 11 : 15;
         Matt. 26 : 39, 42; Luke 22 : 42, 44; John 6 : 38-40;
         Eph. 1 : 1-9, 11 (R.V.), 18-19; 6 : 6; Col. 1 : 9; Heb.
         10 : 7-10; 13 : 20-21.

6 : 11   *Luke 12 : 42; 2 Cor. 9 : 8; Phil. 4 : 19; 1 Tim. 6 : 8*
         (R.V. margin).

6 : 12   Deut. 15 : 2.
         Col. 3 : 13.

6 : 13   *Mark 14 : 38; Luke 22 : 31, 40, 46; 1 Cor. 10 : 13;*
         2 Thess. 3 : 3; 2 Tim. 4 : 18.

6 : 14   *Mark 11 : 25-26; Luke 23 : 34; Eph. 4 : 32; Jas. 2 : 13;*
         (Luke 6 : 36-37).

6 : 19   Prov. 11 : 28 ; Isa. 50 : 9 ; 51 : 6-8.
         Heb. 13 : 5; Jas. 5 : 2-3 (R.V.); (Luke 12 : 21, 33-36).

6 : 20   Exod. 19 : 5 (R.V.) ; Psa. 16 : 6-7 ; 31   19 ; 73 : 26 ;
         Prov. 2 : 7 ; 11 : 4 ; Mal. 3 : 17.
         1 Tim. 6 : 17-19; Heb. 10 : 34; 1 Pet. 2 : 9 (R.V.).

6 : 21   *Phil. 3 : 20 (R.V,); Col. 1 : 5, 12, 27; 3 : 2-3.*

6 : 22   Prov. 4 : 25 ; 22 : 9 ; 20 : 27.
         Phil. 2 : 15; (Luke 11 : 33-36).

6 : 23   Deut. 15 : 9 ; 28 : 54 ; Prov. 28 : 22.
            Mark 7 : 22 ; Rom. 1 : 21-22 ; 2 Cor. 11 : 3 (Gr.) ; Eph.
            4 : 17-18 ; Heb. 13 : 5-6 (R.V.).
6 : 24   Eccl. 5 : 13-20.
            Matt. 8 : 19-22 ; 10 : 36-39 ; Rom. 6 : 16 ; Gal. 1 : 10 ;
            Jas. 4 : 4 ; 1 John 2 : 15.
6 : 25   Psa. 55 : 22.
            Matt. 13 : 22 (Gr.) ; Mark 4 : 19 (Gr.) ; Luke 8 : 14 (Gr.) ;
            Phil. 4 : 6 (Gr.), 19 ; 1 Tim. 6 : 7-9 (R.V.m.) ; Jas. 4 : 13 ;
            1 Pet. 5 : 7 ; (Luke 12 : 22-31).
6 : 26   Job. 12 : 7-10 ; 38 : 41 ; Psa. 147 : 9.
            Matt. 10 : 29.
6 : 27   Psa. 39 : 4-5 ; Eccl. 8 : 8.
6 : 30   Isa. 40 : 6-8.
            Matt. 8 : 10, 26 ; Jas. 1 : 9-11 ; 1 Pet. 1 : 23-25.
6 : 31-32   *Matt. 8 : 20, 22 ; Heb. 13 : 5 ; 1 Tim. 6 : 7-9 (R.V.m.).*
6 : 33   Isa. 26 : 9.
            Rom. 8 : 32 ; (Luke 12 : 31).
6 : 34   *Jas. 4 : 13-14.*
7 : 1-5   *Mark 4 : 24 ; Rom. 2 : 3 ; 14 : 4, 10 (R.V.), 13 ; 1 Cor.*
            4 : 1-5 ; Gal. 6 : 1-2 ; Jas. 2 : 4, 13 ; 4 : 11 ; 5 : 9 ; (Luke
            6 : 37, 38, 41-42).
7 : 6   Lev. 22 : 10 ; Exod. 22 : 31 ; Prov. 9 : 7-8 ; 11 : 22 ;
            23 : 9 ; 26 : 11.
            1 Cor. 2 : 14 ; 2 Pet. 2 : 22.
7 : 7-11   Isa. 65 : 24 ; 66 : 4 (with Prov. 1 : 24-28).
            Jas. 1 : 3-6, 17 ; 4 : 2-3 ; 1 John 3 : 22 ; 5 : 14-15 ;
            (Luke 11 : 5-13).
7 : 12   *Rom. 13 : 8 ; Gal. 5 : 13 ; 6 : 2 ; Phil. 2 : 4 ; Jas. 1 : 25 ;*
            2 : 8, 12 : 5 : 20 ; (Luke 6 : 27-36).
7 : 13   Deut. 30 : 15-20 ; Psa. 1 : 6 ; Prov. 2 : 18-19 (Jewish) ;
            7 : 27 (R.V.) ; 14 : 12 ; Jer. 21 : 8.
            2 Cor. 6 : 17 ; 2 Thess. 1 : 7-9.
7 : 14   *1 Cor. 1 : 26 (R.V.m.).*
7 : 15   *Acts 20 : 29 ; Rom. 16 : 17-18 ; Col. 2 : 8 (R.V.) ; 2 Pet.*
            2 : 1-3 ; 1 John 4 : 1 ; (Luke 6 : 42-45).
7 : 16   *Gal. 5 : 22-23 ; Eph. 5 : 9 ; Phil. 1 : 11 ; Jas. 3 : 12, 17-18.*
7 : 17-18   Psa. 1 : 3 ; 92 : 12-15 ; Jer. 17 : 7-10.
            Matt. 12 : 33-34.
7 : 19-20   *Matt. 3 : 8, 10.*
7 : 21   *1 Cor. 12 : 3 ; 13 : 3 ; Gal. 5 : 19-21 : Eph. 5 : 6 ; Jas.*
            1 : 22 ; 2 : 17 ; 1 John 2 : 4 ; Jude 12, 13 (R.V.) ; (Luke
            6 : 46).
7 : 23   Psa. 6 : 8 (LXX).
            Jas. 2 : 9 (Gr.) ; 5 : 9 ; (Luke 13 : 25-27).
7 : 24-27   Psa. 1 : 4 ; 37 : 10 ; Prov. 1 : 27-31 ; 10 : 25 ; 12 : 7 ;
            14 : 11 ; Isa. 64 : 6 ; Ezek. 13 : 10-14.
            1 Cor. 3 : 10-11, 12-15 ; Gal. 6 : 8 ; Heb. 12 : 27-28 ;
            Jude 20, 21 ; (Luke 6 : 47-49).

INDEX